# The Book of Beer

# The Book of Beer

*Bob Abel*

**Henry Regnery Company** • **Chicago**

**Library of Congress Cataloging in Publication Data**

Abel, Bob, 1931-
  The book of beer.

  1.  Beer.   I.   Title.
TP577.A23          641.2'3          76-6254
ISBN 0-8092-9126-6

Designed by Jan Smith.

Published by Henry Regnery Company
180 North Michigan Avenue, Chicago, Illinois 60601
Manufactured in the United States of America
Library of Congress Catalog Card Number: 76-6254
International Standard Book Number: 0-8092-9126-6

Published simultaneously in Canada by
Beaverbooks
953 Dillingham Road
Pickering, Ontario L1W 1Z7
Canada

To Douglas and David,
more full of sparkle and froth than any beer,
and with good heads, too.

# Contents

Mankind's noblest institution—the British pub—travels well, has been exported widely. Besides Whitbread, The Four Aces features Belgian beer. Of course. It's in Belgium.

# The Book of Beer

# 1/Introduction

*The Romance of Beer*

It will doubtless come as a surprise to many readers to learn that beer is the world's most popular drink after tea—which is, after all, the most popular beverage after water. Few beer lovers know very much about the stuff—the wine drinker has a vast literature whereas the beer drinker has a label—but it is an 86-proof understatement to say that beer, the drink for Everyman, has a long and richly intriguing history. In addition to being twice as popular as wine, beer is a surprising match for the aged juice of the grape in terms of cult and lore and drinkers' mythology. Indeed, whether or not wine outranks beer in longevity—nobody really knows—it does not offer any parallel in the scope of its history, as we will see in tracing that fascinating story from prehistoric caves to the Munich beer hall to the British pubs of France and Belgium and elsewhere—e.g., Paris' The Churchill and Brussels' The Swan and the "instant pubs" of San Francisco.

"Beer is Beautiful" in many lands, an integral part of the culture and social fabric of the nation. On a more practical level, beer is *possible* simply because the grains needed for brewing beer come from hardier stock than the grapes required for the production of wine. Then, too, the common man has usually been able to afford the finest beer in his land. Not so, wine. As a gastronomic treat, beer is best enjoyed as fresh as possible because it is a fragile food. The best wines, on the other hand, improve with age, and grow more costly with age. They didn't create the 1855 classification of first growths—the sancrosanct listing of the top sixty-two chateaus in Bordeaux, cracked only by

Chateau Mouton-Rothschild a decade or so ago—by consulting the people who couldn't afford those wines in the first place.

Over the past ten years, world production and consumption of beer has been sharply on the rise, in some countries nearly doubling. The United States by far leads the world in beer production, but we are hardly among the beer giants of the world in terms of per capita consumption, usually ranking around eleventh in the known universe and *Star Trek* galaxies. However, what is especially interesting, outside this country, at least, is that there seems to be a marked trend toward greater discrimination and taste in beer drinking. To quote the *New York Times* of January 27, 1974:

> Tastes in beer vary from country to country, but they are apparently becoming more critical everywhere. While German beers are almost universally acclaimed, connoisseurs speak highly of Japanese beers, which are drier and less sweet than American beers, reflecting Nordic brewing techniques transplanted to Yokohama a century ago. The Belgians, who are surpassed in European beer consumption only by the Germans and the Czechs, drink a brew somewhere between the light American and heavy German types.

The world's romance with beer goes back to Marco Polo reporting that the ancient Chinese drank it and to the Egyptians and Babylonians, who incorporated it into their religion, and to Pliny the Elder, the most famous grouse of his time regarding the effects of the beverage made from fermented barley. "Alas, what wonderful ingenuity vice possesses!" Pliny wrote. "A method has actually been discovered for making even water intoxicating!"

Then, too, the romance *of* beer includes the great men who led this country to independence, some of whom were commercial brewers and all of whom seemed to have brewed their own beer. Washington was very fond of porter and Jefferson read every book written in English on the subject, the better to brew beer on his Monticello estate. Later on, beer was the drink—that is, for shame, if you liked to drink—recommended by the Temperance crowd. In Australia there was a near revolution caused by a sharp rise in the price of beer just after the end of World War I. But then, beer has long been a very special part of the Australian male mystique and temperament.

In that regard, the author recalls an evening spent in an Edinburgh pub, where he made the mistake of speaking well of English beer. For his gesture of intranational goodwill, he was promptly reminded that Scotland's ales are stronger, tastier, and in all ways worthier than their English counterparts. Only when the author countered with Newcastle Brown Ale (which is owned by a Scottish concern), did the atmosphere grow calmer and cheerier. Thus while you do not bring Scottish coal to Newcastle, you can bring Newcastle Ale to Scotland.

For me the romance of beer includes the Reverend Jonathan Edwards busting his lungs about the hellfire and damnation contained in a glass of "whistleberry vengeance"—a brew concocted from sour beer and "a lot of other perfectly disgusting items"—while most of his contemporaries in the Massachusetts Bay Colony were off drinking the stuff.

I also like the stories about beer drinking that are wonderful even if they may not be true. *Did* a gentleman living in Wroxham, Norfolk, England, in 1810 actually down 54½ pints of porter in 55 minutes? *The Guinness Book of World Records* reports this feat, regards it as exaggeration—how *much* exaggeration, one wonders—but dutifully accepts the beer consumption of a Frenchman, no less, who knocked back a more modest 24 pints in 52 minutes in 1950. The name of this antiwine snob: Auguste Maffrey.

I think they're slightly warped, but I also esteem the speed demons like Peter G. Dowdeswell of Earl's Barton, Northamptonshire, England, who chugged a 2½ yard (a long glass originally used for ground-to-coach drinking) of ale in five seconds on May 4, 1975, a 3-pint yard of ale in 6.5 seconds *the same day*, and then, on June 11 went on to downing 2 imperial pints (40 ounces) in 2.3 seconds. The author has to be impressed with this sort of thing because he once took on the chug-a-lug champion of the University of Connecticut and beat him. Unfortunately, what went down fast came back up almost as rapidly. . . .

Still, I don't feel too badly about that lost moment of glory. Around the turn of the century, King Frederick William IV of Prussia visited Dortmund, where a deputation of the local magistrates waited upon him, one of them bearing an elegant tray with a large tankard filled with Adam, the most renowned of the local brews. When the king learned that the contents of the tankard was the celebrated ten-year-old beer, he graciously declared, "Very welcome; for it is extremely warm." Then he drank the entire tankard without once lowering it from his lips. The members of the delegation, who of course were better acquainted with old Adam, smiled at each other instead of warning the king of his folly. His Majesty was unconscious for more than twenty-four hours.

My favorite beer drinker is an eighteenth-century gent named Jedediah Buxton, an Englishman who kept a record of all the free pints of beer he had received since the age of twelve. His total: 5,116 pints. And those only the freebies.

My second favorite beer drinker is William Lewis of Llandismaw, Wales, who all his long life read from the Bible extensively in the mornings and then drank eight gallons of ale each evening. Holy in the A.M., hedonist in the P.M.

I never sampled the world's strongest beer, EKU Kulminator Urtyp Hell (light), made in Kulmbach, West Germany. It's 13.2 percent alcohol. On the other hand, I don't feel too badly about having missed this treat because this is also the world's most expensive beer, costing up to $1.70 for a half-pint bottle.

I do not collect beer cans myself, but this is a growing hobby—with several books out on the subject including a gorgeous $19.95 portrait of 3,400 American beer cans in color (Great Lakes Living Press). It sounds a little kooky, but it's really fun to look at all these cans and try to remember which ones you've actually emptied at one time or another. It's also quite a comment on the deplorable shrinkage of the American beer industry in terms of brands, a subject we will be attending to in this book.

Getting back to frothier matters, I even enjoy the myths of great water making great beer. These are nice romantic legends, at least these days, since all water used for the brewing of beer is chemically treated to remove the impurities, and that's distilled water in your beer whether its Coors, Hamm's, or Olympia.

And, bye the bye, while I'm a trifle sorry to have dispelled this time-honored myth, I'm even sorrier to have missed the First Annual Aluminum Beer and Soda Can Grand Prix, held at the Polytechnic Institute of New York in April 1976, which proved beyond argument that a utilitarian use can be created for empty beer cans. At least that's the rationale for the event in which a Miller beer can equipped with a soldered flywheel came in first, followed closely by a Carling beer can with a rubber band and a lead pendulum. The soda cans—they were hardly in the race.

Next year I'll be there for sure. . . .

Bob Abel
New York City
April 1976

A display of beer bottle labels from some of the author's favorite foreign brews. One does not notice how attractive such labels can be when the distraction of the beer inside is present. Collage by Ian Smith.

# 2/A Frothy History of Suds

*"Wine, beer, or mead—which came first?*

IN THE BEGINNING, things happened. Man ate. Man drank. And, being MAN, he knew this was the start of something big. . . .

The origin of alcohol goes back at least two hundred million years, to the late Paleozoic era. By then, as far as science can determine, the materials that its generation requires had all appeared on earth. They include water, plant sugar (or starches) and yeast. . . . The form in which man first discovered alcohol, though a matter of some debate, is less perplexing a question than when the discovery was made. Only three possibilities are seriously regarded as likely. One is fermented fruit juice, or wine. Another is fermented grain, or beer. The third is fermented honey, or mead. Most prehistorians, at least at the moment, are inclined to favor the last.

—*Alcohol: The Neutral Spirit* by Berton Roueché, published in 1960 after first appearing as a series in *The New Yorker*

Wine, beer, or mead—which came first? And does it matter, except to those pedants determined to fix which of the three is man's oldest friend? In the informed, but by no means disinterested, opinion of the United States Brewers Association, which, curiously enough, happens to be the nation's oldest incorporated trade association (and more

on that later), beer has *always* been with us. "It just happened," maintains the association each year in its annual almanac-style report. "The beverage occurred when water, mashed grain and minute yeast cells, floating freely in the air, came in contact. The yeast fermented the infusion—and there was beer. [And light heads!] Possibly even before the first loaf of bread."

In another publication, however, the group partially discounts—though certainly doesn't debunk—the Pre-Bread Theory of Beer History. "Although some authorities feel beer may have preceded bread," writes an unidentified spokesman, "an imaginative historian could well visualize a cave-wife chancing to mash some grain in a bowl of water, possibly as a preliminary to making a loaf of prehistoric bread.

"Other matters may have distracted her—could have been her spouse's impulsive attentions or the children wrestling with an intrusive bear—so the bowl of mashed grain was set aside." Now enter the minute yeast cells, floating in the air.

To continue the scenario to its accidentally brewed conclusion: "Her lord and master, mistaking the beverage for water, dipped a gourd into the liquid, tasted it, found it good, and from then on the only problem was for the cave-wife to remember how she had first solved the happy mystery." Of course, being a liberated cave-wife, she soon solved that problem, and mankind had taken a giant step toward its first beer distributorship.

Regardless of its place and cave of origin, a fondness for

beer was soon enough geographically impressive, encompassing these ancient peoples: The Babylonians, Assyrians, Egyptians, Hebrews, African Negro and white Berber races, the Chinese, Incas, Teutons, Saxons, and tribes of Trans-Caucasia. Those free-floating yeast cells sure got around.

Logistics aside, what is perhaps the earliest known usage of beer is affirmed by a series of well-preserved Babylonian tablets that indicate beer was being brewed—and sixteen different types!—in Mesopotamia, the ancient country lying between the Euphrates and Tigris Rivers and noted for its great cities of Babylon and Ninevah (today roughly the center strip of Iraq), as long ago as 6,000 B.C. For that matter, archeologists digging some years ago among the ruins of Ninevah uncovered an Assyrian tablet listing beer among the staples and provisions taken aboard the Ark. Since Noah's account of the Great Flood is regarded as the beginning of recorded history, the translation is especially fascinating. "For our food, I slaughtered sheep and oxen, day by day," the translation runs, "with beer and brandy, oil and water, I filled large jars." Now we *know* that Noah was given to much tippling—"And he planted a vineyard, and he drank of the wine, and was drunken" (*Genesis*)—but his being a beer drinker is news. As one English scholar of beer drinking has sagely pointed out about the Assyrian source: "It seems legitimate to infer from this passage either that Noah was himself a brewer and distiller, or that the liquor trade was already in being before the Deluge."

Good liquor is one of the noblest treasures that Nature in her wisdom has throughout countless ages laid up for the use and happiness of mankind. The evolution of the barley corn and the hop has taken no less than that of man himself. Nature did not keep him waiting. When he was ready for them they were there.

Only the unimaginative can fail to appreciate the blessings that the bounteous fruitfulness of the earth

yields. Such strange people distrust or hate many of the best things, and by their wrong-headed machinations have made them less generally available than they should be.

They credit the existence of luxuries to Satan—with whose affairs they are surprisingly familiar—rather than to a gracious providence. They are doubtless convinced that no fermentable juice lay within the fruit that grew in Eden!

> —Sermon on The Sauce introducing *The Romance of Brewing* by Stanley Strong, privately printed and circulated in 1951

By Mr. Strong's revisionist thinking, it was neither the apple—nor fermented apple juice—that got things shaky in the Garden of Eden. On a less proselytizing plain, to be sure, Berton Roueché, in his information-packed little book, points out that "formal agriculture, whose introduction importantly characterizes the New Stone Age, may have sprung from a desire to assure a regular supply of alcohol." While the use of fermented beverages, including beer, was definitely known among preagricultural peoples, he observes, "no instances are recorded of agricultural societies to which its existence was (or is) unknown." All but three of the many Stone Age cultures that have survived into modern times have demonstrated "an indigenous familiarity with alcohol," according to Roueché, identifying the three sobersides as follows: "the environmentally underprivileged polar peoples; the intellectually stunted Australian aborigines, and the comparably lackluster primitives of Tierra del Fuego [an archipelago at the extreme southern tip of South America]."

Since the shrouds of time—always a convenient rationale for what one doesn't know for a fact—cloak the precise origins of beer, let us content ourselves with the fact that the earliest known written records mention brewing would seem to prove that beer was considered evidence of man's progress toward civilization—not to speak of the civilizing effect one presumes it had on man. As Mr. Roueché indicates, beer may well have been brewed before bread was baked. But to get ourselves away from the shifting sandbars of scientific speculation and onto the more solid turf of history, put most simply, we *know* that beer has been brewed ever since man stopped being a nomadic hunter and wanderer and settled down to farming and growing grain. And it was in the so-called twin cradles of civilization, Mesopotamia and Egypt, both areas rich in cereal grains and both rich in archaeological evidence of brewing, that brewing entered its Golden Oldie stage.

However, before our learning all that is to be learned there—which is considerable—it might be useful, given the world view of beer presented earlier, to examine some of what is known about other ancient cultures. For example, we know that Noah was definitely a vintner (and an occasional wino), and possibly both a distiller and brewer, but were the Hebrews, given their strong moral and religious indoctrination, really beer drinkers? While there is mention of *sicera* in the Old Testament, a Hebrew word later translated as "strong drink" in the King James version of the Bible, some authorities believe that this is the same Egyptian barley wine described by Herodotus, the fifth century, B.C., Greek historian. This theory holds that when the Israelites departed that unpromising land, they brought from Egypt the knowledge of brewing *sicera*. However, it is simply unclear whether or not the descendants of Noah and Ham and Abraham really made beer—*sicera* may have been any alcoholic beverage, other than wine, made from grain, honey, or fruit.

What *is* known is that the Hebrews were making *sicera* shortly after the exodus from Egypt. For example, it is written in *Leviticus* that the priests are forbidden to con-

sume either wine or "strong drink" before they go into the tabernacle, and the term is also used in the *Book of Numbers* and always distinguished from wine. When William Tyndale, who did the first English translation of the Bible, translated a certain passage from *Numbers* dealing with priests of the tabernacle, he did so as follows: "They shall drink neither wyn ne sydyr."

A highly educated man, Tyndale was anxious to bring public attention to the decline of the church and corruption among the clergy, but found "that there was no place to do it in all englonde." Rather than let his work perish, he first published abroad, and his translation, while later greatly admired in England, was sometimes known as "The Cider Bible" because of that "wyn ne sydyr" passage. Later scholars, perhaps suspecting Tyndale of a chauvinistic translation on behalf of English cider—to this day there are cider pubs in England—also perhaps dealt in compromise themselves in opting for the "strong drink" translation of *sicera*. Indeed, Rabbinical tradition dating from centuries before the birth of the English language teaches that the Jews were safe from leprosy during their captivity in Babylon due to their drinking "*siceram veprium, id est, ex lupulis confectum.*" That's a Latin translation, of course, but it refers to *sicera* with hops—which doesn't sound much like "sydyr," doth it? Also doth not sound like sound medical theory.

The two essays in this treatise introduce a new meaning to the word "leaven" of the Exodus, as defined by a technicalist on fermentation who has studied the Oriental leavens in the country of the Exodus. . . . The contention raised is that the substance now rendered as "that which is leavened" (Exodus XII 19) was in reality the Hebrew beer, a substance resembling the present Arab bread-beer Boosa, a fermented and eatable paste of the consistency of mustard, and that the corresponding word, "nothing leavened," in verse 20, was an eatable malt product, probably cakes sweetened by malt. . . . I adduce reasons to show that the manufacture of beer was the earliest art of primitive man; an art exceeding in antiquity that of the potter or of the wine maker, and certainly that of the baker.

—Preface to *The Beer of the Bible*, subtitled (*One of the Leavens of Exodus*), written by James Death, "Formerly of the Cairo Brewery," and published in England in 1887

In Mr. Death's arcane, almost impenetrable, book he makes the argument that the ancient Hebrew term *machmetzech*—"something leavened or fermented—literally, what causes to ferment"—refers to an edible form of "leaven" that was the beer of the Hebrews. He points out that the Mosaic Command pertaining to the "week of unleavened bread" (Passover) specifically ordained abstinence from both leavened bread or any other leavened substance. This latter, he concludes, would include "beer of a pasty consistency"—i.e., his theoretical "beer of the Bible." He puts forth both technical and etymological explanations to support his theory and concludes "that Moses, in referring to the varieties of leaven, specifically mentioned the Hebrew beer. The ancient *Machmetzeth* corresponded to the *Boosa,* 'the beer leaven' of the Arabs of the present day, as differentiated from *Seor,* stale dough, or *Chametz,* leavened bread; as such it is the only specific and distinct Biblical mention of beer." Then, in a somewhat leavening gesture to the reader he observes: "It likewise affords the earliest precedent of teetotalism, if such it can be called."

Having been leavened—or was it unleavened?—by Death's passages, we may as well remain among the English-speaking peoples for a bit more. No one can say, with the same assurance that Mr. Death displays (and why not, with that name—e.g., "This is Death speaking"), how far back in antiquity one would have to travel in an H. G. Wellsian time machine to locate the origins of beer in the British Isles, but the existence of barley in England as early as 3,000 B.C. has been substantiated by archeological research. Scientific examination of handmade pottery of that era has revealed impressions—small dents, really—made by kernels of cultivated barley that must have been accidentally imbedded in the surface of the clay. Then, although the firing of the clay destroyed the actual kernel, its impression was committed to history. Where those early chaps got their barley of course remains a mystery, although such British barley experts as E. S. Beaven and H. A. Hunter—considered international authorities on the subject of barley and its properties and peregrinations—believe that British-cultivated barley had its origins in Egypt or perhaps even further east, and the knowledge of how to cultivate the grain spread across the continent to England over a period of two to three thousand years. So it's hardly inconceivable that there were ale drinkers in England—since the knowledge of how to make alcoholic drink from grain has always accompanied the growing of that grain—at the same time those barleycorns were sneaking into that pottery. (To be continued.)

# 3/The Super Pub Crawl: Myth and Metaphor

The concept of the pub crawl, one must surely suspect, is as ancient as the institution of the pub itself, or at least goes back to the first time two pubs enjoyed enough proximity to enjoy shared patronage also—that is, to inspire one to remove his belly from a particular bar to a similar location at another. London, in my estimation, is the center of the universe when it comes to pub crawling—Dublin ranking second only because while the drinkers are grand, the pubs aren't. However, the finest single boulevard offering a self-contained pub crawl (you do have to cross the street, so watch out for cars and other pub crawlers) is Edinburgh's Rose Street. While not so famous as the magical "Royal Mile" stretching from the Castle to Holyrood Palace, Rose Street is much beloved by generations of college students as the "Amber Mile." I am told that Rose Street once boasted forty or more pubs, and while their numbers have been diminished by time and business vicissitudes, it's still fine pub country. From the Abbotsford, dominated by an imposing dark wooden "island bar," to the renovated Cottars Howff—a smart-looking modern pub with an agricultural motif—to the quietly stated eighteenth century Scott's, Rose Street provides a goodly number of locales to whet your appetite for drinking in comfortable and interesting surroundings.

The pub crawl, then, it is agreed, is a worthy activity with everything to recommend it except the possibility of a hangover. The Super Pub Crawl, however, is a very recent institution—and I *think* that I may have invented it. And,

well, I right now am trying to give it—or else acquire for it—institutional status.

The Super Pub Crawl involves dedication and considerable endurance. It costs money—sometimes as much for transportation as for liquid sustenance. It presumes a plan of action agreed upon by all parties. And it requires reasonably liberal drinking laws, which makes it a mite tough to accomplish in London, with its 11:00 P.M. closing hours, or Edinburgh (10:00, folks) or even Dublin, where the ongoing love affair between the Irishman and his Guinness must endure a temporary divorcing of the ways each night at 11:30.

On the other hand, the Super Pub Crawl offers more than a night on the town. It should provide, if properly constructed and diligently executed, a kind of tour of a city. Indeed, between conception and consumption lies the need for planning—if all the places visited are too much alike, it's a less-than-super pub crawl. That's why all the Super Pub Crawls presented in this book represent hours of presunset planning in addition to even more of predawn drinking. What is needed is clarity of vision—at least until two-three-four in the morning.

A few simple rules do exist. When possible, stick to beer on draft because it's likely to be fresher than the bottled brews, which may have been sitting around too long in the back of the bar and have become stale. Draft or bottled, sample as many different beers as possible. That's part of the fun. Another part of the fun is to explore as much of a

Cartoon by Herbert Goldberg.

"What fools *you* mortals be!"

given city as is feasible and still have a good time. Anyone can drink their way around a neighborhood—so don't muck around with the grand design of the Super Pub Crawl.

A final note of advice: if you're in a place, and you like that place, stay there. You can always start at the next stop the next night out. In any case, it goes against the grain to even imply that the Super Pub Crawl limits your freedom of choice.

There is one limitation, though. You cannot be driving a car, motorcycle, bicycle, or even a scooter during these evening-long outings. He who drives and drinks may literally end up crawling.

(Oh, yes . . . although every effort has been made to make these reports as up-to-date as publication time would allow, we cannot be responsible for the ravages of urban renewal. It was there when we said it was there. As for prices, we will only cite them—as in Jacob Wirth's in Boston and McSorley's in New York—when they somehow, miraculously, beautifully have withstood the ravages of inflation, time, and proprietary greed.)

# 4/The Super Pub Crawl: Manhattan West

The first Super Pub Crawl of record occurred in the mid-1960s, the occasion being the visit from London of a close friend, Richard Gilbert. Then a producer for BBC Radio, and of course a cultured man, he naturally inquired about the status of several citadels of Manhattan civilization he'd visited on his last trip to the Colonies. Being by disposition a perfect host, I could hardly fail to accompany him as he set out one evening to revisit past haunts and haunt some new premises. And thus, without fanfare and—that time—too much expenditure on cab fare, was the Super Pub Crawl created by man—and not out of necessity because in this case pure, raw, unadulterated pleasure was the mother of invention.

That first historic occasion, we started out on Manhattan's Upper West Side, where I live, worked our way southward to the Village, headed east to the East Village, then north via a route of singles bars and other refreshment stands. Once the East 86th Street-Yorkville section had been investigated, we headed homeward—not before, however, the obligatory nightcap had been consumed. In self-defense, we decided to end the evening at a spot nice 'n close to home, one of Manhattan's many ersatz imitations of an English pub. Actually, it's an okay place—but the only stop of the evening not made with great selectivity.

Since we drank mostly beer and remembered to eat at some point in the journey, we had rather a terrific time, one to be fondly remembered. As I recall, we set forth around 7:30 P.M. and rolled home at half-four, as they say in England. We'd spent a few bucks but nothing horrend-

ous, and fortunately I didn't have to work the next day. But more important still—and fortunately for all beer-drinking mankind—the vistas of the plain, ordinary pub crawl had been expanded if not for all time, then at least for the next few future generations. We will, under duress, be modest.

That night, in effect, we'd made a kind of lopsided rectangular trek through the city, but the next time my peerless pub-crawling friend arrived on these shores, we decided to eliminate the East Village bars, which had changed, for the worst, as the hippie scene itself did. Alas, that aspect of the Manhattan Super Pub Crawl wasn't the only one to have changed—New York cab fares had begun their climb to their present unpleasant altitudes after years of sweet reasonableness. Then, too, from 7:30 in the evening till 4:30 in the morning is the equivalent of a helluva long work day, and while Manhattan is a skinny island, it's also a long one. So we decided to geographically divide Manhattan—as does Fifth Avenue—into two drinking zones, and that made our evening's activities more feasible in terms of fiscal outlay, not to speak of physical resources. Also, to always look for the most positive side of compromise, it made for two nifty nights of explorative drinking.

East side, West side, all around the town . . . the Manhattan Super Pub Crawl (West Side Division), as now formally constituted, begins in early evening at the West End Cafe at 2911 Broadway near 113th Street, which is both a college bar (Columbia) and a neighborhood hangout. It's

Dublin's The Long Hall is probably the most glorious example of a Victorian-style pub in all of Ireland. Fine wood and glass, a rare pendulum clock and original paintings by Jack Butler Yeats, father of poet William Butler Yeats, all contribute great atmosphere to this 200-year-old pub. Formerly a macho fortress, The Long Hall now tolerates the female sex.

been described as "a collegiate greasy spoon with an amazingly heterogenous clientele" and part of this heterogenousness is provided by the professional students who frequent the West End, those who never bother to graduate and those who do but stick around for years. Dylan Thomas drank at the West End—one wonders how many New York bars Dylan Thomas *didn't* drink at—but such literary figures as the late Jack Kerouac and poet Allen Ginsberg were the for-real famous regulars.

Situated among the bookstores, clothing boutiques, head shops, and other kinds of retail establishments that provide about as much of a university environment as can be found in New York City, the West End now has a room for jazz, but we'll be there too early for the music, and anyway the place has a tendency to get unpleasantly crowded later in the evening. I perfer to sit at the large oval bar with its gaslights and crossed beams, but the booths on either side of the bar are pleasant enough, too, and well situated for people watching. There are also newer rooms to the rear and side—kind of hodgepodge recreations of an earlier era—but the West End remains for me the front room with its interesting-looking habitues and the feel of a hip, big city bar. There's been a depressing tendency in New York in recent years—beer mugs with ever-higher false bottoms and ever-higher prices—but the West End serves a pretty generous glass of Budweiser at a decent price. Still, the last time I visited there, I overheard a bearded charter member of the Beat Generation lecturing some foreign students on how outrageous the price of beer is at the old West End. O tempora, o inflation!

Okay, exit the West End, cross Broadway to the east side, and then head downtown for a couple of blocks to the Gold Rail, surely the premier student hostel in all Gotham. Close your eyes, and you're in a German beer hall; open them again, and you're in the midst of a logjam of students—and a much younger crowd than at the West

End. I will not risk charges of sexism by pointing out that almost all the females to be found at the Gold Rail are coeds from Barnard but will be content to point out that coeds are sometimes also pretty ladies. Probably more important in the ultimate scheme of things is the pleasant fact that you can buy beer—Schaefer light or dark—by the pitcher here, and it's a big pitcher and one of the best buys in town. Since you're going to be at the Gold Rail before the downtown charge of the entire Columbia football team, by themselves or with dates, you can doubtlessly find a booth and have a pitcher of beer, preferably the dark since it's not sold that way in bottles or cans. This offer of advice will not be repeated at any other refueling stop.

Having left the Gold Rail and an empty pitcher of beer, we recross Broadway and catch a bus (more pleasant than the subway) down Broadway. Our destination is Hanratty's, a place that is admirable for its ability to attract a genuine cross-section of humanity from what is New York's most mixed, diverse neighborhood—the Upper West Side. Hanratty's exists across from the giant West Side urban redevelopment project, which has seen brownstones renovated on the side streets and giant high-rises sprouting up on Columbus and Amsterdam Avenues over the past decade, and it is a truly integrated neighborhood bar—surely one of the most together places in the city.

To get there, we have to pop off the bus at Broadway and Ninety-sixth Street, then walk one block east to Amsterdam Avenue. Hook a right, and there's Hanratty's with its red sign. Generations ago this was a speakeasy and when Prohibition ended, a popular chop-and-ale house. But it had deteriorated into a sad old Irish bar when Bradford Swett, a thirty-five-year-old realtor, took it over in 1970. Today the only resemblance between the old Hanratty's and the present swinging bar and restaurant (no singles swinging, but busy swinging) is the name.

The handsome old bar still has its three large mirrors,

but the addition of a large winerack gives it less of a period look. It was originally painted black, but Swett had it sanded down to the natural wood and then given a rich stain. The original inlaid wooden floor also received a high polish, but otherwise the decor at Hanratty's is Upper West Side Eclectic. Six futuristic lamps resembling a cross between a World War II soldier's helmet and a hair dryer descend over the bar area from the high metal ceiling. There are antique clocks in the restaurant area, contemporary posters, framed photographic prints. No attempt has been made to make Hanratty's a smart place or to render it into a pubby New York bar—some Manhattan watering holes have more pub decor than anything that ever existed in London—but it has a good pub feel, because people who know each other have come to Hanratty's for its relaxed atmosphere. In addition to Bass Ale and Löwenbräu plus domestic beers on tap, Hanratty's has the usual complement of bottled beers. Friends and I have found the draft foreign beers to be uneven, and generally play it safe—and save a little money in the process—by drinking the bottled Heineken. That is, you save money if you're planning to stay the evening.

We don't—not *this* evening—so grab a cab, your first of the night. Our next port of call will be in one of the most rapidly changing neighborhoods in the city—Columbus Avenue in the west sixties and seventies. Just a few years ago this was a pretty depressing boulevard, but now a string of bars, restaurants, boutiques, and a new antique shop every other day extends up the avenue from the Lincoln Center area to West Seventy-ninth Street and beyond. My favorite bar-restaurant (terrific hamburgers) of the several attractive places to choose among is O'Neal Bros. at 269 Columbus Avenue between Seventy-second and Seventy-third Streets, one of three Lincoln-Center-vicinity places owned by actor Patrick O'Neal and his brother, Michael. Since we're probably at O'Neal's to drink, I suggest

we stay in the strongly masculine barroom (please don't step on the backgammon players), but if it's too crowded there, try for a table in the glassed-in sidewalk cafe in front rather than in the two rather ordinary rooms next to the bar. Because of its location, O'Neal's plays host to both the neighborhood and professional types, and indeed, its waitresses are usually highly decorative specimens of the perky creature known as out-of-work actresses. But don't spend all your time ogling the waitresses. Ogle everyone—that's the New York way.

The draft beer is good here, and there's more than a decent selection—Schlitz Light and Dark, Whitbread, Watney, Heineken, and Rheingold—and if your coveting has encouraged an appetite, remember the hamburgers. It's going to be a long haul down the West Side of Manhattan, and you'll need to take food before too long.

The other two O'Neal establishments to the south both have something to recommend them, but the popularity of The Ginger Man as a chic restaurant makes it a poor choice for a bar. But do take a look in—after strolling down Columbus to West Sixty-fourth Street—because The Ginger Man, named after the famous J. P. Donleavy novel (Patrick O'Neal played in a dramatized version of the novel off-Broadway) is a very handsome place that, ironically enough, is *not* a restored old bar. In its other life, it was a garage.

Given the likelihood that there'll be no room here—and besides the food has been quite unpredictable of late, apart from it's being pricey—proceed to Broadway and go south to the third O'Neal namesake, O'Neal's Baloon, at 48 West Sixty-third Street across from Lincoln Center. The Baloon was originally known as O'Neal's Saloon, but due to a quirky post-Prohibition law, O'Neal's had to change the initial S in *Saloon* in late 1967 when the State Liquor Authority, citing the 1934 law, ruled that "a saloon operation is repugnant to the purpose and intent" of the state liquor law. This stirred up a semantic contretemps, with attorneys for O'Neal's arguing that while "saloon" may have long ago denoted a place where gambling, prostitution, and other vices flourished, the word especially as now utilized in New York denotes a drinking place "frequented by moderately wealthy persons of excellent education interested in literature and the arts." Carrying the argument to the doorstep of O'Neal's Saloon itself, William H. Kahn, one of the saloon's attorneys, pointed out that the establishment is patronized largely by operagoers and other esthetes who pursue the arts in Lincoln Center. For that matter, he continued, most of the personnel employed by the center—also patrons of O'Neal's—are college graduates working toward artistic careers.

The State Liquor Authority (SLA) remained unmoved by these arguments, and O'Neal's Baloon was the silly result of just one letter in the sign being replaced. If, as one wag observed, the O'Neals had wanted to really irritate the SLA, there were quite a number of avenues for expression: O'Neal's Quadroon, Octoroon, or Walloon—definite ethnic overtones there—O'Neal's Poltroon; O'Neal's Pantaloon; O'Neal's Frigatoon; and, best one yet, O'Neal's Spitoon.

However, we're here to have a beer, not to wax linguistic, so if the population looks reasonably civilized—it gets absurdly jammed when the shows at Lincoln Center break—by all means drop in and either head for the bar (which I prefer) or else one of the tables in the long glassed-in gallery looking out on Lincoln Center.

To be candid, this Cape Canaveral of culture is not exactly my idea of an architectural triumph, but the spectacle at night of lights and white marble and swirls of people around the illuminated electronically controlled fountain is the kind of urban treat that caused cities to be formed in the first place. So have a beer—Ballantine, Michelob, and Heineken on draft—and enjoy the saloony ambience at the bar of O'Neal's Baloon and the nocturnal light show at Lincoln Center across the way.

Thus far, to recapitulate, we've gone back to college, practiced togetherness with the Upper West Siders, did some pretty people watching, and have drunk in a real New York sight. Now it's time for theater, as if the things we've been doing weren't theatric. Now we're cabbing down to the theater district, and we have to make up our minds which of several intriguing options we're going to give the cab driver as an address. There's the Haymarket, where the kids in the theater go after the show; ditto Jimmy Ray's. There's Barrymore's Pub, very "in" these days. There's also Downey's, a good bar where the Irish coffee is about as authentic as you're going to get in town, but the whole fun here is to do a celebrity march down the aisle and hope that people will wonder who you are. Not our style tonight—we've no time for hijinks *and* histrionics. We could of course just say, "To hell with The Theater! The Theater is dead!" and go sit in a high-backed chair in the lobby of the Algonquin and pretend we're visiting literati. But we may not be dressed for that. Then, too, there's Artist & Writers—known as Bleeck's to anyone who knows—which used to somehow mix some of the Metropolitan Opera crowd and nearly all the reporters and editors of the New York *Herald Tribune,* plus Walt Kelly of *Pogo* fame, John Lardner, and similar world class-drinking artists, but the Met has moved to Lincoln Center and the *Trib* to the valley of dead newspapers, and Bleeck's (the name of a former owner, pronounced Blake's) may be just a little subdued for us, given our mood, at this hour. On any other pubbing venture, I'd say don't miss it; it's part German ratheskeller, part old-time saloon, and both parts are just fine with me ordinarily. But tonight it's unfortunately too far off the path we're beating.

Well, now that we've played "Twenty Questions," let's have the answers. Soon the theaters will be letting out and just as the Baloon can be obnoxious when the Lincoln Center culture sprawl comes across the street, some of the theater area bars don't become just crowded, they become impenetrable. As leader of the group, I am going to risk all and pick "None of the above"—we're going to Joe Allen's, which is ridiculously popular. Not for dinner, mind you, because you have to have a reservation, but surely there'll still be room at the bar and/or at a table alongside. Joe Allen's (326 West Forty-sixth Street) is located on the south side of New York's prettiest restaurant block, between Eighth and Ninth avenues. Still, when you enter the place you may well wonder, "What's the fuss?" Allen's was probably one of the first bare brick-wall jobs in Manhattan, but now that type of decor has become a cliché, which is hardly Allen's fault. A nice feature is the arch work between the bar and larger restaurant to the left, and the quiet decoration consists mainly of framed photographs of theater and sports luminaries. What is indisputable is that Allen's, despite the competition, remains *the* actor's bar in the city. As proof of this, it has spawned branches in Los Angeles and Paris so that wandering or relocated New Yorkers in films, TV, or theater may feel at home. Allen's also has a very well supplied bar, as regards draft beer: Carlsberg, Heineken, Würzburger, Bass, and one domestic beer (Stegmaier) from Wilkes-Barre, Pennsylvania. Good stuff, too.

My first visit to Allen's, I dazzled a friend by indicating a man dining alone in the corner (it was early evening) and saying "Look, there's Harold Prince." I was right, only because I'd once interviewed the famous producer-director. But Allen's is good turf for this kind of celebrity gazing so long as you're cool as they are about it. For that matter, some of the most attractive people here aren't of the celebrity class (not yet), and there's a definite mood of mutual interests and camaraderie. Despite its special New York role, Joe Allen's is, well, I don't see friendly being an overused word.

Time to make tracks to another outpost for the theater crowd, but in this case, mostly people who go to the theater. Two blocks to the west—you can walk it easily enough, although I should point out that it's a bit desolate en route—is the Landmark Tavern at the corner of Forty-sixth Street and Eleventh Avenue. It's situated in a cute little old red building that the wreckers have somehow missed, and is a model for the most tasteful renovation I've yet seen in the city. If we've not eaten by now, no more avoiding the necessary solid part of our crawl; let's sit down in front by the windows or else head for the wonderful back room with its pot belly stove and order a fat hamburger, Irish stew (terrific Irish soda bread comes with this), or something. Hopefully that won't be the case, as I would prefer us to sit at the bar. The bronze plate by the entrance dates the Landmark back to 1868, but an art expert has placed the current aura, if you will, as being closer to 1910. Fine with me. The barroom's a beauty, however old. Mirrors, tin ceiling, dark wooden divider between the bar itself and the dining area in front, with a shelf so you can lean and drink, two sensationally elegant cash registers, a 1930s radio, and oh, yes, what is surely one of the best old mahogany bars in New York. The Landmark is so pleasant to contemplate that even the men's room is worth a visit, whether you need one or not. Also, beer by the pitcher, if you need one—only makes sense if we're eating; otherwise, good-sized steins of Michelob, Ballantine, or Rheingold.

Now, no choice but to hail a cab as we're so far west we're practically in New Jersey. We tell the driver to take us to the Corner Bistro at 33 West Fourth Street, and we hope he knows the one-way streets of Greenwich Village. As we head there, we feel some slight pain at bypassing the White Horse Tavern, scene of our youth in New York, but it hasn't been what is used to be—namely, *the* great Village bar—for what seems like a generation. The Bistro, it's fair to say, succeeded the Horse as the best West Village bar and happily has remained out of the guidebooks. It's a neighborhood bar, and this is surely one of Manhattan's or America's, for that matter, most interesting neighborhoods. It's also a bohemian bar if you can accept the premise of middle-class bohemians. Anyhow, starving artists don't live in the Village anymore because they can't afford the cost of drinks much less the rents.

As a former Villager, I feel as much at home in the Bistro as anywhere in the Village. I still enjoy a stay at Chumley's because it looks exactly like the speakeasy it used to be, as well as for its by-now-ordained 1920s Village literary atmosphere, and I really like the Bells of Hell on West Thirteenth Street because it's as friendly as any Dublin pub; and I know a lot of the regulars—also there's good song here at night. But the Bistro gives me a sense of permanence in Village living. I once declined to move to a far superior apartment on West Fifteenth Street because it was beyond Village borders—in this case, West Fourteenth Street—and I know that some of the Bistro people feel the same lovely inane way.

The Bistro first came into very local prominence when the White Horse became a subway car full of Fordam student-pilgrims and visitors looking for the ghost of Dylan Thomas. But the Bistro never gets *that* jammed. For one thing, sitting down is best accomplished in the back room, and there aren't that many booths there. Also, it has suffered not ever being in fashion in marvelous style. This is a stand-up bar, the conversation's almost guaranteed, and the beer—Rheingold, Ballantine Ale, Schlitz Light or Dark—tastes as good as it's supposed to.

One reason, I guess, that I admire the Bistro is that the Village has always had a kind of volatile bar scene. The San Remo, the Riviera, the Kettle of Fish, Louis' (Looie's to those who went there hunting for chicks), Julius' (a lovely nineteenth-century bar that's now quite gay)—they all had their bright flaming passage across the Village scene. The Riviera is now once again very successful be-

"*I was drinking the one beer to have when you're having more than one.*"

"Gin Lane" engraving after William Hogarth.

Gin became the national drink in England—and the national obsession—during the notorious "Gin Age."

cause of its Sheridan Square location and tourist appeal, but the regulars are long since elsewhere. Accordingly, one doesn't talk about a Village bar anymore as though it's an institution.

Which brings me, however clumsily, to the subject of the Lion's Head, which is almost certainly the most renowned Village bar these days. When my wife and I lived at the corner of Hudson and Charles, a very nice man named Leon Seidel opened a neat little restaurant next door. It was the most relaxed of places, and if at first he had only a wine license, there was always the White Horse for a drink before or later. Then Leon moved the place to Sheridan Square. We moved, too, not long thereafter, to the Upper West Side, to our first semispacious apartment after a year or more of looking for same in the area, and the Lion's Head was soon on its way to becoming a famous writers' pub. Actually, despite the visitations of Norman Mailer and Jimmy Breslin and others, it has always been a haven for struggling writers and *Village Voice* people (the *Voice* was then practically next door) and New York *Post* sportswriters. If you were a regular, it was a great place, and Joe Flaherty in 1968 wrote: "The Lion's Head in Greenwich Village is one of the few existing patches of Thurberesque terrain where one can escape the god-awful decency of one's wife and home. With its wood-paneled walls and mahogany colored liquid, it combines the best dark security aspects of the womb and the coffin. The tenor of the conversation is baritone. In this troubled world, the talk at the Lion's Head is usually about sports."

Given these lyrically Irish metaphors, who is to argue that the Lion's Head isn't a great place? *I* am. I think that unless you know some of the regulars in the barroom, you may as well be next door in the dining room, which is perfectly fine, but it isn't the Lion's Head we're talking about. I can hardly fault the Lion's Head for having become something of a private club (Leon Seidel died in 1969, after having been one of the best guys imaginable in fighting to preserve the character of Greenwich Village) almost from the beginning, but I'm judging it as an outsider, not a member of that club. Still and all, like Mount Everest, the Lion's Head is *there,* so we ought to drop in and see what transpires for the irregulars. Follow West Fourth Street to Sheridan Square and then cross over to 59 Christopher.

The bartenders are nothing if not friendly. Archie Mulligan, one of the presiding Village bartenders, doesn't really look like an aging Archie of the comic strips, as a friend has suggested, and anyway, he's far more competent than that Archie. There is one piece of notable decor—the carved lion's head that once adorned a 1908 insurance building in Newark. But otherwise, the bar is a room of no distinction, nor does it try to be. If these guys wanted creature comfort, they'd be somewhere else.

If you're standing up front, don't get in the way of the dart game (seemingly always in action), but it's okay, and some fun, to watch. To properly enjoy the Lion's Head, though, you *should* try to get into a conversation; then, if you're talking sports, try to get out of it. The beer, it should be said, is lovely—Guinness (served with some care), Watney, Prior Dark (my favorite beer on the East coast), and wonderful McSorley's Ale (more on this a bit later), plus Heineken in bottles. So why am I complaining? I guess it's because there used to be an easy familiarity between regulars and strangers at the White Horse that isn't as dependable here. The bar area here is smaller, to be fair, and I'm sure a lot of people have come here expecting something wonderful that didn't happen. 'Tis a burden of Village bars.

In any case, it has to be across the street for us, now, to Jimmy Day's, because our tour is not over (by far), and this is the home base, a longtime Village resident assures me, of everyone who has given up on the perimeter forts used by Village residents to keep out the outside world. Certainly Jimmy Day's fans aren't keeping out the outside

world when they're cloistered around the large oval bar with its kind of strange but fascinating superstructure, watching the Knicks or Rangers struggle yet again on cable television. But the rest of the time this is a very civilized Village bar with amenities for everyone: pretty ambitious menu (including large portions), plenty of room on either side of the bar, (try for the sidewalk cafe side), and good beer on draft—Bass, Carlsberg, Schmidt's (Philadelphia), Pabst, McSorley's Ale. It's beginning to be a bit perversely disheartening to find McSorley's good ale available other than at McSorley's, but such is the price of fame.

I sure as hell hope fame doesn't happen to Jimmy Day's, which seems to have the right corner location to be inviting to lots of people for a long time. It's smack in the heart of the Village, is large enough to embrace a loyal clientele without their being ousted by outsiders, and seems to have a special charm. For that matter, let's hire a leprechaun to do a number on Jimmy Day's (I'm sure you can find them under "Jobs Wanted, Freelance Leprechaun" in the New York *Times* employment section) so that it'll remain the lively but comfortable bar it now is. That's a romantic notion, I know, but the most popular Village bars can't really avoid the outside world because it's the Village, you see—one of the reasons to visit New York—and if we can put a charm over the place for a decade or two, what's the harm?

However, lest we seem to be avoiding the temporal and the excitement of "now" New York, let's exit smiling and hail a cab to our last Manhattan West neighborhood, Soho (for south of Houston)—home of the artists' lofts, new shops, new restaurants, new bars, new everything except trees. Despite all the new huzzah about this area, it remains ugly as hell. Interesting, but ugly. Some people like to think of Soho as the new Village, a conceit that requires ignoring the fact that the Village is physically a very attractive area of the city, and Soho is attractive because of what is going on there, not because of its grim streets and former industrial buildings now taken over by artists and writers and whoever else gravitates to new bohemias. We will be there at night, though, and Soho is exciting at night, with gallery openings, busy restaurants, and roaring bars. The area's relatively instant celebrity has put loft space at a premium, but that sure doesn't keep the artists and their friends home at night. So see Soho as a sophisticated visitor, and ignore all the press agentry. It's a must place to visit, but you wouldn't want to live there.

Technically Soho is both east and west New York, so let's try to stay west. No problem there. At least I think there's no problem there, because the geography gets a little confusing down here. In any case, let's try for Berry's, 180 Spring Street at Thompson, which is primarily a restaurant but has such a pretty old mahogany bar that it's worth a try. If it's open, and we can get in—if it's open, it's also crowded—there's Watney and Dinkelacker (made in Stuttgart) on draft, and let's hope the crowd isn't so inside-Soho we feel like outsiders. Even if that's the scene you find there, don't blame the owners. Come back another time because Berry's is a good restaurant and shouldn't be measured by the after-dinner crowdiness.

In any case, our penultimate destination is the Broome Street Bar on the corner of Broome Street and West Broad-way. (Ask directions, it's very close.) The decor is Middle-Late Soho—a lot of blackboards and a lot of everything else—the feeling is funky, and the atmosphere is at least as interesting as its London counterpart. (Actually *that* Soho was bohemian, but never artistic.) This is an artists' bar, and the voices are international, and the excitement is real. Even at this hour, we may have to fight for a place to enjoy the McSorley's, Stegmaier Dark, Heineken, and Pabst on draft, but if it's a fight they want, it's a fight they won't get because we can always stand and have our nightcap. On principle, I entirely disapprove of vertical drinking, especially at this late hour, but the Broome Street should not be missed. It has that tingle of energy—not noise, but energy—that people who really dig a place give to that place. It's not enough reason to move to Soho, but it's a thought.

Now the only painful part of the evening, hopefully. Whatever its geography, Soho is out of the way unless you happen to live there. So we must seek out a cab once again. Still, as you see the meter chug-a-lugging its way toward the national debt, don't get morose. You've *lived* as few mortals have lived. If you're corny, you can even tell your grandchildren about it. Just make sure to give them the right directions, in case I'm not available to do so. . . .

*"Hek,"* said the Ancient Egyptian petulantly.

Immediately his retainer brought him a beaker of beer.

This drink would not have tasted like any kind of modern beer, for there were no hops in Egypt to give the fermented barley the distinctive bitter taste of beer. It would have been more like sweet ale, also made from barley, but without the addition of hops. But the method used five thousand years ago, of moulding barley into a kind of malt, and then fermenting it, has not basically changed since. The means of brewing, not brewing itself, has become more sophisticated. . . .

*Hek* continued to be drunk in Egypt for centuries, and existed until comparatively modern times, under the slightly altered name of *hemki*. Even at the end of the last century, a traveller on the Nile recorded that he saw the crew of a ship make an intoxicating liquor from barley and water. The name of this concoction was, the traveller declared, *boozer*.

—from *Beer is Best,* a very pleasant history of beer published in Britain a few years ago. The author is John Watney, of the famous brewing family, and he knows his *hek, hemki,* ale, best bitter, etc.

Despite Mr. Watney's perhaps optimistic appraisal of what that ancient Egyptian beer would have tasted like—it was even then, by the way, also known as *boozah*—there is little doubt that most beers of antiquity would not delight the modern palate (hell, it takes most Americans some time to get used to British beer) because of such peculiar additives as powdered eggshells, crab claws or oyster shells, tartar salts, wormwood seeds, and horehound juice. It seems much safer to presume a modern congeniality toward the wines the Greeks and Romans guzzled rather than for the beers the Egyptians and Babylonians and others quaffed. Palatability aside, however, demand depended upon supply, and in those countries where grapes were plentiful, wine to be sure was (and is) the preferred drink. So at least one historical pattern becomes clear as a dry martini: People who drank, which takes in most folks, naturally brewed or fermented what was in most abundance among the potable raw materials of their soil. Thus, in terms of Europe, at least, beer, despite its attributes as a thirst quencher, has been less popular in the warm, southern countries than in the northern ones (England, Holland, Belgium, Germany, Denmark), which became great brewing centers once barley was available—possibly via those wide-ranging traders, the Phoenicians. That this should be so has far more to do with agreeable soil and climate than it has to do with the respective merits of beer and wine.

For example, the ancient Chinese weren't into wine because they weren't into grapes. However, they regarded their own version of beer as an exotic form of drink and no ordinary staple of their diet. Reports differ on what went into it (originally it may have been fermented millet alone), but by the sixth century B.C., the brew was two parts millet (a seed now sold as a treat for parakeets) to one part rice, heated in clay vessels over a controlled fire, to which was added wheat flour to provide yeast and aromatic plants to add flavor. In all, a sophisticated brew. The *Shi-King* and *Shu-King*—historical records of China's early history dating back more than 3,200 years ago—mention the beer known as *kiu* but do not detail the method for brewing it. What *is* recorded, however, is that it was "yellow and sparkling" and, as is the case today, doubtlessly went well with Chinese food.

Actually, the primitive brewing process was so simple that anyone could have learned it at a glance. In the case of the Egyptians, grain was moistened with water and allowed to stand until it began to germinate, at which time it was dried and ground into a coarse malt. The malt was then steeped in a vat of hot water and yeasted with sour bread dough. When fermentation had taken place, and the yeast had converted the grain sugars into alcohol, the foaming beer was then strained off into jugs.

By the same basic process, beer has been brewed since the dawn of thirst by peoples from the southern tip of Africa to the Arctic Circle. Yeasts and cereals varied according to climate, however. In Africa, the fermentation of native millet beers is still induced by means of milkwood and fermented roots. In the *Kalevala*, the ancient folk epic of the Finns [the *Kalevala* is of enormous antiquity, existing for nearly three thousand years before it was ever put into writing], the saga of the search for yeast is told in the same iambic pentameter as Longfellow's *Hiawatha*:

Courtesy of New York Public Library, Picture Collection.

"What will bring the effervescence,
Who will add the needed factor,
That the beer will foam and sparkle,
May ferment and be delightful?"

—delicious, effervescent article by William Iverson, entitled "Keg O' My Heart," that graced the pages of *Playboy* over a decade ago

Lest you feel it's unfair to leave those thirsty Finns of yore with a flat beer, be assured that their cause was just and their thirst quenched. To quote Mr. Iverson a bit further on in the brewing process: With a mythological assist from Kapo, "snowy virgin of the Northland," the old brewess tries adding ripe pine cones and foam from the mouths of angry bears, with no success. Finally honey is tried, and the beer begins to ferment, "Foaming higher, higher, higher . . . / Overflowing all the cauldrons." [Like bees to honey] the heroes of the Northland swarmed in from all points on the compass, and why not—for this heroic brew was a veritable wonder drug:

> Said to make the feeble hardy,
> Famed to dry the tears of women,
> Famed to cheer the broken-hearted,
> Make the aged young and supple,
> Make the timid brave and mighty,
> Make the brave men even braver,
> Fill the heart with joy and gladness,
> Fill the mind with wisdom sayings,
> Fill the tongue with ancient legends. . . .

Quietly mentioned in the bubbly narrative above is "the old brewess," which is probably no fiction since women, not men, brewed these most ancient of brews. Another nice old Mesopotamian clay tablet—this one written in Sumerian and Akkadian around the fourth or fifth century B.C., but even more intriguing because it reproduced material of more than 1,500 years earlier—reveals that not only was brewing a highly respected profession more than twenty centuries before the birth of Christ, but that women were the master brewers and, because beer had highly religious associations, temple priestesses as well. This was the case until 2,100 B.C., when that male chauvinist king, Hammurabi himself, replaced the women brewers, called *sabitum*, with menfolk. The king, author of the world's oldest set of codified laws, allowed women to continue manning the *Bit-Sakari* (the taverns or taprooms) of his kingdom but imposed strict laws not only upon the manufacture of beer but also upon its sale. Patrons of these Babylonian taprooms drank on trust—that is, they ran a tab—until the end of the harvest season, when they settled up their bill with payments of corn rather than coin. If the female tavern-keeper were found cheating on a patron's bill or accepting less corn than the bill required (because the patron looked like Omar Sharif) or asking for coin instead of corn, she was given a rapid dunking in the nearest body of water. This was no casual punishment, the length of the dunking depending only on the woman's ability to breathe indefinitely under water. No less severe was the punishment for a lapsed priestess found running a tavern or just stepping a lapsed foot into one. In this case, the element of punishment required that the guilty party be able to breathe indefinitely under earth. Bury them alive or drown them until dead—old Hammurabi didn't kid around. It wasn't all laughs, though. A tavern-keeper named either Ku-Bau or Azag-Bau, apparently the prototype for all barmaids who have married well, founded a royal dynasty at Kish in 3,100 B.C.

Still, enough sexist digressions. Returning to this valuable old tablet, irregular in shape and reddish-brown in color—now part of the permanent collection of Manhattan's Metropolitan Museum of Art—it is one of twenty-three such tablets that collectively form a kind of encyclopedia of the times. From them we learn that the Babylonians had learned a good deal about the science of brewing. For example, not only did they prepare malt from barley, but it seems likely that they actually developed strains of yeast for fermentation purposes. Moreover, they provided the antecedent for the utilization of the by-products of the brewing process, which today are a vital economic factor in the manufacture of beer. In other words, just as brewers' yeast is now used as a human nutrient and a supplement to livestock foodstuffs and pet food, and the enriched grains—particles of barley, corn, rice, whatever, which remain after their starch-sugars have been extracted in the brewing process—are returned to the farmer as high-protein feed for his livestock, so, too, was the mash from Babylonian beer used for fattening cattle. But this was hardly the end of it: The brewers produced breadlike cakes from their byproducts, and the temple overseers often paid their workmen with these cakes—a case of bread being not only the staff of life but the stuff of full employment.

As must be obvious by now, separation of church and state was not exactly a working concept in these parts, and brewing, while nominally a secular profession, was irrevocably brought into the spiritual side of things. Thus, as early as 3,400 B.C. the god Anu was used to getting four kinds of beer sent his celestial way via the temple of Uruk, the older neighbor of the more famous temple of Ur. On the distaff side, the goddess Siris was the patron saint, as it were, of beer, but by some sly human manipulation, she was ruled obsolete—made redundant, as the British say— and replaced by a doubtlessly nubile and more attractive goddess named Ninkasi. None of these ecclesiastical hijinks, however, affected the supply of beer for the average mortal, and it's impressive to learn from the ancient tablets that not only wasn't all the good beer reserved for temple ceremonies, but that there was a constant variety of brews as well. It may be that the following categories of beer include the temple brands as well, but workmen and other citizens got to enjoy a dark beer, pale beer, something called *three-fold beer,* beer with a head, and beer without a head. (If you're not impressed with this, try to name six different types of beer produced in America!)

Before moving westward ho! for ancient Egypt, the other Mission Control Center for beer in those days, let us pause to pay homage to one of the real "class broads" of all time, Queen Shu-bad of Mesopotamia herself, who topped the local practice of sipping beer through a straw or reed by using a golden straw long enough to reach from her throne to a large container of beer located in friendly proximity. One of her golden straws was unearthed in re-

cent years and can now be admired at the University of Pennsylvania Museum.

The actual grains of barley floated on top of the bowls [vats of barley wine (beer) stored by the ancient Armenians in underground buildings against the winter], level with the brim, and in the bowls there were reeds of various sizes and without joints in them. When one was thirsty, one was meant to take a reed and suck the wine into one's mouth. It was a very strong wine and, when one got used to it, it was a very pleasant drink.

—Xenophon (435-354 B.C.), Greek historian, military commander and natural-born admirer of traditional wine, writing in *Anabasis* about what may have been the first large drink-in

The great King Amasis himself, observed Sir Wallis Budge, a distinguished British Egyptologist in one of his writings, "is said to have been very humorous in his cups, as he not seldom was." Such was the privilege of royalty, because the sages and priests of ancient Egypt constantly admonished against insobriety.

If thou wilt control thine appetite, thou wilt be listened to; if, having eaten three loaves and drunk two pitchers of beer, thy belly is not full, then thou must fight against it.

—Tuauf, a stern moralist, writing 5,000 years ago

For literally thousands of years, the efforts of scolds such as Tuauf were of small consequence because beer was not only the national drink in Egypt, it was tantamount to a national religion. Beer, as everyone knew, had been invented by the sun god Rā and was most assuredly enjoyed by the patroness of brewing, the goddess Isis. Meaning no irreverence, but quite the opposite, Egyptian artists depicted the gods as getting celestially smashed on the temple brews offered them in supplication. Ramses II had offered 500,000 gallons of wine annually to his subjects as a gesture of goodwill, but his son, Ramses III, was apparently more concerned with goodwill later on than in the here-and-now because he donated 30,000 gallons a year from his royal brewery to the gods. The temple inscriptions attesting to his largess proclaim that he had in his lifetime invoked the goodwill of the gods to the tune of 466,303 gallon jugs of beer, but it is not recorded whether or not the bribe took.

> The King in heaven eats the bread that Rā eats daily, and he drinks what Rā drinks. The bread that he eats never grows stale, for it is the Bread of Eternity; his beer never grows sour, for it is the Beer of Everlastingness.
>
> —Egyptian text, period unknown, perhaps the first reference to eternal shelf life

Far more than any of the other ancient cultures, the Egyptians recorded the big love affair with beer—with temple paintings and carvings, papyri and hieroglyphics—that pervaded their daily life. Everyone drank beer and there was a place for everyone to do so. Royalty and persons of financial and/or social substance had their own private brewhouses whereas persons of ordinary substance collected at the House of Beer establishments which marked the landscape like so many MacDonalds. All this beer, to be sure, was consumed strictly for refreshment purposes, but beer was also a food-beverage. Instead of packing a lunch for their kids in the temple school, Egyptian mothers dropped off a daily allowance of three loaves of bread and two jugs of beer.

In charge of the quality of the nation's beer was an appointed official, the "superintendent of breweries," but more indicative of the high status of beer was its role in many areas of daily life. Beer was accepted as a token for binding official negotiations and for sealing treaties. Instead of an engagement ring, a young man gave a maiden a measure of his beer, and they were betrothed. Beer was accorded wide medicinal powers, and the *Ebers Papyrus*, the famous medical textbook of circa 1600 B.C., included one hundred prescriptions, among the seven hundred listed, which contained beer. Not only was it regarded as a reliable laxative and a cure for the sting of scorpions, but half an onion in the froth of beer was recommended as "a delightful remedy against death."

> Here's beer for your ghost.
>
> —favorite toast of the time

That beer was big business in Egyptian life has been documented by relics and sculpture and mural-drawings not unlike our modern comic strips. But while women did the "donkey work" of stirring the barley mash and preparing the beer, they did so under the authority of the master brewers, who were joined in a kind of guild or craft union, if you will. However, by the age of the Ptolemies—the dynasty of Macedonian kings, who were established by Alexander the Great and ruled from 323-30 B.C.—there was no dispute between Big Government and Big Labor as to who made the beer industry hop. Both the production of beer and its retail sale were under the control of the king.

He supplied the barley for brewing, he took the profits from the beer trade, and he had his own royal accountants handle the books. And when he decided that the lower classes were drinking too much for their own (and his) good, the number of Houses of Beer was sharply reduced. Meanwhile, the royal household, ever an epicurean lot, now got soused on wine instead of on the common beverage.

> . . . persons intoxicated with wine pass out lying on their faces, while those drunk with beer invariably lie on their backs.
>
> —Aristotle, not being philosophical for a change

Although the Egyptians were not famed for being merchants as were the Phoenicians, they maintained a highly active beer trade, and the port city of Pelusium near the mouth of the Nile became known for its shipments of beer to the furthest outposts of the Pharaoh's empire. In 1,000 B.C. the Pharaoh Necho dispatched ships and navigators down the continental coast to explore the rest of Africa, and these seafarers, who sailed around the Cape of Good Hope, could conceivably have introduced the art of brewing to the black Africans. This is, of course, sheer conjecture, but it is more than likely that those tribes which worked their way from the equator to the southern tip of the continent may have learned, or else been influenced by, the Egyptian methods of brewing. Of even more certainty: that the Ethiopians, invaded by the Egyptians with some regularity, were taught how to brew by their conquerors. In terms of documentation, we have learned much about the fabled Queen of Sheba, who ruled Ethiopia around 950 B.C., from the *Kebra Nagast*, the ancient holy work of that land, and her acquaintance with beer was no passing fancy, as they used to say.

Whether or not the Greeks and Romans, both of whom at certain periods of history included Egypt and environs among their empires, gained their knowledge of brewing there is difficult to say. Probably not. The Romans may have learned about brewing beer from either the Greeks or the Egyptians, but both the Greeks and the Teutons were of Aryan stock, and both may well have gained their knowledge of brewing from their original home in central Asia. Regarded as a "wine of barley"—actually it was a blend of wheat, barley, and honey—the earliest Greek beer was called *pinon*, and the Thracian brews made in the northeast section of the country earned praise from such rugged critics as Herodotus, the eminent Greek historian of the fifth century B.C., and Pliny the Elder, the first-century Roman scholar, historian, and naturalist, who was not given to heaping praise on alcoholic beverages.

> The whole world is addicted to drunkenness; the perverted ingenuity of man has given to water the power of intoxicating where wine is not procurable. Western nations intoxicate themselves by means of moistened grain.
>
> —Pliny the Elder

While neither the Greeks nor the Romans came to prefer beer to wine, a countryman of ours named David L. MacIntosh, who wrote a treatise entitled "A Beer View of History" a few decades ago, takes issue with any view of beer as moral pollutant. Quite the opposite. After declaring the Assyrians, Chaldeans (an ancient Semitic people who ruled Babylonia), and Babylonians "barbarous types" who indulged in "abominable atrocities impossible to a people mellowed by good beer," MacIntosh posits that they "were consumers of liquids fully as potent as bath-tub gin and that they scorned the mild effects of beer." As for other genuine beer-loving peoples, the Medes (from Media, the northwestern part of present-day Iran) and Persians "were vastly superior to the people in the city-states south of them. Later they lost their old virtues and adopted elegant and effete Oriental manners and vices." In translation, I believe this means they stopped drinking beer. And what dire destiny befell them as a result?

> It was then that the Greeks, nurtured on brews they had learned about from the Egyptians, showed that a handful of indomitable beer drinkers could overcome the greatest of empires when it had forsaken the contents of the brewing-vasts for exotic and befuddling liquors. In their beer drinking heyday the Persians were invincible, but they succumbed to the inebriate habits of the nations they conquered.

And Mr. MacIntosh is either stubborn or facetious as he sticks to his historical last:

> Originally beer played such a prominent part in their lives, and so many virtues had been ascribed to its use, that in later centuries it was known as MEAD, an evident corruption of MEDE. I am aware that this derivation is not accepted by all etymologists, but who cares?

Is Mr. MacIntosh putting us on? Is his treatise a send up, as the British would say? Perhaps he is writing with beer in mouth as well as tongue in his cheek, because his beer theory of history certainly doesn't stop with the MEADS.

> The Greeks likewise acquired a taste for strange and potent drinks, and when their desire for beer departed, so did "the glory that was Greece." Alexander the Great, had he never been tempted from his boyhood brews by the deadly concoctions of the Persians, would in all probability have added India and China to his conquests instead of dying a drunkard's death at thirty-three.

So it goes.

—Kurt Vonnegut, Jr.

Mr. MacIntosh, who affords us amusement if not enlightenment—Alexander died of a fever, not of cirrhosis of the liver—conveniently drops his central thesis, somewhere between Carthage and Gaul when he considers the Romans, then picks it up again with the ferocious Teutonic races—"beer-swiggers notable for their love of liberty . . . the progenitors of our own colonial settlers." Despite the inconsistency of his goosed-step through history—the Romans didn't pay enough attention to beer and were defeated by the Teutonic swiggers who did little else—he is correct when he exempts the Romans from the beer-loving legions. True, Roman troops did take beer as well as wine with them in their various conquests, and true, Julius Caesar did toast the troops with beer when they crossed the Rubicon. But it is far more likely that beer was considered suitable only for the enlisted men and that Caesar and the other brass drank wine whenever the choice was theirs. Not surprisingly, however, since so many of our words are Latin derivatives, there is general agreement among language authorities that the English word *beer* may safely be traced back, with an etymological stop-off at the High Germanic *bior*, to the Latin verb, *bibere*, meaning "to drink"—which is a terrific generic compliment. *Bibero, ergo sum* is not a famous saying, but who knows what a marvelously bad joke it may have been in its day?

A *Deutscher* and his beer are seldom separated.

# 6/Milwaukee: The Beer (and Brandy) Capital of the United States

(Ray Puechner [pronounced Peekner] is one of two friends I have who double as literary agents and authors. As noted elsewhere, Ray was once one of the wonderful Chicago cranks who harassed Manhattan publishers for their nasty habit of sending rejection slips instead of checks. But those days of open combat are behind him. He has matured, if not mellowed. Widely published in magazines, he is also the author of several books, including a very funny and original collection entitled—are you ready?—*The LSD & Sex & Censorship & Vietnam Cookbook*. He should have won a Pulitzer Prize for that title alone.

Ray now lives in Milwaukee, his home town, and runs his agency. He still writes about as much as before, which makes for a busy life. I thank him for taking time out to write something for a friend.)

For truly colossal figures, however, one must inspect per capita brandy consumption. Wisconsin consumed 422.8 fifths for every 100 citizens last year—more than the next three states combined. Runnerup Nevada tossed off a modest 173.6 fifths; Minnesota 173.5. California, which produces about three-quarters of all the brandy consumed in the nation, drank a miserly 70 fifths per 100 people.

—"A Spirited Look at our Brandymania" by Don Oleson, a December 21, 1975, article in the Milwaukee *Journal*'s Sunday magazine

Milwaukee is a neighborhood tavern town. In some areas there may be as many as six taverns within two square blocks in a residential area. Chances are, no matter where you are in the city of Milwaukee, you don't have to walk more than two blocks to the neighborhood bar.

The taverns are nearly all known by the names of the proprietors: Ray and Vi's, John and Ellie's, etc. The regulars report as faithfully as they report to work. It's a ritual. Most sit and drink tap beer in twelve-ounce glasses. Pabst, Blatz, Schlitz, and Miller are the most common beers on tap.

Chances are the owners live behind the tavern, that there's a dog wandering around, maybe a couple of kids too. Behind the bar, along with the usual racks of potato chips and pretzels, will be some obscene-looking sausages floating in liquids, which people eat; maybe a basket of hard boiled eggs, too. Very often there's an old Nesco roaster, or a small grill, for roast beef or hamburgers. Many Milwaukee bars serve some kind of food.

Customers, mostly blue collar workers, and mostly men, unwind by drinking brandy and beer. This is one fact which distinguishes a Milwaukee drinker from nearly all others—the boilermaker here is brandy and beer, not whiskey. The preferred brandy is Coronet, a mild grape brandy. Ask for it any other place in the country and see where it gets you. Something like eighty percent of sales of Coronet are in the state of Wisconsin and about ninety percent of that in Milwaukee County.

Once, in Clearwater Beach, Florida, I watched a guy

When the Civil War began, Milwaukee was in good shape for it—one saloon for every ninety-five adults. Each outpost of civilization had its loyal clientele, as witness this band of derby hatters *(above)* lined up outside the institution known as The Cannibal's Rendevous. This forlorn-looking young man *(right)* was a "bucket boy"—he rushed back and forth to the nearest saloons to make sure that none of the folks who worked for his company would suffer from a parched throat. Today's steel companies provide no such amenities.

order Coronet and beer. The bartender didn't know what Coronet was. The drinker settled for Christian Brothers from a dusty bottle on the back shelf. I asked the guy if he was from Milwaukee. "No," he said. "Menomonee Falls." I almost hit him—Menomonee Falls is a suburb.

Some of the old-timers might have wine and a glass of beer or peppermint schnapps and a glass of beer. The peppermint schnapps is really like a cordial; few people outside this area, however, know of it.

Most bars have a pool table, and 8 Ball is the game. Here, though, the rule often is: one and three. Instead of shooting the eight ball straight in, it must be played by banking it once or using three banks on the cue ball.

Dartball—baseball played with darts—is popular. Many taverns have leagues, as for pool players. Even churches have dartball leagues, and there'll be beer on tap there, too.

In summer some bars will sponsor softball teams. It's a good excuse to drink beer before and after (and sometimes during) a game.

You don't just drop into neighborhood bars; you belong. And you don't ask for mixed drinks there. A mixed drink in a neighborhood bar is brandy and sweet soda or brandy and water or whisky and sour. Order a Manhattan or Martini, and they'll tell you to take a walk.

Friday nights many of the neighborhood taverns serve fish fries, another peculiarly Milwaukeean practice. The whole family comes. Pike, perch, or haddock will be the fish of the day, and they'll be a lot of it for about $1.50. All over town.

The neighborhood bar here two blocks away, the Ritz Bar, has a modest reputation for good, inexpensive food. On Friday nights they pack them in for fish fries. During the week, there's food all day: steak sandwiches, half a chicken, shrimp, chili, and things like, ugh, cannonballs. That's what'll be called in, "Give me a cannonball:" if you order raw beef on rye—a cannibal. It's an interesting bar really. They'll mix any drink there, have things like Dortmunder Dab on tap, even bock beer in season. In bottles, practically anything.

There are some super bars in Milwaukee, too, big bars which open at 6 A.M. and run until 2 A.M. The most interesting of these is probably still the National Liquor Mart on the south side. Folks in the neighborhood call it, for some unknown reason, The Synagogue. (Probably some ethnic slur there; it's a Polish neighborhood.) There's also Hooligan's. People on social security can drink all day in those places, also younger drinkers who are on the way down.

At almost every bar, too, they shake dice. It can drive you nuts.

There are a lot of bars where the younger set congregate, like O'Reilly's on North, on the east side. They drink a lot of beer there, too; and since the drinking age in Wisconsin was reduced to eighteen, fewer kids drive out to beer bars and get drunk. They stay in town and get drunk, still mainly on beer. It's cheaper.

Beer, when you get down to it, is part of the social scene. At company picnics, church picnics, art fairs, and ball games, ponies and half-barrels are on tap. Beer and bratwurst. Beer and bowling. Beer and baseball.

It's cheaper to buy a case of beer than a case of soda water. And the many beer depots here will deliver free of charge.

And if you're a dedicated beer fan, you can tour Pabst, Schlitz, and Miller breweries here and get free beer at the end of the tour.

Beer, it probably did make Milwaukee famous.

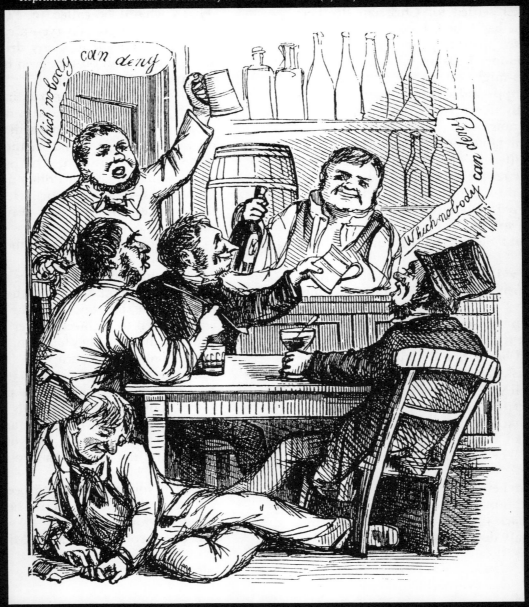

Reprinted from Bill Wannan's *Folklore of the Australian Pub* (Sydney: Macmillan Co., 1972), p. 129.

# 7/A Frothy History of Suds

*". . . It was the custom during German beer-brawls . . . for the contestants not to leave the table. . . ."*

The Romans, who—like the Greeks—believed their culture superior to all others in the known world, brought their political and social systems to the lands they conquered, but geographic considerations plus local custom prevented any wholesale transplant of Roman life. In any case, the Roman conquerors may have added nothing to local brewing knowledge simply because the peoples of what are now Spain and southern France and the Celtic people, including the Britons and the Gauls and other ancient peoples of western and central Europe, already had their breweries stoked. In point of fact, although the Egyptians may have had some knowledge of hops as a brewing adjunct, it was the brewers of primitive Spain—*Hispania* to the Romans—who are first credited with having brewed beer that would keep for some time, and it may have been a knowledge of hops, garnered from Africa via the Moors, that allowed them to help preserve their beer. Pliny the Elder, who apparently tried to write about everything in the known world, gave *caelia* and *cerea* as the names for the brews concocted by the aborigines of Spain. However, the Latin name for beer, *cerevisia,*—which meant *gift of Ceres*, Goddess of Corn—came to dominate because *cerveza* is today the name for beer in Spain and Mexico and *cerveja* in Portugal. According to Pliny, who wrote more than once on "the exquisite ingenuity of mankind in gratifying their vicious appetites," corn was used in many lands in making beer—"All the nations who inhabit the west of Europe have a liquor with which they intoxicate themselves, made of corn and water." But this is a matter of some dispute.

Kourmi, made from barley and often drunk instead of wine, produces headaches, is a compound of bad juices, and does harm to the muscles. A similar drink may be produced from wheat, as in Western Spain and as in Britain.

—Dioscorides, a Greek physician, writing in the first century, A.D.

Despite his abstemious lifestyle, Pliny, who had served in the army in Germany—he was colonel of his calvary regiment, no less—must have had a stein or two of beer during his time there if only because it would have been hard to avoid. Beer, or ale, was the national drink of the various Germanic tribes, and they drank it daily and in awesome quantities. Tacitus, the Roman historian much admired by Pliny, also observed the Teutonic tribes at first hand—he lived there for sixteen years—and he recorded that they would drink for a day and a night and would settle their drunken quarrels not by "mere hard words, but more often by blows and wounds." This knowledge led the great Roman to suggest a line of military diplomacy whereby Germanic vice would lead to Roman victories: "You have only to indulge their intemperance by supplying all they crave, and you will gain as easy a victory through their vices as through your own arms." He was wrong. The Romans won some victories against the Germanic hordes—Caesar, in Gaul, drove two invading German tribes back across the Rhine—but in the fifth century Attila, the "Scourge of God," brought his Huns in from Asia and united the Teutonic tribes under his banner, and his 'ale 'n hearty warriors, sobered up for battle, proved more than a match for the sophisticated Roman legions. He lost the siege of Orleans to the combined armies of the Romans and the Visigoths and retreated to Hungary. But in 452 he drove into Italy, devastating everything and everyone in his path, and Rome was spared only by the personal mediation of Pope Leo I, who charmed Attila out his warlike ways with large sums of money. After each victory, Attila's Huns and the various other Teutonic warriors would have huge brewings to celebrate their success at war games, and anyone who has visited one of the giant beer halls of Munich during *Oktoberfest* (more on this later) will appreciate the endurance of this tradition. "Drink? Die! Drink not? Die anyhow! Therefore, drink!"—old Bavarian proverb.

Speaking of endurance, it was the custom during German beer-brawls—and it didn't require a military victory to get the boys into a drinking bout—for the contestants not to leave the table, regardless of the demands of nature, during the length of the contest. Since these would last three hours or more, and the gents involved were drinking continuously, this bladder control may be more of a tribute to their endurance and stamina than any feat on the battlefield. The beer they drank was made from both malted and unmalted barley, aromatized by myrrh and flavored with various herbs and even bark and leaves, and a stronger beer was also brewed from wheat and honey. The Germans regarded their "liquid bread" as food as well as drink, and both the words bread and brewing are of German extraction. At some point in history *bior* became *bier*,

and I suppose that the invention of the men's room ("*Herren*") meant that it was okay to relieve one's bladder, but little else has changed as regards the lusty German appetite for their favorite beverage. "Beer that is not drunk had missed its vocation."—Meyer Breslau, from a speech in the Reichstag, 1880.

Through the ages, as we have seen, beer drinking has been put to many purposes, not the least of which was to get very drunk, break heads, and sing as noisily as the human throat would allow. However, there has also been a ceremonial use of beer. The Egyptians used it to seal treaties and bind business deals. The Roman soldier toasted his emperor, and Teutonic warriors toasted their leaders and each other—"*Gesundheit!*" means "Good health!" It wasn't until the seventeenth century that the toast got that name, as a result of the practice of dipping a piece of warmed bread into wine to improve its flavor, but the custom goes back thousands of years to when nomadic tribesmen, celebrating a fine kill, saluted each other with their local brew. Of all the ancient peoples of premedieval Europe, the Saxons of northern Germany were surely the toasting fools of all time since a Saxon warrior would demonstrate his great affection for his *schatzie* by drawing a dagger across his forehead, allowing the blood to drip into his cup, and then drinking the fortified brew. Almost needless to add, this could be a hard act to follow if the fellow's lady-love required constant reaffirmation of his love.

Nowhere, however, did the toast become the beer drinker's delight more than in the ancient lands of Scandinavia, where the Norsemen measured a man's prowess by his skill with the sword and battle-axe and his ability to down giant silver-banded drinking horns containing as much as a gallon of ale—malt brews were called both *ol* and *biorr*—without end and sometimes without coming up for air. To the Norseman, whose daily food requirements included six meals, each accompanied by a soup of bread and beer, drinking was often an occasion for toasting, and always vice versa. They were given to toasting their departed loved ones, toasting a bountiful harvest, toasting the newly married, toasting the birth of a new Norseman. Any meeting, whether secular or religious, was called an *ale* because that was the obligatory refreshment served and contracts drawn up at an *ale*, whether held in church, the royal court, or the neighborhood beer house, were not only considered completely legal but were believed especially binding on the partying parties involved in the transaction. In fact, "beerhouse testimony" became a part of their legal language and enjoyed, logically enough, considerable weight in any kind of litigation.

No one can really say when these all-purpose drinking customs actually began—Scandinavian culture goes back a very long way—but graves dating back two thousand years or more that were unearthed by archaeologists in Denmark and Sweden contained not only jewel caskets and other personal items but drinking horns and bronze flasks containing traces of their ancient brew. At the living end of this you-*can*-take-it-with-you philosophy was the *grave ale,* naturally—at least in Denmark—where ale was consumed on the spot by the mourners to keep the departed's ghost away. But don't think for a moment that these hearty warriors feared that death would put an end to their beer drinking. No, according to the ancient Norse legends—the reciting of which was also cause for much serious imbibing—any warrior worth his sword and drinking horn could expect to ascend to Valhalla, where the voluptuous Valkyries, Odin's armored maidens, would greet them with ale horns filled to the brim. Heaven, to these Norsemen, was a place to fight and carouse through eternity, drinking ale from the skulls of their enemies—the beer unlimited, and always on the house!

Courtesy of Carlsberg Breweries.

The famous Elephant Gate to the Carlsberg Brewery in Copenhagen bears the motto, *"Laboremus Pro Patria,"* which, translated, says "Let us work for our country." The Danes, an obliging people, regard the consumption of beer as a patriotic activity.

**GENUINELY A PLEASURE**

*Irate Barman:* Can't you find better work than hangin' round here all day
cadgin' for drinks?
*Bill the Blotter:* Work—d'yer call it? It ain't work—it's a 'obby!

# 8/Beer Just South of the Border: A Good Story, Hardly Told

(One of the joys of working in book publishing, which I did for seven hyperkenetic years, is the good people you meet. Gary Blumberg, who contributed this swell piece on Mexican beer, was my author—editors refer to their authors via the possessive pronoun—at two publishing houses and became a close friend. At one point the friendship had to thrive on a long-distance basis, since Gary was living in Mexico for two-plus years, but despite the Mexican telephone system, thrive it did. Gary and I produced four books while he lived there. Since I've never been to Mexico, and his letters from there indicated a rich familiarity with the local brews, I figured the least I could do to exploit the friendship was to force him to write part of my book for me. He didn't seem to mind . . . and his generosity is my section on Mexican beer.)

By any reckoning, the biggest-selling beer in Mexico is Carta Blanca. There are Carta Blanca breweries in every city of consequence throughout the country. In quality and sales volume, it could be compared to Budweiser in the States. It's main selling point is price. They spend tremendous amounts of money on advertising and promotion, right down to decaled folding metal tables and chairs. Soccer players and bullfighters endorse it. Of all the beers which get exported to the States and other countries, Carta leads by far—which, alas, gives the world a false (or at least limited) impression of Mexican beer.

Before the early 1930s, those hearty souls who even ventured into Mexico—a postrevolutionary land of bandits, impassable roads and murderous water—had a standing joke: If the water doesn't kill you, the beer sure will. Then, after Hitler came to power in Germany, a German (don't know if they were Jewish or not) family named Klöster emigrated to Monterrey, Mexico, and founded a brewery. Klöster is one of the best beers available today. Their headquarters remain in Monterrey, Mexico's most industrial city; the original Klöster is dead, and his descendants all bear Mexican surnames. But this was the event which put Mexican beer on the map—it created a new standard and popularity in the country.

Tecate is an unusual beer. It comes only in the can. It is the one beer which, when you order it in a restaurant or bar, is automatically accompanied by a plate containing cut-up limes and a mound of coarse salt. Lime juice is sprinkled around the rim of the can, salt sprinkled on top of it: You drink. It's great. In the hot, coastal regions of the country, Mexicans drink any beer with lime and salt—but Tecate is consumed in this manner anywhere, don't ask me why.

Another big one is Bohemia, brewed in Monterrey by the Klöster folks. It is, in every way, premium. Pour it in a glass, and the head'll stay intact for a half hour. It is available only in bottles. In reputation, I'd compare it to Michelob. In quality, I'd give it ten more stars than Michelob: It's heavy and heady, like the German and Danish beers, rather than light. Mexicans don't like light beer, which is why Carta Blanca is not noted there for quality.

Then, there are the *Equis. Dos* and *Tres,* signified by XX and XXX on the cans or bottles. XXX is stronger and heavier, hovering on eight percent alcohol. XX is standard yellow-amber in color, designated *clara,* while XXX is available in *clara* or *obscura* (an almost chocolate brown like the rare American bock beers). You can almost cut the head with a knife on this latter. *Equis* is how you pronounce the Spanish letter *x,* and this is how you ask for it by name. The *tres equis obscura* is top of the line.

On the regional and local scenes are beers which are hard to obtain outside the regional distribution and which are, for my money, superb. Take Yucateca Negra, from Yucatan, brewed in the capital city of Merida. It is nearly black in color, thick in consistency and very tasty. Outside the region it can cost as much as $5.00 per case—in Mexico, there are twenty-five bottles per case. A major ingredient in this beer is rice; the Yucatecos (people of Yucatan) are Indians. Mayans. Rice plays a large part in their diet and culture. They combine rice with hops and yeast and barley and come up with this fantastic beer. It is *very* heavy and rich.

Another one, along the northern Pacific coast, brewed in Mazatlán, is Del Pacifico. It, too, is heavy and rich, and cheap if bought within the distribution area. Sadly, Mazatlán is a popular spot for gringos, who go right on drinking Carta Blanca because they don't know enough Spanish to read signs or ask for the superior local product.

Note on Klöster: every Christmas season, they come out with their own bock beer, packaged *a la Navidad,* and call it Noche Buena. It's expensive. It's good.

While beer is the workingman's drink in this country, it is not the poor man's drink in Mexico. He can't afford it; inflation, since mid-1973, has skyrocketed beer prices in Mexico. The campesino and peon still drink their home-made raw tequila and pulque, as a liter can be had for as little as 4 pesos ($.32 US). Even cheap Carta Blanca was, when I left Mexico in December 1974, about $1.20 U.S. per six. Beer is for people who work. No Mexican who wants to get a glow buys beer unless he can buy a lot of it. But it is the most popular alcoholic beverage in the country next to tequila.

Beer is consumed early in the morning and throughout the day. It is common to see men drinking *cerveza* (beer) along with their eggs, beans, tortillas, and chili. Alcoholism is number one social disease in Mexico, too.

More than a few Mexican recipes call for beer, especially along the Gulf Coast (Veracruz, Tampico, et al). You can find them in *The Art of Mexican Cooking* by Jan Aaron and Georgine Sachs Salom (Doubleday).

Beer remains the most popular liquid next to milk for washing down hot chili recipes. It serves this function along with the tortilla—a neutralizer, and it works. Only gringos try to cool the hot with water (which makes it agonizingly hotter).

To sum it up, beer in Mexico was poor before the 1930s. The Klöster family brought German methods to Mexico, and Mexican beers now rank among the world's finest. I've talked to Europeans in Guadalajara: Germans, French, what-have-you, as well as Canadians, and they all agreed that Mexican beer eludes international fame only because of the sorely limited export activity on Mexican breweries' parts.

# Tequila & Beer

# 9/The Super Pub Crawl: Manhattan East

Mr. John Modi, who knows how to produce an encyclopedia or completely renovate a kitchen, accompanied me on this pub crawl. He was chosen, out of many, many applicants, several of whom were more nubile than John, because of his wit, intelligence, perspicacity, *and* drinking capacity, plus—and no mean talent—his ability to spot a fine old tin ceiling that hasn't been botched up in the restoration process.

We were on our best behavior because this was, after all, the East Side. Manhattan's much bruited East Side. There is a folk legend on the West Side that the natives there get the bends when they cross Fifth Avenue, but of course this is merely jealousy having a psychosomatic reaction. What is true, however, is that West Siders ask East Siders to produce a passport when they are found sneaking across the border. If they don't have one, or they've left it at home because they haven't been to Europe this year, they are nonetheless graciously received.

Our evening began in an unlikely locale, but east without dispute. A cafe named Fanelli's at 94 Prince Street, which would seem to be a strange choice until you consider the possibility that Fanelli's may be New York's oldest bar. We broached this possibility with one of the owners, and he pointed to a liquor license over the cash register on the back-bar—all dark wood and mirrors, the wooden part reaching up all the way to the tin ceiling—and said, "You see that license over there? That goes back one hundred years, and we was around before that. This bar is about 140 years old." This was, of course, stated with very genuine pride, and one must report immediately that Michael Fanelli runs a fine establishment, oldest in New York or not. (Actually Fraunces Tavern, which was George Washington's headquarters in New York, is probably the oldest surviving establishment to serve drinks, but that's hardly a bar.)

Fanelli's consists of two rooms. One is a cafe back room, and nothing more, and one is a barroom with etched windows in the door, old photographs of prize fighters on the wall opposite the extraordinary old bar, and a tiled floor which belongs very comfortably in this room. There is a serving bar at the end of the room, used for lunch during the day and to support a cluster of drinkers at night. The crowd, and there is a crowd, is part Soho habitant, part warehouse employee, part truck driver, and part old-time resident—from before the local renaissance. Still, while the clientele may be somewhat (and only somewhat) different these days, Fanelli's withstands the fads of fashion in beautiful fashion. Everyone knows the bartenders, and the bartenders know everyone—the distinction is important. Why else would Schaefer and Rheingold remain at thirty cents a shell glass. And nicely served, too, because when we switched to bottled Ballantine Ale, we were given new glasses. Moreover, there seemed to be some kind of ebbtide in the size of the crowd at Fanelli's, but it was always good-natured and good-mannered—when someone jostled you a bit in reaching for a new drink, he or she said, "Ex-

McSorley's Old Ale House, said to be the city's oldest bar, is the subject of a book and was a *cause celebre* for Women's Lib a few years back.

cuse me," which is not so common as one would like to think. One suspects that Fanelli's, having had style for so long, rubs off a little on its customers.

As we left, John said, "You know what this bar reminds me of?" To prove that great minds run along the same beer tap, I responded, "The White Horse in the old days." John nodded, a bit unsettled, naturally, by this latest display of disgusting clairvoyance on my part. But our sensibilities were more than just mutual: long life to Fanelli's.

Our next port of entry was Phebe's, which is at 361 Bowery (Fourth Street), a neighborhood now shared by the winos and the Off-Off-Broadwayites. Walk it or cab it—it's not very far. Phebe's is the oldest of the growing number of places in this area, and remains very popular, very relaxed and very easy-to-take. We weren't ready to eat, so we just looked into the large dining room to the right and behind the bar, and it looked very pleasant. Our pub crawl was still in its infancy, though, and we settled down at the bar and ordered beers. There is Ballantine, ale and dark, plus Heineken on draft, which is a very nifty threesome so far as we were concerned, especially since I worry about the continuing availability of Ballantine Ale since a large company (Falstaff) has taken it over.

The barroom is most attractive, and, in one regard, spectacular. It's a big room, with white-washed walls, theater posters, accoustical tile ceiling and some tasteful light fixtures and spots. What's *imposing* are the giant wine racks on the wall behind the bar, filled not with wine but with booze as well—rye, bourbon, vodka, Lancer's, scotch, red wine, German wine, and everything else which a bar uses. I love to study the bottles on the back-bar in places to surmise what people most order at any bar, but at Phebe's you'd have a hard time doing this because the impression is that everyone drinks everything—in the best Off-Off-Broadway tradition.

Phebe's is best enjoyed before the theaters in the area open and after they close, and since we'd caught half of the performance, John and I voted to exit during intermission curtain and continue our journey uptown to the far reaches of the Upper East Side. Not very far uptown, however, because we were just five minutes away from the legendary McSorley's Old Ale House, which is another contender for most ancient bar in the city—a verified 122 years old.

Just off Third Avenue on the north side of Seventh Street (the Bowery becomes Third Avenue along about here), McSorley's claims not to have changed in all those years, but of course this is not true. Women are now allowed in McSorley's, and John and I both confess to having some mixed feelings about this rite of passage. McSorley's, the subject of a charming book by Joseph Mitchell and of reams of newspaper and magazine copy, used to be reliable for its ale and porter—no hard liquor—the same wonderful memorabilia on the walls, the famous pot-bellied stove, the same tables and chairs, the same cat (or so it seemed), and its all-male ethos, which guaranteed among other things, both quiet conversation and, if you were alone, entrance into a conversation. I've had some good ones here, some nutty ones here, and a few that defy ready categorization. Since the great Female Lib event that unlocked McSorley's doors to them—and I do not for a second disagree with the principle of that event—McSorley's, in the four times I've been there, has been noisier because dating couples make more noise than we stolid drinkers. I wish it were the way it used to be, when Mother Fresh Roasted, a peanut vendor whose husband had died of a lizzard bite during the Spanish-American War was welcomed for an occasional ale, but that was all. The young women—mostly college kids—who come there are often attractive, certainly good-natured when it comes to using the same john as the regulars, and seem to enjoy McSorley's all to hell, but it's not the same, chums, it's simply not the same. A delicate balance between masculinity and civility has been lost. McSorley's was all male, but despite the male college students who congregated there, it remained a gentleman's preserve. No more.

This having been said, in some sweet sorrow, I should add, I would order you not to avoid McSorley's on pain of death. It's still wonderful and old, albeit a bit giddy these days. In 1966 ale and porter were thirty-five cents a stein, now the "daily bargain" offers two for eighty-five cents, which is damned fine progress in terms of inflation. The ale's made by Rheingold, surprisingly enough, and the porter by Stegmaier. There's also India Pale ale, made by Ballantine, in the small seven-ounce bottles. This pale ale is an acquired taste, because it's bitter (English bitter, remember?), but by the second bottle it's either been acquired or else you hate it. And there's Mackeson's Stout, which is fine stuff. John and I hadn't intended to eat yet, but watching everyone munch on thick sandwiches and chomp on Cheddar or Liederkranz, we both ordered a sandwich and some cheese, which is served with crackers, nice thick slices of sweet Bermuda onion and hot mustard—light on the mustard, it's *hot*—and constitutes a small meal by itself. So, if you just want a hearty snack at this hour, stay with the cheese. Contrary to rumor, however, the Liederkranz does not make you "kissing sweet" the whole night long.

It was still early, as Super Pub Crawls go, so we took a walk up Third Avenue seven blocks and stopped in at Lüchow's Bar, which is the first door as you approach the famous German restaurant on Fourteenth Street. This is not a normal fueling stop on a pub crawl, but we wanted some calm after McSorley's, and we wanted to continue the sense of tradition we'd been imbibing, along with India Pale Ale and porter, at McSorley's, so Lüchow's was an estimable choice for this purpose.

To be perfectly candid Lüchow's doesn't swing like it did in recent years, when the former owner Jan Mitchell prided himself on serving thirty-two kinds of beer. But then America is different, and an absolutely huge restaurant like this one has to find ways to survive. But we didn't bring you here for a lecture on restaurant economics, we brought you here for, as John put it, "a nice breather from McSorley's." Lest that not be attraction enough, there's the best Würzburger in town, plus some other well-kept draft beers—the bartender informed us that any beer found flat the morning after is thrown out—and at least ten kinds of bottled beer, all of it either foreign or premium domestic brands. Then, too, while I was mulling my Würzburger in relaxed appreciation John was admiring the room—the terrific German chandeliers, the original nineteenth-century woodwork, the luxuriant sense of space and most of all, the magnificent bar itself. At one end there's a large buffalo's head, and the other the head of a musk-ox, but everything else is European civilization at its best—the numbered wine cabinets beneath the back-bar, the glistening display of glassware of many varieties, plus the liter (1.06 quarts) beer mugs, all along the bar, and the well-preserved wood, all a tribute to the axiom (rendered here for the first time) that what's old and good should stay that way.

John next wanted to go to an old haunt of his, Connelly's, but I had to inform him that some bank has decided the location would be better served by something other than a fine old Irish watering hole and restaurant, and to make amends I told him I'd take him to a place he'd surely never seen. (By the way, I'm reporting only on the places we liked, not the ones we walked in and then walked out of, or else had a beer and left less than enchanted.) He took serious issue with the premise that there was a fine bar on Manhattan Island he hadn't seen, if not visited, but the virtuous are always right, at least this once.

Once upon a year, I worked for a controversial little magazine called *The Realist,* and Paul Krassner, the editor, who never fought with anyone, had kind of a squabble with his wife, with her doing most of the squabbling. Being there and being fond of both of them, I decided that Paul and I should go out for a drink and let some calm settle in behind us. Real man-to-man stuff, you know. Only Paul doesn't drink. Of the two of us, only I drink. Nonetheless, as we were morosely wandering along East Eighteenth Street, we passed a bar, and even if Paul didn't need a drink, *I* did. So we went inside for a beer and Coke or something. The Coke didn't cheer him up, but the bar cheered me up immensely. It was the Old Town at 45 East Eighteenth, and I can only hope this rave review will bring it more business as you have to get there fairly early in the evening or you don't get there at all.

There is nothing extraordinary about the beer here, or the owners apart from the fact that the place has been in the same hands for over ninety years, but the place itself is one of the best-kept (and not intentionally) secrets in New York. John cheered up immediately. One can mourn the loss of bars like Connelly's, but the only grace to be received from that is to try and make sure it doesn't keep happening. He started admiring the loving care that has been given the bar, while I drew his attention to the high-backed wooden booths (highest backs I've ever seen). He countered by saying the back-bar must be one of the largest in the city. I countered by saying the white tile floor was in great shape. He countered—well, we had a very fine counterculture forty minutes or so there. But then the Old Town was closing, and we were headed to Pete's Tavern, the last really old hostel we would visit this evening.

I used to take dates to Pete's—which is at 129 East Eighteenth Street, on very pleasant Irving Place, and about ten/twelve minutes from the Old Town—and my impression then, which hasn't changed over the years, was: great bar, rotten restaurant. As a result, I haven't eaten there in some time, so I may be way-off about the food these days, but happily the bar's still one of the most attractive rooms in the city. In fact, John was in his glory here because the elaborate stamped tin ceiling merited his attention, as did the dark mahogany walls which, he pointed out, were dark

Photograph by Byron, The Byron Collection, Museum of the City of New York.

The bars of yesteryear had handsome exteriors, too, as witness the outside view of Wessel's Saloon, no longer to be found at Madison Avenue and 34th Street but once upon a gentler time the midtown headquarters for admirers of Dortmunder Beer and Carstairs Whiskey.

red before generations of wood stain rendered them just dark. The tin is carried down the wall behind the spacious cash register area, at the end of the bar, of course, and I went over to ask the cashier if the sign above the bar, "Oldest Original Bar in New York City—Opened 1864," meant what it said. A very friendly woman, and not the least bit disputant, she admitted she'd never heard of Fanelli's, but did take exception to the notion that McSorley's had been continuously in operation longer than Pete's. "Maybe the sign should say 'Continuously Operated' rather than 'Original,'" she conceded, "but Pete's has never been closed since the day it opened." Then, showing a little, just a *little*, fire, she went on: "Where was McSorley's during Prohibition? There was a flower shop here during Prohibition—right where you're standing—and you walked through it and then went downstairs to a speakeasy. . . . Tammany Hall was nearby, you know." She was right, of course, about Tammany Hall being close—at Fourteenth Street and Irving Place, as a matter of fact. But I later found out that the customers didn't exactly "go downstairs," hell, they entered through the refrigerator in the flower store and went downstairs to a rathskeller famous for the Tammany Hallers and other political tribesmen it hosted. But she fought the good fight, she did, in her quiet way. Although I still think Fanelli's is older, since it never closed, either.

When I got back to our table, John had noted that the red checkerboard tablecloths, out here, at least, are now plastic, but he also directed my attention to the real old-fashioned Wurlitzer juke box, and that was another plus. Not so the draft beer—only one kind of domestic beer on draft when we were there. But there is Miller, Bud, and Heineken in bottles, and you don't have to be unhappy. Enjoy Pete's—it's not everything it should be, but it's more than most.

The original East Side Super Pub Crawl Plan, as endorsed by the mayor and the Board of Estimate, was to do a bit more on Third Avenue and include Tuesday's—because it used to be Joe King's Rathskeller and still has a lot of the old decor—and Once Upon A Stove, which is as much an antique museum as it is a bar and restaurant. But we vetoed this part of the grand plan because Tuesday's is putting in an absolutely rotten-modern discotheque where generations of college students used to have a ball in most amiable 1920s surroundings, and because this particular night, Once Upon A Stove was already closed. So uptown it was, by cab because neither one of us was about to walk to the nearest Lexington Avenue subway stop.

Charlie Brown's Ale and Chop House, in the Pan Am Building, is (1) not named after the comic strip character, but rather the owner of a Victorian pub still standing in London's Soho, and (2) absolutely uninhabitable during the cocktail hour when executives and the secretaries or other office females they're sleeping with have their post-work tryst. These guys miss more trains than they catch, certainly—the place has been called "A dark hole of the junior executive set, the pleasure dome of finkdom." But by the time we're hitting it, either the guys will have decided to stay in town and are feeling very cozy, or else the singles will have settled in, or else both of the above. And yet Charlie Brown's will be calm and relaxed and interesting enough to merit a stay for a while. Restaurant Associates opened this dashing commuter's bar in the mid-1960s, and it has never dimmed in popularity because it has a captive clientele and is really a pretty fine (not authentic, just handsome) rendition of an English inn, except that no English inn ever had wall-to-wall displays of Victorian sex *behaviour*. We might want something to eat again but not here, and let us content ourselves with one of the English brews at the bar. They're expensive, so one will do. Try Whitbread for a change.

Now, well-rested and restored, especially since we don't have to worry about leaving a pliant female for a late train, we walk uptown a few blocks to the new location for

Costello's at 225 East Forty-fourth Street. The original James Thurber 1930s drawings on eleven beaverboard panels, restored a few years ago, are now framed and hung on the walls, and the shillelagh Hemingway broke over his head to prove what a tough son-of-a-bitch he was to John O'Hara, again hangs over the original bar, itself replanted in this new location, but of course this is now a different bar. I was privileged to know Walt Kelly, creator of *Pogo* and the only giant among contemporary comic strip artists, and he once regaled me with stories of the drinkers on the Costello's-Bleeck's axis, but Walt is gone now, and all those wonderful characters he talked about are also gone now, and Costello's is inhabited mostly by *Daily News* people and a cadre of British and Australian newspapermen. That's all right—if they're there, the place is exceptionally lively, and if they're not, it's a bit of a dreamy, even haunted place. But don't worry—they'll be there when you're there unless there's a subway strike or the earth has opened up.

I am told that the popularity of Costello's lies with its being considered an "Irish pub" by these English and Australian journalists, and if that is so, well, then, we should get over to the Green Derby on Second Avenue and get into an American-Irish pub with Irish waitresses, Irish music, and a young very Irish (still) crowd. The Derby opened in the early 1960s, went through a kind of silly singles stage, and has now (hopefully permanently) returned to its original purpose—being an Irish outpost in America. I have a special fondness for the Derby because they used to have an article of mine framed—a *True* piece about my wife and me in Ireland, where she charmed Irishmen unused to the sight of females in their midst into getting at least very temporarily used to the idea. I don't think it is quite so special now because there has been so much competition in this authentic Irish department (the owners themselves have five other spots in Manhattan). Still, it's Irish, all right, and if we're a mite hungry by

P. I. O. Photos, Ltd., London. Courtesy of Whitbread & Co., Ltd.

now, we could do worse than to have a bite here, and if we're still a mite thirsty, we have a foin choice of potables to handle that problem. However, and I shouldn't be telling you this, the night John and I were there, we had a Beck's or two—'tis German, y'know—instead of Harp, which is Irish and also very good. In any case, our attitude was very Irish: If ye think Beck's be better than Harp, then drink Beck's, ye nit!

Then, because I am a compulsive about the truth, we left the Green Derby and walked over to Clarke's at Third Avenue and Fifty-fifth Street—formerly P. J. Clarke's but minus the P. J. now because of all the competitive P. J.s that sprang up in the 1960s—because to ignore it would be to fink out on the premise of a Super Pub Crawl. I respect Clarke's (but I don't like it) because it looks the way it did when it was just another neighborhood Irish bar in the 1890s. John pointed out that the best part of the decor, actually, is the stained glass covering over the men's room. I respect it also because it serves good beer, especially the Guinness Stout; because the office building behind it was built *behind* it; and because it is sensational for people watching.

On the other hand, I don't much like Clarke's for an equally good list of reasons. Even twenty years ago, Clarke's was slightly ultra-dig among people whose problem was that they were not really ultra-dig, and the trend has not diminished in the interim. So you're watching people you might not care to know, even though as a friend wrote about Clarke's, it's an "Irish bar owned by an Italian and inhabited by the best-looking Protestant and Jewish career girls you'll ever see in one place." This is still true, I cannot deny it, but Clarke's is somehow awfully phoney, too damned crowded, and too expensive for the small glass of very good beer—yes, a terrific selection: McSorley's, Michelob, Whitbread, Heineken, Löwenbräu (Dark and Light), Guinness, and Pilsner Urquell. What to do? Me, and John too, we'd avoid Clarke's if we weren't

doing this tour for you, but if you haven't seen it, you should. It's unique, I fear, and that may be compensation enough.

Slightly depressed, slightly exhausted, and slightly disgruntled, we pondered our next move. It had originally been to go to Friday's—the launching pad for singles bars on First Avenue. But frankly the thought of another overcrowded bar, even if every third female looked like a younger version of Sophia Loren, seemed oppressive. We'd done our share for humanity, hadn't we? We'd been nice, really nice, all night long. And now it was 2:00 A.M., and while we didn't want to go home, we didn't want to do the singles scene, either.

Well, we had to do something, so we did take a cab to Friday's. It wasn't terribly busy at this hour this weekday night so, in good conscience, we could ignore it. And then we stopped off at Maxwell's Plum, which is elegant and famous and terribly successful—normally the bar is seventeen deep—and had an overpriced Michelob there while the bartenders made it perfectly obvious that they wished we'd go away so they could do the same. We were perfectly happy to accommodate them.

It was getting on past the wee hours now, and we had two more stops on the master schedule. However, just up the street from Maxwell's rude delight on First Avenue is a place called Flanagan's, which I seemed to recall is owned by the Green Derby people, so just for a lark we stopped in there to make better plans for the rest of the rapidly shrinking evening. And struck gold. Flanagan's was a veritable Irish feast of live music, dancing, good cheer, and much conviviality at the bar. Moreover, where Maxwell's bartenders had been bored, if not almost nasty, the young bartender here couldn't have been nicer. He served our Bass Ales as though we were his first customers of the evening, and when we switched to Irish whisky for a change of pace, he bought us another round on the house. When we asked him questions, he answered them with friendliness and candor, and we were so busy enjoying the atmosphere at the bar that it was about half-an-hour before we realized that Flanagan's was indeed a singles bar but without the "Hey, look me over!" hysteria that seems to characterize too many bars of this type. So let us *not* label Flanagan's as a singles bar; it's just a fine, friendly bar for creatures of both sexes.

"We made a real discovery," John said, sounding like Columbus, as we left Flanagan's. Yes, we had, and that is part of what the Super Pub Crawl is all about.

The final pub on my list was Gleason's, a very popular singles bar over on York Avenue that should have quieted down to a loud roar at this hour of the evening, but York Avenue is far east. And besides, we'd had some good singles action at Flanagan's, so why risk our luck? In any case, I had several Alternate Selections to choose among, and one of these, Martell's, is the favorite pub of my wife and myself on the East Side. So a cab to Martell's at Eighty-third and Third Avenue seemed the sensible approach to ending the evening on a high note.

Martell's used to be a Yorkville bar when that area was solidly block-to-block German, and when the singles scene first happened, Martell's was among the leading lights of the galaxy, but the competition from downtown proved to be a singular (ahem!) blessing because while Martell's still embraces a dating crowd, it's become a very low-key, relaxed place to eat or have a drink. If you haven't had some sustenance since back at McSorley's, be advised that Martell's hamburgers are among the best. If that's not the case try to sit at the bar, where there's a fascinating magazine rack on the wall that divides the bar area from the tables in the front room with all sorts of odd, interesting publications.

Martell's attracts all types of people, and has been known to host a celebrity in one of the dining rooms or else outside in the glassed-in area, but people don't patronize Martell's in the hopes of seeing anyone other than the people they're with or else meeting there. Since we were ending up our pub crawl, it was only fitting we switch back to beer, and Martell's has a prime selection: Michelob, Carlsberg, Heineken, Budweiser, Whitbread, and Schmidt's. There wasn't time to have one of each, so we opted for Carlsberg, which is always a treat. Then a Whitbread to wash it down.

Can't say we didn't end the night in style. . . .

*". . . Ale consumption in medieval England was in the drunken neighborhood of eight quarts a day."*

Like the Danes and the other marineering marauders who sometimes descended upon them for a spot of mayhem, plunder, and adventure, the Britons of pre-Christian history drank ale, but unlike the Danes they got in their cups only on festive occasions because they were a nomadic people who had yet to settle down and cultivate the land. Their diet was simple—milk and venison—and when they did make a fermented liquor, they used barley, honey, and apples, all of which were accessible to these wandering tribes. Far more popular than ale, however, were *metheglin,* or mead, and cider, since the honey for mead and the wild crab apples for cider were everywhere available. Either drink could be made by the campfire, whereas a regular supply of ale could be possible only when the inhabitants settled down in a particular area and began the practice of agriculture. This occurred first in the southern districts and of course their proximity to Europe would also advance their knowledge of both agriculture and brewing. The wheat they grew was partly used for brewing, honey providing the fermenting agent, and the barley they cultivated and grew was now put to the use it has enjoyed since time immemorial.

Still and all, when Caesar invaded Britain in the middle of the first century A.D., to Roman eyes it must have seemed a primitive place indeed, but during the three hundred and fifty years of their peaceful occupation, population centers gradually developed and hamlets grew into villages and towns. As they had done elsewhere, the Romans built roads connecting these outposts of civilization, and among the first amenities along these roads were *tabernae* (taverns or, to the locals, alehouses), where alcoholic beverages were sold, including three kinds of beer: mild, clear, and Welsh. In Wales itself, ale remained a luxury, especially the spiced ale which was twice as expensive as the common ale and four times as costly as mead. In Scotland, where the wild Picts and Scots resisted any Roman intrusions, the natives drank not their famous whisky, which was just getting started in Ireland, and probably had to content themselves with what one observer has called "their own peculiar mixtures." Ale was not one of these, however, although it seems strange that the Scots, coming from Ireland, did not make it since home-brewed ale was in common use in Ireland during this period. Later on, however, the Scots would more than make up for their late start in the ale sweepstakes.

> Kings may be blest, but Tam was glorious,
> O'er a' ills o' life victorious.
>
> —Robert Burns' *Tam o' Shanter,* in which Tam gets blind, swacked, potted, juiced, and also inebriated

At the start of the fifth century with the Roman Empire crumbling, the troops were called home to help defend Rome herself, and this was the cue for the Anglos, the Saxons, and the Jutes to invade England. Actually the Anglo-

Saxons, as they were later known, were invited in to help take care of the Picts and Scots, who were threatening from the north, but having accomplished this, they decided to stay for a few thousand years. By this time the system of alehouses was well established and could be identified by their ale-stakes, long poles such as those traditionally utilized by the Romans as a shop sign with an evergreen bush hanging from the pole if the establishment also sold wine. The managers of these alehouses—progenitors of the publican—paid rent to the landowner in the form of physical labor and foodstuffs, including a quantity of ale often brewed right on the premises.

If these places hadn't existed, the Anglo-Saxons would surely have built them, because the availability of ale was a matter of no small importance to them, being a large part of their religion and an even more sizable part of their diet. With the Anglo-Saxon takeover, ale became the national drink of England and was consumed at every meal and in such quantities that one estimate of per capita ale consumption in medieval England was in the drunken neighborhood of eight quarts a day. Since brewing ale was the responsibility of the women of the household, it was only seemly that the menfolk take up any slack in the consumption and use of it, and that they did. Beer was a substitute for legal tender, being sometimes used for rents and tolls. As in Scandinavia, the business transacted at an "ale" was entirely legal and, again as in Scandinavia, any excuse for a fraternal drinking bout was not only self-evident but self-sufficient. These were organized, well-attended, highly motivated affairs and if any participant in these heady sessions defaulted (crapped out, as they say), he was fined on the spot in malt, which was quickly converted into more ale so that another intoxicated evening could be planned. This brotherhood in beer was, one must concede, a fail-safe system to avoid staying home with the wife and kiddies.

In Wales, where beer had lagged in popularity because of its costliness, it now assumed such importance that the royal brewer ranked above the royal physician—and little wonder, since the devil was thought to be behind many illnesses and a blending of herbs, religious incantations, and that good strong ale was usually the medicine prescribed for devilish diseases. But when it came to ale for nonmedicinal purposes, no one ranked above the king since he had the right to sample every new cask deemed ready to drink. Moreover, during the great ale orgies at the royal courts throughout England, one drank in the order of one's station at the court, and so the king and queen always got first gulps of the evening's ale. However, since these evenings generally proved to be long, hard, dazed nights, no one was conscious enough at the end to complain about the privileges of rank and royalty.

The earliest fragments of English literature describe convivial ale-drinkings at royal courts. *Beowulf* describes how the hero slays a monster which had been eating King Hrothgar's warriors. Much jollification naturally ensues. Hrothgar's queen, bidding the guests to be merry at the ale-drinking, offers the jewelled drinking-horn to the company in order of precedence. As it passes round, stories of brave deeds are told, "at times a minstrel sings, clear-voiced in Heorot," there is music and social merriment, until at last the tables are cleared away and the hall is turned into a dormitory.

—from "The Story of Beer," an absolutely first-rate series on beer that appeared in Britain's *Geographical* Magazine in 1955

Eventually the Anglo-Saxons, who didn't want to relinquish those pagan beliefs that included an ale-filled heaven, succumbed to the brandishments of Christianity, but if anything this seemed to inspire them to greater performances in this life in order to ensure that they wouldn't go thirsty in the next one. The Church did not smile upon such conspicuous consumption, and the first Christian king in England, Ethelbert of Kent—a sixth or seventh century monarch—laid down rules for the running of alehouses. The Church's concern also concerned the Church, and punishment ranged from no supper—St. Gildas the Wise ordained this for monks who, "through drinking too freely, gets thick of speech, so he cannot join in the psalmody"—to a lot of penance. "Those who get drunk through ignorance must do penance fifteen days; if through negligence, forty days; if through contempt, three quarantains [120 days]," decided St. David.

What is deliciously ironic about all this ecclesiastical concern about ale drinking among the priesthood is that the monks and the nuns, both in England and on the continent, were by far making the best malt beverages. Although it seems likely that German monks were using hops for their astringent (pungent-bitter) taste—to counteract the sweetness of the grain and sugars—and for their preservative values before this time, much of the literature on beer credits sixth or seventh century nuns experimenting in a convent kitchen in northern Gaul with their discovery for use in beer and ale. Just to give credit where credit may be due, however, the Germany school has medieval era Bavarian monks substituting hops, the extract from the flowers of a little plant known to botonists as *humulus lupus*, for the bark and tree leaves that were then also used for tanning animal hides (and, therefore, a mite stiff on the taste buds), and that hops emigrated from Germany to Norway to the Netherlands and Flanders. Only when a group of Flemish immigrants settled in Kent during the reign of Henry VIII, did the British get wise to hops, and then they were highly suspicious, if not down-

Reprinted from *Löwenbräu München* (Munich, 1969), p. 14.

Scene in an old brewery.

right hostile, toward this little relative of the mulberry bush. Be that as it may, the religion-beer connection in Britain was being as solidly linked as the old pagan-beer relationship had been, and the abbots of England were becoming as famous for the ales developed in their monasteries as the Benedictines of France were for their liqueurs.

In particular, the ale of Canterbury, seat of the Christian Church in England, was both much admired and much consumed, as literally many thousands of gallons flowed down monkish gullets there each year. Nor was the great quaffing of ale limited to Canterbury, which may have been especially fortunate in the quality of its ale, but was by no measurement unique in its habits. According to the historian of The Monastic Order in England of this time, "The cannons of St. Paul's had each an allowance of thirty gallons per week, and those of Waltham six bottles a week—each sufficient for ten men at a single meal." Since men of the cloth were forbidden in the eighth century by Ecbright, Archbishop of York, "to eat or drink in taverns," they did their drinking at home, and as historian David Knowles observes in some wonderment: "Doubtless we must reckon with the total absence of tea and coffee, of fresh fruit and vegetables during most of the year, but even so, these quantities are on a heroic scale."

It is reported that in your diocese the vice of drunkenness is too frequent. This is an evil peculiar to pagans, and to our race. Neither the Franks, nor the Gauls, nor the Lombards, nor the Romans, nor the Greeks commit it. Let us then repress this iniquity by decrees of synods and the prohibition of the scriptures, if we are able.

—the famed great West Saxon missionary, Winfrid, more popularly known as St. Boniface, "Apostle of the Germans," writing in the eighth century to Cuthbert, Archbishop of Canterbury

Religious dictates notwithstanding, ale drinking had such a hold on the laity that the only penance they suffered was a severe hangover. Ale was a part of everyday life among all segments of society. In the small villages, brewing was now sometimes the province of one member of the community, and he and his wife were entrusted to provide good ale for their neighbors. Bad brewing was repaid with a dunk in the village pond but no one harbored a grudge because the local alehouse was a gathering spot and meeting place for inhabitants of the village, and these were the earliest pubs. This didn't mean that home-brewing had become a lost art, however, and when an impoverished couple tied the knot, the wedding feast—a "bride-ale"— was paid for by the ale the bride and her mother brewed for that occasion. Along with money relatives and friends also brought gifts to set the young couple up in housekeeping, and in return for their generosity were guaranteed a good drunk. And while the pagan religion had been given up, those old-time "ales" were conveniently translated into Christian bacchanals, and there were Whitsun ales, Easter ales, and ales for every saint in Christendom.

[The pepul come] with candelys burnyng, and would wake, and come toward night to the church of their devocian . . . afterward the pepul fell to letcherie, and songs, and daunses, with harping and piping, and also to glotony and sinne.

—tenth century account of what sounds like a pretty full evening

Despite all this devotion to deity, though, the church—not only in England but throughout northern Europe—continued to chide the populace for its alcoholic activities. For example, King Edgar, who ruled England from 959-975, limited the number of alehouses to but one per village. More maniacally, he further tried to limit drinking by one of the dumbest ideas of all time. He ordered pegs placed within all drinking vessels used in public establishments—the pegs being regularly spaced and the clever theory being that as the drinking vessel was passed around, as was the custom, no one should drink more than the distance between two pegs. The expression "to take someone down a peg" no doubt originated from this historic ordinance and certainly must have been, in the estimation of some of his countrymen, most applicable to the king himself. To show that the idiocy of officialdom did not long deter the progress of an Englishman to his favorite alehouse or pub, however, we find that in 1215—to jump a bit ahead of our story—when the British barons forced King John to sign the Magna Carta granting civil and political liberties to all citizens of the land, there was included in this great document the standard for a proper measure of beer, evidence that the Englishman and his ale would not be soon parted.

Bryng us in no befe, for ther is many bonys,
But bryng us in good ale, for that goth downe at onys.
Bryng us in no eggys, for ther is many shelles,
But bryng in good ale, and gyfe us nothyng ellys.

—old English drinking song, very phonetic, and if it doesn't make sense at first, let a small child read it to you

Further, that beer and cheer were more than phonetic bedfellows was in evidence throughout the land: It was being brewed in the home, in the alehouse, in court, on baronial estates, at the various colleges of Oxford and Cambridge, and at the cathedrals, churches, monasteries, convents, abbeys, priories, and all defined nooks and crannies of the Church. As yet there were no commercial breweries of any consequence, if any, because neither the king nor the Church was about to loosen the reins of this important activity—ale provided taxes for the Crown and consumer income for the Church, which in some areas ordained that beer could be bought nowhere else. If this seems high handed, and monopolies are seldom high minded, the locals may have taken some solace in the fact that the religious orders were ever striving to produce a beer that was consistent in its strength and quality. This involved the constant control of ingredients, measurements, and temperature, and the brews produced came to be identified in terms of alcoholic content by one, two, or three $X$s, the latter being the one (five to six percent alcohol) with the most monasterial wallop. The practice of identifying the strength of beer by a number of $X$s continues, in some nations, to this day—a case of $X$ hitting the spot, and $XX$ zapping it even harder.

# 11/Brew-It-Yourself

I have a friend who used to throw an occasional party at which the only alcoholic beverage served was his home-made beer. Sometimes it was sublime. Other times, it was . . . well, shall we say "uneven." The only thing consistent about these parties was the way the beer was poured. Once one of the large bottles was opened by my host, he kept gently—and continuously—pouring. "Can't let the sediment out of the bottle, and don't want the beer to cloud," he explained to the uninitiated.

Since I have no kitchen skills, I have never tried to make my own beer. However, according to a *Wall Street Journal* article by Stanford N. Sesser a few years back, there are an estimated half-million home brewers in the United States. Most of these are law-abiding citizens except when they're brewing their own beer, because brewing your own beer is sort of against the law. Which is sort of like being sort of pregnant.

Well, do these normally law-abiding citizens defy the Internal Revenue Service, risking five years in the pokey and a $5,000 fine, to make their own lager, pale ale, brown ale, oatmeal stout, sweet stout, milk stout, pilsner, et cetera, plus a certain degree of danger—home brews have been known to blow up—just to save some money? Well, yes, as we'll learn a bit later on in this section, the home-brewed stuff costs as little as one-sixth of what you'd pay for a quart of beer in the store. But there are other ingredients in their story. To quote the *Journal* piece:

While the final product can taste like anything from the greatest of German brews to a year-old bottle of salad dressing, it has one uniform characteristic: The alcohol content is at least 50% greater than that one of the commercial suds. "Let's put it this way," says a Seattle businessman. "If you want to get high, you don't have to guzzle it the whole night. It gets a party going a lot faster."

Then, too, home brewing can be a family activity. According to the *Journal*, one New York couple gives bottles of the family beer to friends at Christmastime instead of sending cards. The element of romance is also not to be underestimated. I'm not referring to the illegality of the practice. No one at the IRS recalls anyone being prosecuted for making his own beer, and the law remains on the books as a prohibition against moonshiners using beer ingredients to make their favorite "white lightning." But I am referring to the notion that you can do it yourself better than the commercial brewers. Some home brewers recall their parents' stories of what they did in the family bathtub besides bathing during Prohibition, and now they have *their* secret suds. Home brewing is also an entertaining hobby because one graduates from the simpler recipes to the more advanced beer curriculum as soon as the challenge of the first brew has stood the test of taste. One may also regard home brewing as something of an underground-type hobby in which the camaraderie of making one's own brew is shared with fellow brewmasters via a magazine, *The Purple Thumb,* published by a gentleman named Sidney B. Taylor in Portland, Oregon—who is also the *Journal* source for that 500,000 home brewers estimate. Mr. Taylor, when asked why people make their own beer, mentioned the "crackpot" contingent—those folks who "make their own beer because they suspect the breweries are out to poison them." So, whatever their reasons—crackpottery or pleasure of the palate or whatever—brewing as an industry is very much at home with a lot of Americans.

In an uncustomary act of generosity, I am going to turn over the rest of this section to a good friend of mine from Australia—and therefore by definition a beer lover—Craig McGregor, author, novelist, journalist, globe trotter, *bon vivant,* and maker of his own potables. Craig and I were originally going to collaborate on this book, but the combination of a peripetetic Australian and a (then) job-locked New Yorker proved to be an awkward team. Craig was in England when I was in America, and I was in London when he was in California. However, he contributed a few excellent pieces to this book, and they are all included.

Once upon a time brewing beer was something you did yourself. In England until the nineteenth century, more beer was brewed at home than in the breweries. Everyone who had a home, from the country squire to the farm laborer, knew how to do it. Much the same was true in the United States, but during Prohibition home-brewing acquired a nasty reputation, no doubt because this was the only beer available for people to drink—and much of it was awful. Since the repeal of Prohibition it has been strictly illegal to brew beer without a license: the breweries can be trusted to brew beer, but you can't. In the last ten years, however, more and more Americans have begun to brew their own beer, either secretly or in open defiance of the law. The stage has been reached in some states where there are now chains of stores selling all the equipment, malts, yeasts, hops, and how-to-do-it books anyone needs to start making his own brew, and no action has been taken against them. It would seem that people have begun to take the right to brew beer back to themselves.

And about time.

However, before you begin to brew your own beer or start making use of the recipes in the chapter, you might be well advised to check out just what the strict legal position is in your own state. Home brewing is prohibited throughout the United States by federal law, but it is one of those federal laws more honored in the breach than in the observance. Your local state regulations might prove more troublesome. Some states specifically prohibit home brewing, some are vague about it, and some don't care. (Oregon has no local law prohibiting it, and there are 5,000 Oregonians brewing their own beer.) As long as you don't start selling your beer or give it to minors, it's unlikely that anyone will bother you. Home brewing is undoubtedly carried on in every state in the Union; the only decision to make is whether you do it on the front porch or in a room out the back.

At this stage the West Coast (especially the San Francisco Bay area)—hops are grown in the Northwest and, therefore, readily available—is the heart of home-brewing country. Berkeley, for instance, has three stores supplying home-brew materials and equipment within two miles of each other. In fact, says Peter Brehm, manager of the Wine and the People store on University Avenue:

> Berkeley probably has the highest concentration of home brew stores in North America. It's always been a very sophisticated wine and food town—next to Palo Alto, I guess. Plus you have the college and the whole hip movement here—they don't want to wait around for a year or two making wine when you can do your own beer in a month and a half, or even less.

Brehm, who had a beer-drinking German grandfather, got into home brewing as a hobby.

I was a wine freak at first, had all the equipment, but people kept telling me to try making beer and when I did I was amazed at the results. It was really good, I found I really liked it! So then it was taking up more and more of my time, and I figured it was about time I started a business of my own. So I opened the store. It's not illegal to sell the supplies—it's food. I guess I could be busted for being an accessory before the fact, but nothing's happened. . . .

Brehm says the home-brewing industry is growing "at a phenomenal rate—it's unbelievable the number of people who are getting involved." A former economic consultant, he believes just how big the industry grows depends upon government regulations and what the commercial breweries do. "If they keep on doing what they do, I think home brewing has a bright future!" he says, grinning, then adds:

Apart from Anchor Steam Beer and a couple of other breweries, up in Wisconsin mainly [see Brian Boylan's contribution—B. A.], there just isn't any good beer in the U.S. Anchor Steam uses quality grains, but I don't think that's done throughout the industry. This carbonating process: it makes beer pleasing to the eye, but as far as getting down to creating good beer, it just doesn't have it.
  Also, you can brew a really good beer because these days you can get the very best materials. I'm getting grain from the Anchor Steam brewery, and I've got a load of their hops in the back of the truck. So you can make the best beer being produced in the U.S. You can get good cultures for yeast from Germany and England. And I can help people out when they're beginning, because I've done it myself.

Brehm looks around his store. Big kegs are lined along the back, huge bottles, row after row of bins containing different yeasts and hops ("Choice Yankee Hops"), and cans of labeled malt extracts (light dried malt extract, dark dried malt extract, malt extract with caramel, "UK bitter"). On the tables near the door, piles of books on beer and wine making. And along one side, row after row of the imported beers that have inspired so many Americans to try brewing their own: Dortmunder, Würzburger Dark, Kirin, Watney, Guinness Stout, Mackeson, Heineken, Pschorr-Brau.

It's not difficult [says Brehm] but given one hundred people you're going to have some really wild mistakes. For instance, one guy called in here, took one of those five-gallon glass jugs there, and did his primary fermentation in it. He put a stopper in it, and left it in his kitchen. Well, about four o'clock in the morning there was this massive explosion, and he found the whole thing had just blown up—BANG! There was nothing left of the container, just a few glass pieces, you know, and of course the walls and the floor and the ceiling were just covered with beer. His hydrometer, and glassware around the sink, all of it obliterated. It would have killed him if he'd been in that room! But generally people don't make mistakes as wild as that. . . .

Why else do people brew their own beer? One Californian home brewer, David Greenberg, has a straightforward explanation: it's cheap.

I'm brewing right now and mine's costing me fourteen cents a quart for Irish stout, and about twelve cents a quart for lager. Lager is a little cheaper because you use less malt and sugar. That's a pretty average price. Some people can knock down the price

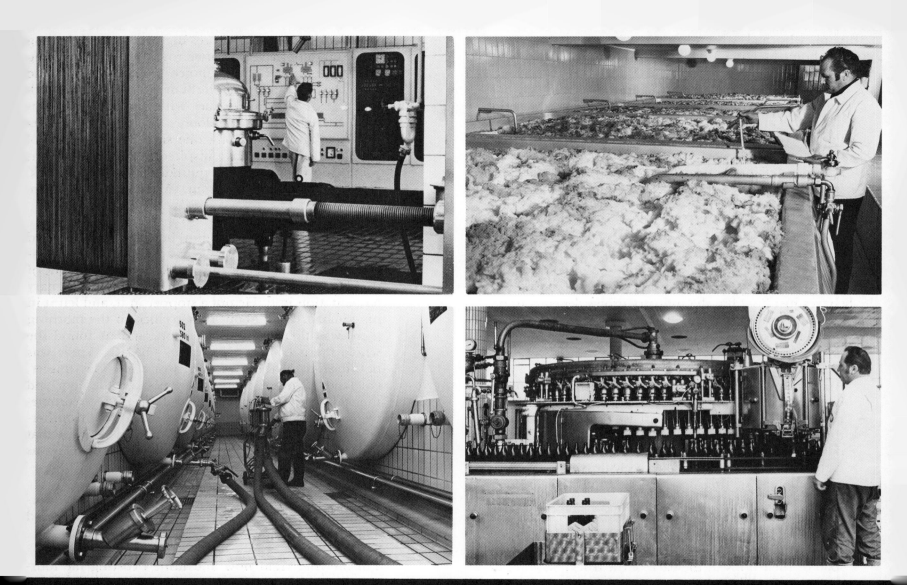

In the cold storage room *(top left)*, the still cooking, hot beer brew is cooled down to fermentation temperature. Under a high deck of foam (a big, foamy head), the sugary brew ferments in the fermentation cellar *(top right)* into new beer. In seven days here alcohol and carbonic acid are generated. For eight to ten weeks the beer rests in large tanks in a storage cellar *(bottom left)*. During the secondary fermentation here its taste matures and its concentration of carbonic acid increases. Up to 70,000 bottles are filled every hour with one modern bottle filler *(bottom right)*.

even more by buying their grains and sugar in bulk, but I'm not up to that scale yet. But if you're brewing, say, five gallons at a time you can get it down to at least fifteen cents a quart. That's a fraction of the price of American beer, and if you buy imported beer, it's about one-tenth of the price. That's not allowing for buying the equipment, but once you've bought that, *you've got it.* And as you keep on brewing and brewing, it gets cheaper, because you don't make so many mistakes.

[Any other reason?] Well, a lot of people are dissatisfied with American beer. It's kind of watery, tasteless, low in alcohol. When people have sampled some of the foreign beers, they really liked them a lot, and then they go into a store in the U.S. and it costs seventy-five cents or more a bottle. They'd like something that tastes like that but doesn't cost so much. So they make their own.

How do you go about brewing your own beer? Here is an elementary guide to the fine art of home brewing, starting with the equipment you will need and ending with some basic recipes for different types of brew. But remember: you and your palate are the best guides to what to do. In the end, every man is his own best brewmaster.

**Equipment**
● A supply of hot water. This is not essential, but it's useful.
● A large vessel, at least two gallons in capacity, for boiling up the beer wort (unfermented beer). You can use a fruit canner, a large stainless steel or enamel pot, an electric or gas boiler, or even a large saucepan. *Don't* use a lead container. Stainless steel is best, and easy to keep clean.
● An even larger vessel, holding at least eight gallons,

for primary fermentation. The old-fashioned method was to use a pottery or stoneware jar, but a cheap plastic garbage bin is just as good. You can buy one in any dime store. It doesn't even have to have a lid—a sheet of plastic large enough to fit over the top will do just as well.
● For the secondary fermentation you will need a third container which doesn't have to be nearly so big. Glass or plastic jars, fitted with corks and fermentation locks, are just the thing—especially if they fit in your refrigerator. A glass jar lets you see how the settling process is going before you bottle the beer.
● Ah yes, the bottles. The returnable sort are probably the best—get them from your local bar. You will need corks as well: the traditional sort, or plastic caps, will do. You might even want to buy a bottle capper, which makes everything easier.
● A sieve or strainer for straining the wort. You can line it on the inside with muslin or terrycloth.
● Five or six feet of plastic tubing. You need this for syphoning the beer off into the bottles. You can add a few inches of soft rubber tubing at one end to make it more flexible; plastic funnels are also a help.
● A stirring spoon. It should be stainless steel or made from nonresinous wood.
● An immersion thermometer of some sort. This is not absolutely essential if you are making the simplest of simple brews, but for more sophisticated beers it's a help.
● A specific gravity hydrometer and jar. Again, this is not absolutely essential, but it's a great help. Get the jar as well as the hydrometer; it is very hard to read a hydrometer properly during the secondary fermentation unless you have the jar.
● Kitchen scales, a measuring jug . . . and a refrigerator, if possible. Then you're ready to go.

**Keeping Everything Clean**

Beer and beer wort are beautifully suited to raising bacteria, especially the bacteria which will ruin your beer. If you visit a commercial brewery (it's a good idea: quite apart from learning how the big breweries operate, you invariably get some free samples of their product!), you will notice immediately how spotlessly clean everything is. You must be just as careful. Take all the hygiene precautions you normally do, but you need some extra ones as well.

For a start, you need to sterilize all your equipment after using it. The most popular sterilizer is sulphur dioxide, which you make up to a ten percent solution—one part sulphur dioxide to nine parts water. Others use chlorine or household bleach, but remember to rinse it away. Chlorine can ruin the taste of an otherwise good beer. Sterilize everything, then rinse it in hot water as well. A dishwasher is just fine. Make sure that *every* part of each beer bottle is sterilized. Boil the caps in hot water.

Between brewing sessions, you might want to keep your containers clean by filling them with warm water and baking soda. Store them on clean, dry shelves, preferably out of the reach of children, dogs, and other predators. Take a tip and always rinse our your beer bottles as soon as you've drunk the beer—otherwise they become moldy and much harder to clean.

If you think all this is overemphasizing cleanliness, just remember that unclean equipment is probably the single major cause of bad home brews. It's a pity to spoil an eight-gallon brew of beer just because of slipshod hygiene.

**Ingredients**

The basis of all beer is malt. You can mash your own barley malt extract, but most home brewers simply buy it off the shelf. Malt gives beer its characteristic body and flavor, and a high quality malt (for example, some of the imported ones, especially those which are imported from Europe for home brewers) should help you make a high quality beer.

Sugar is another essential. It is impossible to make a fermented drink without using it in some form or other. Ordinary white granulated sugar is just perfect for the job; there is really no point in using confectioner's sugar or any such fancy variety. Some home brewers like to use treacle and golden syrup instead of sugar, but this depends upon your taste; you might like to try it with a stout. One thing, though, remember that the more malt and sugar you use in your beer, the more alcoholic it will be. Just how alcoholic you want it to be is up to you, but don't be silly about it.

Hops give your beer flavor and bitterness and, if you use enough, a delicate hop aroma. You *can* make beer using other herbs, but hops are traditional and hops *are* best. They are almost invariably added during the boiling of the wort (unfermented beer), and as well as imparting flavor, they help sterilize the wort. Hops are expensive; in point of fact, they are the single most expensive ingredient you will use. For this reason, some home brewers use cheaper varieties of hops, such as hop extract or compressed hops, during most of the boiling period and then add the natural loose hops at the end. Or, if you want to use normal hops throughout, you still might find it a good idea to hold some back to throw in during the last five or ten minutes of boiling. This ensures that you have a good hops flavor in your beer, because the boiling process drives off much of the hops quality. Or you can add a few drops of hops oil to the beer in the second stage, when it has been in the jars two or three days.

Yeast provokes the primary fermentation of your beer. Get the bottom-fermenting variety if, as likely, you are going to make a lager beer; you can use the top-fermenting sort if you decide to branch out into British ales. Don't use baker's yeast or wine yeast; what you want is dried beer yeast.

What else do you need? A little salt helps in the fermentation process; use plain salt, not the iodized variety. Dark and stronger beers use more salt, while British ales use less or else use gypsum instead. Citric acid, or the juice of a lemon, also helps fermentation. If you're a specialist, or become one, you might decide to make use of beer finings or gelatin since both help settle your beer during the lager period and should produce a nice, clear finish.

## Simple Beer

Here is an extremely simple recipe for beer which is suitable for beginners, but which you should only use as a jumping-off point to much more sophisticated brews.

### BREWING

Boil up two gallons of water, 3½ oz. of hops, half a teaspoon of salt and 3½ lbs. of malt together for about thirty minutes, using whatever container you have decided to use for beer wort (see the Equipment List). To keep your beer clean, have the hops suspended in a stocking or wrapped in some cheesecloth.

Then take 2 lbs. of white sugar, a level teaspoon of citric acid and a pint of water and boil it in another container. Keep it simmering for about 2 hours. Then add enough cold water to bring it up to a gallon.

Mix this in with the malt and hops mixture you have boiled in the other container. Add enough cold water to bring the whole mixture up to 5 gallons. Pour into your primary fermenter, plastic garbage pail, or whatever.

Leave it to cool. When the temperature is down below 70°F., add two teaspoons of dried yeast. Cover the fermenter with a plastic sheet and leave in a warm room to ferment. Leave for a few days, until the fermentation has stopped; you can judge this by the fact that the beer has become clear, except for a surface scum which you can skim off. Next, dissolve 5 oz. of sugar in one pint of water, add it to your mixture, and siphon the brew off into bottles. Cork or cap the bottles tightly.

It's a good idea to leave the bottles standing upright for four to six weeks so the beer can age a little. If you get impatient, you can sample a bottle or two. A still better idea is to start on your next brew.

## Lager Beer

This time try a more sophisticated beer. The following recipe comes from the Wine-Art shops which now exist in major cities in the United States and Canada; it should give you a fine, flavorful lager beer suited to most American tastes.

### INGREDIENTS

    6 gallons of water
    1 2½-lb. pale malt extract
    2 oz. compressed hops
    ½ oz. loose (finishing) hops
    4 lbs. sugar
    1 teaspoon of citric acid
    Lager beer yeast
    1 teaspoon gypsum (optional)
    1 teaspoon yeast energizer or 2 teaspoons of brewing
        salts
    ½ teaspoon beer finings
    1 teaspoon heading liquid
    1 teaspoon ascorbic acid
    1¾ teaspoons salt
    Note: save two cups of the sugar for bottling later on.

### BREWING

Bring about two or three gallons of water to a boil in a stainless steel or enamel kettle. Add the salt and the citric acid, and when the water boils, add the malt extract. After the wort has been boiling fifteen minutes, add the compressed hops broken up. Boil for one and a quarter hours more. Add the finishing hops tied in a cheesecloth, turn the heat off, and strain the wort over the sugar (less the two cups saved for bottling) in your primary fermenter. An ordinary household strainer or several layers of cheesecloth will do. Add the balance of the cold water necessary to bring it over the six-gallon mark by about half a gallon. The finishing hops are left in the wort for a time. Cover the primary fermenter, and let cool to about 70°F.

When the temperature is 70°F. or lower, add your yeast. Your gravity should be about 1.035-1.040. Add water or sugar to adjust the gravity.

In one to three days, when the head has built up and the gravity is down to about 1.028-1.030 or so, skim the foam (especially the dark gummy resins) off the top of the brew, and remove the hops.

In eight to fourteen days or when the gravity is down to 1.010, syphon into your secondary fermenter. Add yeast energizer or brewing salts. Dissolve beer finings in one-half cup of water, boil, and add to brew. Attach fermentation lock.

Place the lager in a cool place, refrigerator, or wherever it will keep between 38° and 48°F. Store for four weeks to three months or until gravity is 1.000.

Syphon into primary fermenter. Dissolve two cups of corn sugar into a small amount of the beer to make a syrup (boil beer and sugar for about three minutes, stirring it), then allow to cool. Then stir it gently into the main brew along with the heading liquid and ascorbic acid.

Syphon into beer bottles and cap.

Store for ten to fourteen days at 60°-70°F. Chill and serve.

Using the basic lager brewing method just described, it is possible to vary the ingredients and thus produce your own version of some of the famous international lagers: Bohemian (Pilsen), Dortmunder, Austrian (Vienna), Dark Lager, Bavarian (Munich), Kulmbacher, and bock beer (spring). The chief variation is in the malt/sugar ratio. Table 1 gives the details for these famous beers; it is taken from Fred Eckhardt's *A Treatise on Lager Beers* (Published

## Table of Starting Gravities

| Beer | malt malt extract lb. | corn sugar lb.* | total malt/ sugar** | start gravity | probable alcohol |
|---|---|---|---|---|---|
| Light Lager | 2½-3 light | 3-4 | 5-7 | 1.032-40 | 5-6% |
| Bohemian (Pilsen) | 5-9 light | 1-4 | 8-10 | 1.040-48 | 5½-6½% |
| Dortmunder | 5-10 light 1 crystal | 1-4 | 9-12** | 1.050-60 | 7-8% |
| Austrian (Vienna) | 2½-7 light 1 crystal | 1-4 | 8-10 | 1.040-48 | 5½-6½% |
| Dark Lager | 2½ dark 2½ light | 2-4 | 7-9 | 1.038-44 | 5½-6% |
| Bavarian (Munich) | 2½ dark 2½-5 light 1 crystal | 1-4 | 8-10 | 1.040-48 | 5½-6½% |
| Kulmbacher | 2½ dark 2½-5 light 3 crystal 1 black malt | 2-5 | 14-18** | 1.050-70 | 8-10% |
| Bock beer (spring) | 5 dark 2½-7½ light 1 crystal 1 black | 3-6 | 16-19** | 1.060-80 | 9-11% |

\*   Deduct 1-lb. of sugar for the five gallon batch. Sugar totals include 1-lb. (2 cups) for priming prior to bottling.

\*\*  See the section on high gravity beers for adjusting the sugar-malt ratio in high gravity beers.

by Hobby Winemaker, 2758 N.E. Broadway, Portland, Oregon 97232), which is an indispensable guide to the home brewer who decides to get serious about his task.

British beers, ales, and stouts are easier to make than lager, but the home brewer in America is handicapped by the difficulty of obtaining the right ingredients. However, as more stores catering to the home brewer appear, it is becoming easier to try your hand at traditional ales. For those interested, probably the best book on British home brewing is Ken Shales's *Brewing Better Beers* (published by The Amateur Winemaker, North Croye, The Avenue, Andover, Hampshire, England). Then, too, most of the books on home brewing published in America also have their recipes for British bitter and ales and stouts and the like. In fact, *Home Brewing Without Failures*, by H.E. Bravery, is British in origin and available in an inexpensive paperback (Arc Books) edition.

## Queensland Home Brew

Finally, out of deference to those who find brewing even the simple beer not simple enough, here is a still easier recipe that defies climate or rank amateurs to spoil it.

It comes from Queensland, on the tropical east coast of Australia, and is a very hardy type of brew well suited to hot climates such as California's. It's heavier than lager, lighter than English bitter, and roughly ten to twelve proof. It's supposed to have originated with two old Queensland bushmen, who whiled away the time outback proving you could brew beer in a hot climate with few ingredients and no equipment—if you were thirsty enough. After they put down the first brew to ferment, the sun beating down on their little iron shack, the less experienced of the two bushmen said:

"What do we do till she's ready?"

"Well," said the old hand, "I suppose we could play a hand of cards."

INGREDIENTS
  1½ gallons of water
  2 lbs. of light malt extract (D.M.S.)
  4 lbs. of white sugar
  4 oz. of hops
  1 heaped teaspoon of salt
  4 tablespoons of top-working yeast

BREWING

Put all the ingredients except the yeast in a two-gallon container, saucepan, or what have you. Boil for half an hour. Allow to cool. Strain through a cloth into a six-gallon container. Bring up to six gallons by adding cold water, pouring it through the straining cloth, which still contains the mash to make sure that all sugar and malt is extracted from the mash.

Add the yeast—dried brewers' yeast is probably best. Allow to ferment for five to seven days, skimming off the froth that results; dried froth that is allowed to sink back into the brew will make it taste sour.

When all the frothing has ceased and there is no sign of sweetness left in the brew, it is ready to bottle. Siphon into bottles, and add to each bottle one level teaspoon of white sugar. Cap the bottles, making sure you shake the bottles to mix the sugar in and to test that the caps seal properly.

Ideal fermenting and bottling temperature for this brew is 68°F. But it will still make a good beer at 50°, and even temperatures in the high 80s find it undaunted—just faster.

And here is a song to go with the beer. It was written by Don Henderson, who can make a song or a home brew with equal ease:

### Five Cents a Bottle

At a small town in Queensland
  No matter where
Those that don't know
  Don't even care.
Don't care at all
  Till after they hear
That the local inhabitants
  Brew their own beer.

CHORUS:

(and)  It's five cents a bottle
     and that is the rub
    That's less than we pay
     for a glass in the pub.
    Five cents a bottle
     the brew was a beauty
    Five cents a bottle
     with the excise duty.

The first lot they made
  was a bit of a risk
You sometimes got poisoned
  before you got full.
But the brew was improved
  by making some tests
On daredevil friends
  and unwitting guests.

CHORUS:
(and)  It's five cents a bottle. . . .

One day it happened
  Caught by The Law
Fined and instructed
  to make beer no more.
Add on the fine
  Subtract the excise
Six cents a bottle
  is still a good price.

(I spoke with the Proprietor of the Wine-Arts Store located on Saw Mill River Road between White Plains and Tarrytown, New York—apparently the nearest supplier for home brewing in the New York metropolitan area—to learn if home brewing is flourishing here. He reported that there was a steady growth in his trade. He also mentioned that there is no New York State law "specifically prohibiting the making of beer at home." Asked for his opinion as to the best book for beginning brewers, he named *The Art of Making Beer,* which is available as a quality paperback (Hawthorne, $2.95). Of the various books I've looked at—from a professional bungler's point of view—I've liked Leigh P. Beadle's *Brew It Yourself,* which is also available in an inexpensive edition (The Noonday Press, $1.95). The writing is clear, and the author has some opinions. The latest edition also tells you how to make soft drinks.—B. A.)

# 12/In Pittsburgh, *Don't* Ask for a Boilermaker

(Stuart Brown, our Pittsburgh correspondent here, is a former television newsman [KDKA] now working for the Pittsburgh *Post-Gazette*. We met when he was trying to get a book placed on the Tony Boyle murder case. The project began as a fine article in *Philadelphia Magazine* and then went through several stages and, happily, ended up being published by W. R. Norton in fall 1975 under the title, *A Man Called Tony*. It got fine reviews, which makes me feel good. It doesn't bother Stu, either.)

In Pittsburgh, you've got to remember that you're in what even the natives—or is it especially the natives?—call a shot-and-beer town. The usual custom around mill-type bars is to ask for a short and a beer, not what's commonly called a *boilermaker* elsewhere. And nobody does funny things like I hear they used to do elsewhere, such as dropping the shot glass full of whiskey into the beer glass. That's bad for the dentalwork.

Those who specifically ask for a Seagrams and an Iron say, "Seagrams and ah-rnn." It's Pittsburgh-phonetic, and it works. "Ow" and "eye" sounds here are usually pronounced "ah"—as in "Sahth side" for "South side" and "Stu Brahn" for me. But enough of this 'enry 'iggins crap.

Pittsburgh is a great place for beer, and the best of the local products is probably Iron City, made by the Pittsburgh Brewing Company. The company also makes Tech, Mustang Malt Liquor, DuBois Premium and Export, Gambrinus, Augustiner, Robin Hood Ale—how do you like that one!—Mark V, Old German, Old Dutch, and Old Export. That's an impressive list of products, but Iron City is what the company's known for here. There used to be some stiff competition from Duke Beer, which was made by Duquesne Brewing, but it's operated by C. Schmidt in Philadelphia now, and Iron City seems to rule the city.

But the competition was kind of nice, though. In fact, when the new sports stadium opened in 1970, there was a big fight because Iron City felt it had proprietary rights on the beer concessions in the stadium. When somebody discovered that Budweiser was also being sold in the stadium, Duke and Iron City went at it draft by draft, and the whole thing wound up before the city council. Pittsburghers take their beer and politics seriously. Iron City sponsors the games on station KDKA; and when the Pirates' general manager moved the team to another station under Duke sponsorship, the baseball announcers refused to go along. We've had a lot of boozy fights here, going all the way back to the Whisky Rebellion in the 1790s.

There are a number of good places to drink beer in downtown Pittsburgh (called The Downtown), including the Press Box and the Pewter Mug on Market Square. But the most atmospheric of the lot is my favorite, the Oyster Bar, on the edge of the square. It's just a big long bar, and it's what this shot-and-beer town must have been like back in the days of unpaved streets.

The Oyster first opened its doors in 1870, and now it's known all over the country—an estimated 18,000 persons go through its swinging doors each week. "We get all

kinds in here," says one of the managers. "Thieves, perverts, lawyers, and judges." The Oyster is also a favorite haunt for professional athletes, newsmen, and steelworkers. Famous visitors have included Jack Dempsey, Gene Kelly, and Hubert Humphrey, to mention gents from three walks of life.

What the Oyster offers is fast-moving bartenders and a fish sandwich and beer for 95¢. There's no formal menu, but they serve—besides these enormous whiting fish sandwiches—oysters from Chesapeake Bay, clam rolls, and mountains of french fries. Besides the good cold local beer, they also feature butter milk! Somehow that doesn't seem quite kosher for a place like the Oyster Bar, but I learned that drinking buttermilk with the fish sandwiches became a habit that arose during Prohibition, and the place still sells 1,400 gallons of buttermilk a month.

The Oyster also sells more liquor than any other tavern in the Pittsburgh area. It's always jammed with guys who drop in for a fish sandwich and a beer morning, noon, and night. They're lined up along the fifty-foot aluminum bar which is decorated with old group portraits of Miss America contestants. This was the passion of the now deceased owner, Silver Dollar Louie Americus, who used to attend the Miss America beauty pageants on a regular basis. Silver Dollar Louie put together quite a collection of Miss Americas on his walls.

In addition to being a fine quick drop-in tavern, this is an ideal location for touring imbibers because Market Square, the oldest part of the city, has undergone a revival of nightlife since the late 1960s. So there are all kinds of offbeat shops, jazz joints and more formal cocktail lounges in the area. But mostly there's the Oyster Bar.

Germany has changed since the days of the Weimar Republic, but Munich beer halls haven't. The title of this drawing:
"The spring cure for the Municher is strong beer in a *bräuhaus.*"

# 13/A Frothy History of Suds

*"In point of fact, Munich beer is older than Munich."*

On the European continent, as the influence of the Holy Roman Church grew, so did the science of brewing, an essential activity at every large, well-provided monastery. According to an account of the planned expansion of the monastery of Saint Gall in Switzerland in the year 840, the new building plans called for three separate breweries, each adjacent to a bakery so that the raw materials for beer would be right at hand. Each of the three breweries was intended to produce a different kind of brew—a strong beer made from wheat or barley for the exclusive use of the monks and important guests (recommended allocation: one gallon per day), and two beers for ordinary pilgrims and the poor, both made from oats. The various monastic beers varied, of course, according to area, but until the thirteenth century most of them made some use of oats because it was a more abundant crop than either wheat or barley. In due course, especially in Germany, the fame of the beers produced by certain religious orders grew so wide that they exist to this day—for example, such still highly regarded brands as Augustiner, Franziskaner, and Paulaner.

Ah, Germany. Lest we seem to have left German beer in the sloshy hands of Attila the Hun and his fifth-century Vandals, Ostrogoths, Gepidae, and Franks, let us hark back to what, along with English ale, has formed one of the two dominant brewing traditions of the modern world. In 812, Charlemagne, King of the Franks, conqueror of other tribes, and now ruler of the Holy Roman Empire, issued his *Capitulare de villis*—a kind of executive order on the running of all royal establishments, including the breweries. Not only can we learn how the royal breweries were operated as a result of these edicts, but we can be assured that Charlemagne, who had subdued the fearsome Saxons and then persuaded them to submit to baptism and become his faithful vassals, would understand the importance of beer in his kingdom. Leader of men, warrior, diplomat, learned man—he spoke Latin and could read Greek—Charlemagne wanted the best for his empire in all respects, and brewing meant not only potential pleasure, but great potential commerce as well.

Among the duties of the administrator of the royal households at Aachen and Ingelheim in the west of Germany was the hiring of "good and competent craftsmen at the manor, among them brewers [brewmasters, as we know them today] capable of making good beer." Charlemagne was a just and wise ruler, built many churches, and in general tried to spread Christian culture (which included beer) and consolidate order (which advanced beer). When he died, his successors proved to be weaklings, but the work begun would have its own historic flow. The towns and cities in the South were followed by larger towns and great cities to the north, and one, the Cathedral City of Cologne, became a great brewing center under the monopoly market granted the Archbishop of Cologne. (It's always intriguing what congenial bedfellows the Church and Commerce can prove to be.) In the far North, where the leading coastal cities, such as Hamburg, Bremen, and Lübeck, had in 1338 formed a loose coalition of free cities

Reprinted from *Löwenbräu München* (Munich, 1969), pp. 12-13.

for mutual protection and commercial cooperation, brewing became a major industry and these cities became known for their exports of Rhine wine, linen, and local beers. That they were shrewd traders can be substantiated by this one example. The brewers of Bremen sold beer to inhabitants of the Frisian Islands northwest of the city, receiving a large ox for each tun (a cask holding 252 gallons) of their beer. The ox's skin, alone, was worth a tun of beer back in Bremen.

With Germany still centuries away from becoming a unified nation, the regionalism that still characterizes German brewing—even today there are no national brands as we know them—developed during this period and Hanover, Dortmund, Frankfurt, Muenster (also famous for its cheese), and the walled city of Nuremberg were leaders among the hundred or more cities known to all within drinking distance for their beer. However, the high reputation that German beer seems always to have enjoyed perhaps obscures the fact that there were no uniform standards of quality control during this period (apart from the individual monasteries), and the brews would vary from city to city and brewing to brewing.

In some cities on the Rhine a beer is made now, and it is a pity that good fruit [grain] is spoiled in such a manner; the people derive only half the benefit from it, for the reason that before a cask is half emptied, the other half has spoiled and has become sour. The cause of this is that not enough malt is used and too much water, and that it is not boiled, not to speak of the fraud that instead of hops some take willow leaves, others kaminvuss, in order to color the beer.

—Jacobus Theodorus Tabernaemontanus, a Doctor of Medical Science, writing in 1613 (but under his real name?)

Old soldiers never die, they just hang out at their local bastion.

A magnificent beer hall in Frankfurt, Germany. Missing from this 1881 lithograph are the traditional German barmaids who carry a minimum of three one-liter (1.06 qts.) mugs in each hand without losing their heads (yes, pun intended if not achieved).

Regardless of those wise in the ways of *tabernae*, the average German was more thirsty for beer than discriminating about it, and whenever a city was large enough to justify a fairly elaborate town hall (*Rathaus*), it almost always included a wall-to-wall basement beer hall (*rathskeller*) for the citizenry to come simultaneously fill up on beer while filling up the municipal coffers. This early example of togetherness was so vital to local civic spirits—not to speak of the local economy—that towns with few or no breweries couldn't afford to stand on false civic pride, but instead imported their beer from the nearest large supplier. "There is no bad beer, some kinds are better than others."—old German proverb.

In the wake of the ravages of the Thirty Years' War, the northern cities lost their importance as brewing citadels, and beer hegemony passed on to the cities of the South—Nuremberg, Augsburg, Würzburg (the famous beer bearing that name was first brewed in 1643 within the walls of the castle of Würzburg), and, most especially, Munich—the city now synonymous with German beer.

In point of fact, Munich beer is older than Munich. As far back as 815, beer was being brewed on a small scale in "*Kirchsprengel Oberfoehring*," which is today a suburb of modern Munich. The beer was shipped as far as 25 miles away (no small distance in those days), to the Court of the Bishop of Freising. Not only did the Bishop enjoy a regular supply of beer, he also enjoyed an income from the tolls at the bridge that spanned the Isar River—a financial bonanza that greatly annoyed the local ruler, the Bavarian Duke Heinrich der Loewe, known to his people as "Henry the Lion." From the Duke's point of view, this was the right bridge in the wrong place, so he seized it and demolished it. Of course, no bridge, no tolls, so he built a new bridge about an hour's walk upstream, "hard by the monks"—there was a small monastery there—and the settlement he founded there was to become Munich, one of the indisputable beer capitals of the world.

Duke Henry displayed additional capitalist savvy by establishing both a mint to coin money and a marketplace in which to spend it. At this time in Bavaria only the royal households and the monasteries were allowed to brew beer for sale, but no one at whatever station of life was ignorant of the fact that "table beer" was being brewed as often as homemade bread was being baked. At some point in this uncharted period—still the Middle Ages, remember—brewing became more the function of a "common brewer," who got the needed raw materials from the king and provided beer for his subjects. Don't assume the king switched brands, however. And these commoners began to expand like a good yeast.

By the advent of the fourteenth century, brewers, like masons, carpenters, and other master craftsmen of the day, had formed their own guild, and your neighborhood *München* brewer had to serve an apprenticeship for a specified number of years and then a term as a journeyman brewer before being accorded the status of a *Braumeister* (brewmaster) and being permitted to function on his own. This was no small achievement, since by the late 1330s there were still only a dozen or so brewers—Löwenbräu, or "Lion's Brew," began in a small Munich alley in 1383—authorized to produce their own beer. Among other things, this made the local beer a product of quality and made the *bierstube* a place for all the various guild members to congregate. People who ran stalls in the marketplace also liked their beer; therefore, not only would the brewers talk shop, but so would the shopkeepers. Add to this crowd the passing pilgrims and travelers needing succor for their thirst, and the *gemütlichkeit* level grew in direct proportion to the decibel din. What grew as well was the fame of Munich beer.

As noted earlier, there was no municipal enforcement of quality control among the brewers through all this period, nor were there statutes governing the contents of beer and what amount of *bier* constituted a true measure. The first

Munich edict regarding beer was issued in 1363, and both the Brewers' Guild and the city fathers—in this instance, Dukes Wilhelm III and Ludwig VII—called in 1420 for regulations governing the manufacture of the local product. A "Pledge of Purity" statute applicable to Munich was enacted in 1487 by Duke Albrecht IV, to be followed by others pertaining to all of Bavaria, imposed by the jointly reigning dukes Wilhelm IV and Ludwig X, in 1516 and 1520.

> Furthermore, we wish to emphasize that in future in all cities, markets and in the country, the only ingredients used for the brewing of beer must be Barley, Hops and Water. Whosoever knowingly disregards or transgresses upon this ordinance, shall be punished by the Court Authorities confiscating such barrels, without fail.
>
> . . . Furthermore, should there arise a scarcity and subsequent price-increase of the barley (also considering that the times of harvest differ, due to the location), WE, the Bavarian Dutchy, shall have the right to order curtailments for the good of all concerned.

—part of the Bavarian Pledge of
Purity (*Das Reinheitsgebot*)

Speaking of Ludwig X—just think, between 1420 and 1516, there were dukes Ludwig VII, VIII, IX, and X—and Wilhelm V, they personally resented the profits the monasteries were still taking in from brewing beer. So they established the first official state brewery to take over that action, and of course, the royal brewery catered to the royal palate. In Wilhelm's case, at least, the state *hofbrauerei* produced a number of dark beers for him, from among which his favorite was chocolate-brown in color and decidedly sweet. This type of beer had originated in the town of Einbeck, and via some mysterious linguistic assimila-

tion, *beck* became *bock*, which means a young male goat. And since goats are associated with Bacchus, the Roman wine god, the traditional symbol for bock beer, illogically enough, became a goat's head. (Or did *bock* derive from Bacchus in the first place?)

Well, all undiplomatic assumptions aside, we do know that bock beer—still a springtime favorite of Bavarians—reflected the usual Germanic logic in its consistent contents and quality, as did the other German brews. Basking in the reflection of their true brew, if you will, the members of the Munich Brewers' Guild were held in very high regard by other members of the community. And small wonder, since anyone who wanted to become a brewer *had* to join the guild and agree to be governed by its precepts and regulations. Once accepted as a brewer, the guild member had to purchase a "brewing deed" from the ruler of the country, no less, which ceased to be valid when the brewer ceased to be alive. That was half of the bureaucratic involvement with brewing. The "brewing prerogative," a local affair, was bestowed by the city authorities on the actual premises, and it could be bequeathed or sold along with the premises themselves. Thus, we see that beer and brewing were of more official concern in Bavaria than perhaps anywhere else at any period of modern history.

By the time Ludwig I mounted the throne of Bavaria, beer had become such an important drink with Bavarian workers that when in 1848 the king raised the price of one *pfennig* a drink, riots broke out that nearly cost the king his throne. It was an Irish dancer, Lola Montez, who drove the king to this extreme measure. [See Max Ophuls' movie of same name.] Ludwig was quite a ladies' man, as one can see by visiting the Gallery of Beauties at Schloss Nymphenburg where portraits of his many lady-loves still hang on the walls. After the beer riots, Lola was forced to flee the country, but she found refuge easily enough in the United States where tales of her royal romances were a decided asset to her stage career. She lies buried in a Brooklyn cemetery. I don't suppose anyone thought of using a keg of beer for her funeral urn, but it would have been appropriate.

—Betty Wason, in *The Art of German Cooking,* published in 1967

Courtesy of New York Public Library, Picture Collection.

"A beer, a beer—my kingdom for a beer!"

# 14/Let's Get Cooking—with Beer!

Sacrilegious though it may seem to the devout drinker, beer—minus its properties as thirst slaker and pick-me-up and relaxant—can be used to unusual and good effect in cooking. Everyone knows about wine in food, but beer happens to be, if not as versatile a culinary ingredient, a very intriguing one probably familiar only to ethnic-style cooks or very sophisticated ones—those who enjoy experimenting in the kitchen. Indeed, *Carbonnade Flamande,* the Belgian dish included in the following list of recipes, is a classic recipe that is known to the great chefs of the western world.

In a less prestigious role, perhaps, beer adds a pleasant hoppy flavor to soups, stews, marinades, cakes, and breads. We do not speak of subtle dishes here, because beer goes particularly well with robust meals (stews and beef) and with meat dishes which are braised. Be careful when using beers in soups—it's important not to use too much. For that matter, to quote the late culinary expert, Michael Field, from a *Holiday* magazine article:

> Cooking with alcohol in any of its drinkable forms can frequently transform a prosaic dish into a masterpiece, or almost as frequently ruin it. Paradoxically, cooking with alcohol, once shorn of its mysteries, proves to be more a matter of cooking *away* the alcohol rather than cooking *with* it. For in food the taste of alcohol is harsh and unpleasant. In part, the usefulness of wine, beer, spirits and liqueurs in cooking depends on knowing how to control the alcohol in each of them.

Thus forewarned, let's get cooking with some of these disarming recipes. It's hard to ruin anything so long as you stick to the recipe—if there's beer left over in the can or bottle, don't waste it. Drink it—with *savoir faire! Con mucho gusto,* too.

Most of these recipes use the lager beer available everywhere in America. For lustier tastes, you might want to substitute ale, dark beer, or even stout.

Home-baked bread is always tastier than the store-bought variety, and there's that great aromatic moment when it comes out of the oven. My wife has substituted beer for water in one of her favorite bread recipes, and the result is a very hearty bread which stays moist long after it's emerged from the oven. No kneading needed here, and the fermenting action of the yeast shortens the time needed for the bread to rise.

**Bread**

1 cup milk
1 tablespoon salt
1 cup warm beer
2 packages of yeast
3 tablespoons honey
2 tablespoons butter (or margarine)
4¼ cups unbleached flour

Pour milk in saucepan and boil until milk is scalded. Cool to lukewarm. Add the honey, salt, and butter. Dissolve the yeast in beer. Add the milk mixture.

Sift in flour. Stir 30 or so times. No need to knead the mixture. Let rise for about 1 hour until double in bulk. Stir down another 30 strokes. Divide dough in half. Place in 2 well-greased 1-pound pans. Bake at 375°F. for 45 or 50 minutes. Remove from pans and let cool.

Try these griddlecakes for a weekend breakfast, and you'll find that kids have discriminating tastebuds, too. Again credit the yeast for lightening the frying batter and helping to produce something light, fluffy and delicious.

### Beer Griddlecakes

¾ cup bread crumbs
2 eggs, well beaten
¼ cup light cream
1 teaspoon baking powder
1 cup beer at room temperature
3 tablespoons salad oil
¾ cup sifted flour
1 tablespoon sugar
½ teaspoon salt

Combine the bread crumbs and beer, and let stand for about ten minutes.

In a large mixing bowl, combine eggs, oil, and cream and mix well. Sift together the flour, baking powder, sugar, and salt, and add to egg mixture along with beer compote, alternately in thirds. Preheat an electric griddle to 390°F. Grease lightly, and drop the batter on to the griddle ¼ cup at a time. When medium brown on bottom and dull beige on top, turn them over and brown other side. Serve with generous pats of butter and hot maple syrup.

Serves 4-6.

Beer and cheese go together like old friends—which they of course are. This is an indecently easy dish to prepare for a brunch or luncheon party. Sounds a mite caloric, but a half-cup of beer contains only fifty calories, even before the alcohol burns off.

### Welsh Rarebit

1 cup grated cheddar cheese
1 teaspoon of French mustard
½ cup beer
Dash of Worcestershire sauce

Carefully combine and melt all ingredients in a saucepan over a low heat. Don't overcook or the cheese will go stringy.
    Serve on toast.
    Serves 4.

This has proved to be a reliable dip for any party occasion or to take the edge off a starving group. It's not only simple to prepare, it's attractive and colorful and has a different enough taste (the beer) to cause rave comments.

### Raw Vegetable Appetizer

4 ounces cream cheese
1 crushed garlic clove
½ cup sour cream
4 ounces blue cheese
3 or 4 tablespoons beer
Cut up: carrots, cucumbers, celery, green pepper, zucchini, cauliflower, turnips, and green beans.

Combine the cheeses, which should be at room temperature, with garlic and beer. Blend until smooth, then add sour cream. Serve in a bowl surrounded by the vegetables.

This magnificent Victorian-era bar and back bar are one of the many interesting exhibits at the Beer Museum in Barnesville, Pennsylvania. It's open from June 27 to August 24 each year.

Some beer bread and salad on the side, and you've got yourself an economical one-dish meal here. Improvisation has proven successful—for instance, substituting a dark beer (Löwenbräu does fine) for a zestier taste.

### Vegetable—Bean Soup

4 beef bouillon cubes
2 cups small white or red beans
1 cup diced ham (or any leftover meat)
1 teaspoon prepared mustard
4 tablespoons onions, chopped
1 cup chopped celery
Salt and pepper to taste
1 hambone
1 12-ounce can of beer
2 tablespoons brown sugar
3 tablespoons catsup
2 cups chopped carrots
Water, enough to cover

Soak beans overnight in water.
Drain and put in large pot. Add the hambone, beer, and water to cover completely. Simmer for about 2 hours. When the beans are tender, add the remaining ingredients and simmer for an additional 40 minutes.
Serves 8.

Another meal in one dish. The cabbage makes for a nice flavor, but our preference is for the sauerkraut—gives the soup a more piquant flavor. (Beer and sauerkraut are key elements in a number of zesty German dishes.) The experience in our household is that this is even better the next day, so save some, gourmands permitting.

### Beer Soup

Beef bones (large quantity)
2 large onions
1 small cabbage or ½ can of sauerkraut
¼ teaspoon white peppercorns
¼ teaspoon worcestershire sauce
1½ cups of barley
1 small clove of garlic
2 large carrots
1 quart of beer (ale is best)
1 tablespoon malt vinegar
2 tablespoons oil

Slice onions into rings and brown in oil with pieces of garlic in large soup pot.
Add half the beer, then the soup bones, barley, and peppercorns.
Add water till the bones are covered; bring to a boil, and then let simmer for 3-4 hours.
Dice carrots and add to soup.
Slice cabbage and steam in separate pot with 1 tablespoon of vinegar. (If you use sauerkraut, just add the strained contents of the can to the soup about 5 minutes before serving.)
Pour in rest of beer and Worcestershire sauce. Then add the cabbage. Simmer for another 5 minutes. Serve with chopped parsley or grated cheese.
Serves 6.

Beer acts more as a catalyst than as a flavoring, because of the yeast and enzyme action. This pork chop dish is a perfect example of that—the interaction between the beer and/or ale (try the latter for a more pronounced sauce) and the fruit help produce a really different, exotic flavor.

## Pork Chops

4 center cut pork chops
1 large onion, sliced
2 tablespoons flour
Salt and pepper to taste
6 apples
2 tablespoons butter, or margarine
1 cup beer or ale

Pare, core and slice apples; add onion, salt, and pepper.

Place in buttered casserole. In a small pan, melt butter, blend in flour; add beer all at once. Stir constantly until thickened.

Trim fat from pork chops; place on apples and onions in casserole. Pour beer sauce over all. Bake in moderate oven (350°F.) for 1½ hours.

Browning pork chops before baking will add to their appetizing appearance.

Serves 3-4.

"Have it your way . . ."

Don't go out to Burger King or McDonald's, but instead see how beer helps transform a mundane little hamburger into a surefire gourmetburger. And there's something to bite into between the two halves of the roll.

It won't cure them of McDonald's, but it's a start toward teaching the children that there *are* other things in life worth eating.

## Hamburger Deluxe

1 pound lean ground beef
1 teaspoon salt
1 clove minced garlic
2 tablespoons catsup
8 hamburger rolls
¾ cup quick-cooking rolled oats

2 tablespoons minced onions
1 teaspoon Worcestershire sauce
½ cup beer

Cut rolls in half. Combine all other ingredients. Spread mixture on roll halves. Salt and pepper them, and put under broiler for 8-10 minutes.

Serves 8.

This is one of those foolproof dishes that lends itself to all sorts of experimentation. Check the fridge for whatever vegetables are sitting there minding their own business, and get them into the casserole. Using a foreign lager seems to add a slight but discernible edge of hoppiness, but our best results have been with either Canadian or British ales (Labatt, Molson, Bass).

## Chicken and Sausage Casserole

1 chicken cut up into 8 pieces
1 tablespoon salt
5 tablespoons oil or margarine
1 pint beer or ale
½ cup flour
⅛ teaspoon pepper
8-10 link sausages

Coat chicken in flour and sprinkle with salt and pepper. Heat 2 tablespoons oil and sauté onions until transparent. Remove from pan.

Brown chicken in rest of oil. Then add chicken, onions, and sausages to casserole. Pour beer or ale into pan and scrape up the bits that remain in the pan. Pour into casserole.

Cover and bake in preheated oven at 350°F. for approximately 50 minutes. Ten minutes before serving, uncover and cook at 425°F. to brown.

Serves 4.

We called this Flemish favorite a classic, and a classic it is. Although it uses a lot of beer, relatively speaking, this is a dish stalwart enough for the test. It cooks for hours and tastes better for it, the onions, beer, and spices blending to produce a sauce entirely original in taste. One warning: Stick with American lagers on this one as you don't want the higher hops content and maltiness of foreign brews interfering with what is, surprisingly enough, quite a subtle flavor.

## Carbonnades A La Flamande

4 pounds beef (rump or round)
½ cup flour
5 cloves garlic, minced
3 cups of beer or ale
½ cup parsley, chopped
2 teaspoons thyme
1 tablespoon salt
6 medium-size onions, sliced thickly
½ cup margarine or oil
3 tablespoons brown sugar
½ cup wine vinegar
1 large bay leaf
Freshly ground pepper
2¾ cups beef broth

Preheat oven to 325°F.

Cut slices of beef into bite-size pieces. Lightly flour and sauté them in hot oil until lightly browned. Place them in large casserole. Add the onions and garlic to oil in pan and sauté until golden. Add to casserole with sugar, vinegar, parsley, bay leaves, thyme, salt, and pepper. Add broth to frying pan and scrape up all remaining bits, and then pour into casserole. Add beer; cover and bake for approximately 2½ hours.

Correct seasoning and serve.

Serves 6-8.

This recipe, we've found, improves any fish fillets (sole, red snapper, lake trout) because it not only complements the delicacy of the fish flavor, but prevents dryness during the cooking process and helps it remain moist and tasty.

## Fillet of Flounder

4 flounder fillets
1 minced shallot
1 tablespoon butter
½ cup heavy cream
6 large mushrooms, sliced
½ onion, thinly sliced
1 cup beer
1 tablespoon Hollandaise sauce (prepared mix or homemade)
Salt and pepper to taste

Place fillets in pan, and cover with beer; add onion, shallots, and mushrooms, and cook 10 minutes.

Remove fish; add cream, butter, and Hollandaise sauce to beer sauce left in pan. Simmer slowly for 6 minutes. Place fillets in fireproof dish, pour sauce over it, and broil until golden brown.

Serves 4.

Boiling shrimp is the practice in most seafaring nations; they have been doing this for centuries. Why? Because it enhances the flavor, of course. Why else do something for centuries!

### Boiled Shrimp

2 pounds shrimp
1 garlic clove, minced
½ teaspoon thyme
Juice of ½ lemon
Dash of cayenne pepper
24 ounces of beer
1½ teaspoons salt
2 bay leaves
1 tablespoon chopped parsley

Wash shrimp thoroughly. Do not remove shells.

Combine above ingredients, and bring to a boil. Add shrimp, and bring to boil again; reduce heat, and simmer uncovered for 3 minutes. Drain, shell, and devein shrimp.

Serve hot or cold with favorite sauce.

This is not your typical gooey chocolate cake. This is Adult Chocolate Cake, unless you happen to be cursed with an inordinately sweet tooth. If so, this isn't for you because the beer offsets the sweetness of the sugar, with the sugar reducing the bitterness of the beer.

This is eaten in two ways in our family—frosting for the wee folks and no trimmings for the adults. And absolutely don't mess with amount of the beer here—that just-right taste balance is easily unbalanced with too much or too little beer.

### Chocolate Cake

1¾ cups sifted flour
½ teaspoon baking soda
⅓ cup butter or margarine
2 eggs, separated
¾ cup beer
1 teaspoon baking powder
½ teaspoon salt
1 cup sugar
2 squares (2 ounces) unsweetened chocolate, melted and cooled

Mix and sift flour, baking powder, baking soda, and salt together 3 times. Cream butter until soft. Add sugar gradually, beating after each addition until light and fluffy. Add egg yolks one at a time, beating until well blended. Add chocolate and beat until smooth. Add flour alternately until smooth after each addition. Fold in stiffly beaten egg whites.

Pour into 2 greased 7-inch layer cake tins. Bake in moderate oven (375°F.) for approximately 30 minutes or until done. Cool and spread frosting on it if you wish.

Serves 6-8.

Pumpkin pie is controversial in some families. Try it with beer; it does lighten the filling and adds another dimension.

## Old Fashioned Pumpkin Pie

1 unbaked 10-inch pie shell
1 cup sugar
½ teaspoon cloves
1 teaspoon cinnamon
½ teaspoon ginger
1 cup light cream
1½ cups pumpkin, canned
½ teaspoon salt
½ teaspoon nutmeg
½ teaspoon allspice
2 eggs, beaten
⅔ cup beer or ale

In a bowl, combine the sugar, salt, and spices. Add the eggs, pumpkin, cream, and beer, and blend thoroughly. Pour into the unbaked pie shell.
Bake at 350° (preheated oven) for about 1 hour.
Serves 6-8.

Time-tested. Fail-safe. Never last more than a day. An absolute favorite with kiddies and grown people both. You can make the dough ahead of time and freeze it, to be used when you need it. Not only are they light and delicious, but they have a pleasant and different aftertaste.

## Cookies

½ cup shortening
2 cups brown sugar
2 tablespoons warm beer
3½ cups sifted flour
1 teaspoon salt
1 cup chopped walnuts
½ cup butter
2 eggs
1 teaspoon vanilla
1 teaspoon baking soda
1 teaspoon cinnamon

Cream the shortening and butter. Add the sugar slowly, and beat until light. Add the eggs, beer, and vanilla, and mix thoroughly.
Sift the flour, baking soda, salt, and cinnamon, and combine with the above mixture. Blend well and add the nuts.
Make 4 rolls out of the dough, and wrap in tin foil. Refrigerate overnight.
Slice the dough thinly, and bake in 400° oven for ten minutes.
Makes 6 dozen cookies.

The author of this book heartily disapproves of punches in which eight different kinds of booze got into the mix. He is of the theory that all that fruit and sweet syrups are not good for people. However, if you want to try a pretty safe punch that is certainly not too sweet, you got it. It gets the desired effect, but isn't deceptively lethal.

**Beer Punch**

2 teaspoons brown sugar
⅛ teaspoon ground cloves
1 cup cranberry juice
1½ teaspoons ground cinnamon
1 cup orange juice
6 12-ounce cans beer

In a 4-quart saucepan stir brown sugar, cinnamon, and cloves. Add orange juice and cranberry juice, and cook until hot, stirring to dissolve the sugar. Stir in beer, and continue cooking until hot but not boiling.

Serve in a warmed punch bowl. Garnish with tiny red apples or spiced crab apples.

Makes about 20 4-ounce punch cup servings.

This "soup" is actually a spiced drink. And is related to English spiced ale and to the original wassail. Not always to everyone's liking, but different enough to evoke much discussion.

**Hot "Beer Soup"**

4 cups dark beer
2 tablespoons flour
6 cloves
Juice and rind of ½ lemon
1 tablespoon butter
1 tablespoon sugar
1 cinnamon stick
2 egg yolks

Pour beer into saucepan, and let stand at room temperature for about 3 hours or until it is flat.

In another saucepan melt butter, stir in flour and sugar, and cook the mixture very gently, stirring until it turns a caramel color. Do not let it burn. Heat the beer, and slowly add it to the flour and sugar mixture, stirring until the mixture is well blended and smooth.

Add cloves, cinnamon stick, and lemon, and simmer for 15 minutes. Discard the cinnamon stick and cloves.

Beat egg yolks and 2 teaspoons water, and beat in a little of the hot soup. Add the mixture to the rest of the soup, and blend the mixture thoroughly. Serve it in heated mugs.

Serves 4.

For anyone anxious to experiment further, there is an excellent range of recipes in *The Beer Cookbook,* by Berneita Tolson and Edith McCaig, which may well establish beer as a culinary ingredient to rival wine, and a much cheaper one, too.

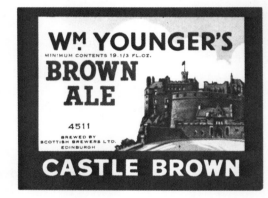

Of the three beer traditions already going great guns—the German, the British, and the Scandinavian—the first two would eventually influence the way beer is brewed in most of the advanced nations of the world. However, lest it seem that a few nationalistic monopolies have existed on beer as a way of life, it must be pointed out that beer has also long been important to the Czechs and the people of the Low Countries.

During the Middle Ages, some German beer drinkers, instead of praising their own brews, extolled the light, dry, wheat-based brews of Bohemia, a Slavic country in central Europe, once part of Austria, now part of Czechoslovakia. In one particularly dramatic incident, the thriving sale of Bohemian beer by the cathedral chapter of Breslau—a city directly north of Bohemia—proved such a threat to local brewing interests that, well, to quote William Iverson, to whom I am indebted for this information: "brewers and councilmen joined forces to make the trade illegal, thus touching off the *Pfaffenkrieg* or 'Parsons' War' of 1380. Denied their traditional right to sell beer of any origin, the clergy closed the churches and refused to perform all sacraments."

Today the fame of Bohemian beer, at least in this country, lies primarily with Czechoslovakia's *Pilsner Urquell*, the beer created in 1842 when a band of 250 Pilsen families pooled their rights to brew beer—brewing rights, unlike those in Bavaria, were passed down from generation to generation—and started a cooperative known as the Citizens' Brewery. Their beer became so famous that "pilsner" became a generic name for light, dry beer before trademark legislation existed to prevent this kind of commercial usurpation.

To add to their troubles, there was a dispute among members of the cooperative, and several groups of shareholders went out on their own. One of these produced a beer called *Prior*—Latin for "first"—to dramatize their claim of being the first brewers to use the original pilsner brewing formula. Both brands—*Prior* and *Urquell*—prospered until after the first World War, when the feud was discontinued and the two brands merged back into the old *Pilsner Urquell*. During the 1930s, an American beer distributor named Arthur Kallman, son-in-law of one of the Pilsen brewery's owners, did a healthy business importing that beer into this country. But World War II put an end to the supply of any Czech beer, and Kallman went looking for an American brewer who could reproduce this excellent beer. The Adam Scheidt Brewing Company in Norristown, Pennsylvania, proved suitable for his needs, and Prior was reincarnated. Later on, C. Schmidt & Sons acquired this small brewery, but happily Prior is still marketed and ranks as one of America's true premium beers.

The truth of the Gambrinus legend seems to point more precisely to a man who actually lived: one portrait of Gambrinus labels him as "King of Flanders and Brabant." We do know that a famous Baron of Brabant was a certain Jan Primus, who was not only a noted warrior and a local hero, but also renowned for his capacity. He is said to have quaffed 72 quarts of beer at one sitting. In addition, he was President of the Brussels Guild of Brewers from 1261 to 1294, with his portrait hanging in the great hall. If you say Jan Primus fast enough and figure out that a man of that name was the champion drinker of his time, you have the right kind of start to launch a patron saint of beer called Gambrinus.

> —*Falstaff's Complete Beer Book* by Frederick Birmingham, sponsored by the San Francisco-St. Louis brewing company, which also provided some nifty color photographs of antique beer steins from its St. Louis International Museum of Brewing. Well worth a visit. Same goes for Birmingham's book.

As indicated by Birmingham, "Gambrinus" may be the stuff of legend—and God knows that anyone capable of knocking down seventy-two quarts of beer at one sitting is *unreal*—and there seems to be confusion about his legitimacy. He may have been Dutch rather than Belgian. By the beginning of the ninth century Brabant was an important and prosperous state, formerly part of Charlemagne's empire, and is today the central and metropolitan province of Belgium. North Brabant is the largest province in Holland, bounded on the south by Belgium. One of the early rulers of Brabant was John I, and one Dutch scholar has explained that Gambrinus evolved semantically through a *geleerdenvergissing*—"error by men of learning"—from "Jan Primus" (John I). On the other hand, the earliest biographer of King Gambrinus—a gentleman named Aventinus—decided in 1554 that the patron saint of beer

for all Christendom was born in 1730 B.C., exactly 2234 years after the world got started. As Birmingham notes in his amusing discussion of the Gambrinus legend, "The Egyptian god Osiris is also believed to have invented beer, but Aventinus smooths this over by saying that Gambrinus was the consort of Isis, who was the wife of Osiris, and that this bit of mild adultery gave him some claims on the beer invention of her husband, not to mention the lady."

Apocryphal or not, the Gambrinus legend is one of the better ones and has enjoyed wide currency and fame. Andrew Campbell, the English author of a very readable book on beer—now, alas, out of print—begins his own consideration of the legend by quoting part of a Dutch student song—*Gambrinus, Koning van Bravant/De wijsger die het Bier uitvant*—that is still sung at beery gatherings. Most scholars believe that "Gambrinus" is a nice, folksy legend as legends go, but that his achievements—among which are said to be the invention of two highly popular types of Dutch beer—are just so much historic foam. Still, as Campbell concedes, "that does not prevent paintings, carvings, and statues of him being displayed on the Continent, or choruses being chanted in his honour, or figures dressed to represent him taking part in pageants, or from restaurants being named after him."

Gambrinus is usually depicted in a secular setting, sitting astride a barrel, holding a foaming tankard of beer in his right hand. On the other hand, chiseled in stone in the ancient Andecho Monastery in Bavaria is the inscription—a visible legend, if you will—"Holy St. Gambrinus, pray for us!" Accordingly we can at least rest easy with *that* small bit of reality in tracing back the Dutch and Belgian traditions of beer because it is known that beer was introduced in the Low Countries, sometime in the tenth or eleventh centuries, by monks who were spreading both the Word of God and the good news about beer. And certainly

Gambrinus, patron saint of the brewer, here represented by an unknown Dutch master of the sixteenth century.

the news about beer was received with both enthusiasm and avidity because today the Belgians are among the champion beer drinkers of the world—we'll rank them later on in the book—and export their beer, which is generally not available in this country, heavily to the Common Market countries, trailing only Denmark as the world's leading beer exporter. As for the Dutch, Heineken and Amstel are famous on the Continent and Heineken is exported to well over one hundred countries. Moreover, the exporting business in both countries got off to a very early start—by the twelfth or thirteenth centuries, certainly—since both the Netherlands and Belgium were producing more beer than their people could consume. Beer was shipped to other nations through the German cities of Hamburg and Dantzig since neither Amsterdam nor Antwerp—today the world's third largest port—had developed as major seaports as yet. Delft, today famous the world over for its chinaware, was already famed as a beer capital by the thirteenth century, and in Belgium all the leading cities could boast of a booming beer trade. Brussels produced *Faro* and *Lambiek,* Antwerp *Seef* and *Matus,* Ghent *Uitzet* and *Tripel.* In that latter city, Jacob van Artevelde became the most famous brewer of this time—i.e., "The Brewer of Ghent"—not because of his terrific beer but because of his leadership in the liberation of Flanders from the French during the fourteenth century.

In both countries, beer drinking enjoyed the same kind of associations it did in Scandinavia, England, and Germany. This was particularly true in the Netherlands where almost every family or social occasion required the accompaniment of large amounts of the local beer. *"Kinderbier"* was served at christenings and *"Leedbier"* (Sorrow Beer) at funerals. When a building was completed, there was an obligatory ceremony, known to this day as "Wetting the Roof," in which the carpenters and builders would wet their whistles with *"Richtbier,"* the most literal translation of which is "Ready Beer." When the building was ready, so was the beer, and one assumes that a carpenter fell off the roof now and then.

State occasions, on the other hand, were nowhere so carefree and casual. Elaborate beer mugs manufactured and designed especially for these occasions were put to use and some of these, having survived the ravages of time and the wear-and-tear of politicians, kings, and diplomats, are on display in the wonderful old guildhalls and other medieval buildings of Holland, Belgium, and Luxembourg. They can surely be seen in the buildings that form the most beautiful public square in all Europe, Brussels' *Grand Place,* which, with its spectacular *Hotel de Ville* (city hall), imposing *Maison du Roi* (a state building in which the king gave his State of the Nation addresses), and lovely guild buildings, all dating back to the Renaissance, is one of the most extraordinary sights anywhere, especially when illuminated by floodlight at night.

Yet, perhaps the highest tribute to beerdom in these countries was the practice, in the Netherlands, of families nicknamed after beer or brewing—names which then stuck. "Even family names testified to the universality of the beer trade," notes Andrew Campbell. "Apart from the well-known Brouwers and Bruwers, both of whom are to be found in South Africa [settled by the Dutch and the English], the ancestors of the Bestbiers and Biermans, likewise flourishing in our country, gained these soubriquets because of some early link with the 'Trade.' "

Courtesy of New York Public Library, Picture Collection.

"Hollanders drinking beer," probably 15th or 16th century, although the Hollanders, judging by their capacities, were positively Roman in their appetites.

WHITBREAD

THE ALMA

WASHINGTON

16 51

WASHINGTON · CROMWELL

WEST COUNTRY

WHITBREAD

The EAGLE

RATTLEBONE INN

WHITBREAD

CHURCHILL

PLATE of ELVERS

WEST COUNTRY ALES

The ROYAL OAK
WHITECROFT

BEAUFORT ARMS

MUTARE · VEL · TIMERE · SPERNO

WEST COUNTRY BEERS

# 16/Beers of the World— Worth Knowing About

The fact is, beer is having a virtually worldwide boom, with consumption in many countries double that of ten years ago.

It outsells sake in Japan. It is nearly as popular as wine in France. It is a hero of the Soviet Union. It is practically the staff of life in West Germany, where they call it "liquid bread."

. . . They call it ale, pilsner, lager, porter, stout, bock, bitter. The labels, colors, strengths and tastes vary. But they brew it in big cities everywhere, as well as remote corners ranging from the Australian outback to the backwaters of the Amazon. And they drink it on rooftops in Tokyo, rathskellers in London and sidewalk cafes around the world.

—January 27, 1974, New York *Times* article by Robert D. McFadden

The following is intended to be a minisurvey, a semi-census, whatever you wish to call it. If the title of this survey presumes too much, I wish to explain. I have tasted perhaps two-thirds of the ninety or more beers imported into this country. Of the others, one is a diabetic beer, and many others are brands within brands. When I was stationed in Germany, the local brewers were just fine, the beer from Munich and Würzburg magnificent. In truth, I never had a bad glass, stein, liter mug of beer in Germany. A friend of mine, very knowledgeable in the ways of brew-ing, says the Germans are now mucking around with their beer, that they are "using hop extracts instead of hops, so that you are losing those delicate notes—like truffles—in the flavor." If this is so, it is sad news because I have always found German beer a very superior product. During *Oktoberfest* and *Fasching*, there were special brews made, one darker and thicker than the other, and I loved them all. Now, on visits to Germany in more recent years, I find the really heavy dark beers are too sweet for my taste, but the lights still all seem first rate to me. In fact, the beers in Europe are generally aged longer than ours before bottling—e.g., Heineken, Tuborg, Beck's—and unless they're going to be exported, they're usually not pasteurized. As my friend says, "The reason you like draft beer instead of the pasteurized bottled stuff is that you lose the delicate flavors when you pasteurize it, you lose some of the qualities that aging adds."

I spoke with Fritz Maytag, president and brewmaster of Anchor Steam Beer in San Francisco about this, and he added the important observation that "it's difficult to ship beer without losing some of its quality. That's one of the reasons the beers in Europe are so good. The breweries are smaller, they serve a limited area—so the beer is fresh and it doesn't need to be modified so that it can be shipped 5,000 miles." I asked a bit further about this modification process, and he responded: "There are all sorts of things you can do to beer to make it stable, biologically and physically, and none of them are good for the beer. The same applies to German beers which are imported into the Uni-

How This Book Came to Be Written: In the 1950s, the government sent the author to Ansbach, Germany, to defend democracy against the Cold Warriors. Here he is, doing just that. He identifies himself as the "grinning idiot" at the left end of the kneeling beer steins. In the photograph below, he has entered his More Mature Period. *True* Magazine wanted him to go to Ireland and have his wife get thrown out of a pub (which you can read about elsewhere in this tome). Instead they had a great time. When the article appeared, *True* and Guinness Beer celebrated the event by hosting a St. Patrick's Day walking race. The author trained intensely, performed gallantly, but lost out to a swift bartender with unnaturally long legs. He drowned his remorse in an afternoon of 'Black Velvets' (Guinness and champagne).

ted States; they have to be pasteurized, shipped across the ocean, stored, retransported—exactly what's wrong for beer."

Of course, what this means for most of us is that a little ignorance may be preserving a lot of bliss. I'm glad that my palate isn't as sophisticated as the one Fritz Maytag owns—he speaks of sometimes tasting imported beer as "stale beer"—but I *have* found that my appreciation of English beer has changed markedly as a result of quite a lot of time (six months) spent in London over the past five or six years. I once thought all British beer was fine. The temperature didn't bother me. We're talking about a country without central heating in its pubs, and if the beer is served at room temperature, well, that's in the middle-40s, which is a *good* temperature for beer. Americans who complain of the "flat, warm" beer there are just too used to the freezing, highly carbonated beer here to appreciate the subtleties of British beer. However, I have found that the trend of the large British brewers in England to "keg beer," which is chemically carbonated, has inspired me to seek out the beers made by the smaller London brewers and the various regional brewers, wherever you can find them in London and environs, and to marvel at the differences between British beers. Last summer I sat in a pub that served Fuller's in two varieties of bitter—London Pride and Extra Special—and you could taste the difference, really delight in the difference, between the two brews. One was very good, the other was even better, hoppier, lustier, really a drink for kings. These days, as a result of agitation from British beer lovers who disdain to drink the keg beers, more and more of the excellent regional beers are becoming available in those London pubs that don't belong to a major brewer, and it is a lovely development you can read more about elsewhere in this book.

I've of course gained a lot of knowledge about beer from traveling in places other than England and Germany—

Jamaica's Red Stripe, for example, is designed as a terrific thirst quencher and does just that—and from talking at length about beer to travel writers and beer importers and brewers here and beer connoisseurs and other folks who, like me, are best categorized as beer nuts. Now having told you perhaps too much in the way of autobiography, let's do our survey of world beers.

## Africa

The beers here are French inspired, and not very inspired, therefore, in the North African countries, and are brewed either in the German or British tradition elsewhere. Guinness has a large brewing plant in Nigeria, producing a stout designed to be drunk at much warmer temperatures than the Dublin-London variety, and in Kenya, brewing is the largest industry. The white South Africans drink rich, German-type beers, but also, because of the hot, dry climate, enjoy their domestic lagers and ales. South African blacks, on the other hand, drink a beer made from a maize-meal mash that, I'm told, tastes sort of like sour porridge. It's less alcoholic than a beer made with hops and is regarded as food as well as drink. Between the white and black South Africans, beer consumption is double what it was a decade ago—which may be a result of two kinds of heat there, one of them political.

I've not tasted any of these African brews—Kenya, for example, has Allsopp's Pilsner and White Cap; Uganda has Nile Beer; South Africa, Whitbread (from Britain), Castle, Lion, Glucko—so how about a few comments from travel writer Mack Reynolds:

The Dark Continent, in general, is no haven for beer bibbers. Tangiers' *Pils* is possibly the reason why the Prophet forbade alcoholic drinks to the faithful. And *Zenith*, of Oran, Algeria, although labeled *Bière de Qualité*, isn't much better. *Stella*, in Egypt, has the strange quality of being both heavy and weak. Malta does better with a branch of England's Simmond's breweries, and in Niarobi, Kenya, *White Cap Lager* is a worthwhile product of Taylor's. . . . South African brews of the British type are good, but the French areas produce no better beers than Metropolitan France—which is a hard thing to say.

In fairness to African beers in general—and to Reynolds—this was written a few years ago, and I'm sure that with the industrial nationalistic pride that now characterizes the Third World countries, the beer is being improved. In Angola, once the civil war was over, the first thing the winners did was to nationalize the brewery and boast about what a better beer they were going to produce!

### Asia

Funny thing is, they always feature Japanese beer in Chinese restaurants, but with our trade with China beginning, that situation may change. The official policy of the government is that its citizens don't drink very much, but one journalist who visited a commune there recently reports that his "hosts enjoyed their beer keenly and were clearly accustomed to drinking it in large quantities." The best known Chinese beer is Tsing-Tao, and it is now being exported and gaining in popularity abroad, but there are other brands (White Cloud is the name for one, in translation, that's popular in Canton), and maybe one of these days we will be able to sample some with our Chinese food. Beer, incidentally, goes better with Chinese cuisine than does wine because the latter seems to get overwhelmed by the rich sauces. And with the spicy Szechuan and Hunan dishes, it's practically a necessity.

Kirin is the leading beer in Japan and, as noted elsewhere, the third largest-selling beer in the world. I used to think that the Germans taught the Japanese to make beer during World War II when rice was too precious as a food commodity to be used for beer, but that's pure bushwah. I spoke about the origins of Japanese brewing to Susumu Moriya, manager of the Kirin office in New York City, and he said that Kirin did hire a German brewmaster in the early part of the century, but he left the country during the First World War because Germany and Japan were then enemies at war. After that, Japanese brewmasters began to appear on the scene, and the beer they developed was more Danish than German in flavor. True enough, Kirin does remind me of Tuborg and Carlsberg, which is a very flattering comparison, it seems to me. In Japan the other leading beers are Sapporo, Asahi, and Nippon, but Kirin constitutes over sixty percent of the market there—it would have to, with that ranking in the world market—with its beer, stout and black beer. I've not had these latter two, but I have drunk the other three Japanese beers with consistent pleasure.

In the nearby Philippines, the leading beer by far is San Miguel, brewed there since 1890, and a beer that has won a number of international prizes—e.g., *Prix d'Excellence* at the 1958 Brussels World Fair—and is definitely deserving of your attention if you can find it served anywhere or in your local beer emporium.

South Korea has OB Beer, Diamond, and Crown, and I'm sure a lot of American GIs are familiar with them. I'm not, but I hear that OB is tolerable stuff.

Australia is covered a bit later in the book, but suffice to say that in 1966 someone brought out a product that purported to look, taste, and smell like beer, but had no alcoholic content. That someone thought their product was so good that it would provide real competition for the Australian breweries. It didn't. Beer is such a national religion in this country that when there was a beer strike some years ago, the government almost fell.

In nearby New Zealand, there are some excellent beers.

Leading brand names include Lucky, Waitemata, Nelson, Harleys, Steinecker, but the only ones I've ever tasted are D. B. Lager, which seemed all right, and Speight's Ale, which was grand.

Taiwan has one kind of beer—named Taiwan, naturally. The Hong Kong Brewery in the city of that name produces Mon-Lei Beer, which I've not had. It's sold in this country, and I suspect it will start showing up with Chinese food fairly soon. Singapore's Tiger Beer is famous throughout the Pacific and has done in several generations of sailors from around the world. I've only sampled it once—in a London Pub catering to Australians—and it seemed appropriately named.

Of the various Pacific Islands, I only know about Tahiti's Hiñano Lager, because actor (now playwright) Gardner McKay once told me about it. He spoke fondly enough about it, but when you're making TV films aboard a schooner, any beer is bound to taste good, I suspect.

In India and other Asian nations beer is simply not a factor of any consequence.

## Europe

### AUSTRIA

The Austrians love beer, wine, rich food, all kinds of coffees, and—most of all—sumptuous desserts. They have always struck me as a slightly decadent people. They seem to have nothing better to do than sit around eating and drinking in fairly prodigious quantities. Their leading beers include Goesser (light and dark), Schwechater, and Puntigam, all of which I've tasted and found to be slightly sweeter versions of German beer—or was it that rich Austrian pastry I was washing down with the beer?

### BELGIUM

This is real beer country. The Belgians, who are not famous for their beer in the United States, are well known for it in Europe since they export a lot to surrounding nations. They are always up there among the leading per capita beer consumers of the world, and their beer is very interesting to the American palate. You might find it slightly acidic to the taste, although Caulier is a fairly sweet, full lager with a head that hangs up there quite awhile. Louvain in Brabant is the country's largest brewery, and its Stella and Palten lagers are well worth a try. Other leading brands include Cristal, Brug, Jager Pils (Belgium's version of pilsner), Wiels, and Juliper Urtyp. I have a random acquaintance with all these with no particular preferences among them, but I do recommend Lambic, which is matured at least two years and then bottled and served like champagne. This is a barley wine, really, as is Bush Beer made in Lournai. That one has the same alcoholic content as a table wine—around 12 percent—so it should be drunk with appropriate manners, just as you would a wine. You might find it too sweet for your taste, but have at least two before you make up your mind as it does grow on you.

### CZECHOSLOVAKIA

Pilsner Urquell, of course, justifiably famous for its golden appearance, clean, full taste, and fine head. I also like the light, but discernible, hoppy aftertaste this excellent brew leaves in your mouth. But the Czechs, who lead the world in per capita consumption of beer, have some choices other than Urquell. Abzug and Schenk are two other worthy pilsners, and there are those who think that Graetzer is the best of all the various pilsner-type beers. It's a nice debate to get into, although I have met old-time connoisseurs of Czech beer who maintain that it's not anywhere as good as it was before the Communist takeover of that country. If so, then it's a matter of degrees of excellence, and what we're getting now is still pretty okay with me.

Courtesy of Tuborg Breweries.

This splendid vehicle *(top)* was a service car for draft beer installations in Denmark. The old horse dray *(bottom)*, she ain't what she used to be. These Tuborg horse drays with the famous umbrella—a Tuborg symbol since 1881—used to deliver the goods to thirsty Danes.

## DENMARK

If you have some fond acquaintance with beer, you're surely acquainted with both Carlsberg and Tuborg, now one company. They merged a few years ago to avoid ruinous competition. Some beer experts favor Carlsberg, others Tuborg. I think the Carlsberg lager-type beer may be a little more delicate to the palate, but I'm sure I'd flunk a taste test between the two. In America we get Carlsberg Export Gold Beer, Special Dark Lager—great!—and Elephant Malt Liquor, which is, to my taste, far superior to any malt liquors made here. In Denmark, of course, there are other Carlsberg brews, including a porter and Carlsberg Hof, which is an extremely subtle beer, very dry, yet intriguing, in taste. Similarly, Tuborg sends us only a partial sampling of its output. In Denmark the company makes the following brands: Green Label, Gold Label, Fine Festival Brew, Strong Dark, Imperial Stout, Luxus (luxury) Gold, and KB. I've had all but one of these (the KB), and it's an abundance of riches. The Luxus Gold is indisputably one of the world's greatest beers. Interestingly enough, however, there are regional beers which outsell both Tuborg and Carlsberg in their areas because the Danes are very partial to pleasing the inner man and thus drink what *pleases* them most, not just wet and cold as is usually the case in this country, where we simply don't revere beer as much as the Danes do. Ceres is popular in its area, Viking on *its* turf, and Odense Pilsner in another area. In Helsingor, where Hamlet's castle stands, there is a beer called Hamlet's Castle. There are also Hamlet and Ophelia Beers, which the slight literary strain in my make-up prevented me from trying, but the same brewery's (Wiibroes) Wiibroe Gold and Kronborg are both fond memories.

## GERMANY

When I was in the service, I was stationed in a small town in Bavaria, Ansbach, which was rather charming, especially once a year when its famous Bach Festival transformed a place of 30,000 men, women, and cows into a sophisticated little Mecca for music lovers. There were in this small town four brewers, offering twelve brands of beer and *all* were good. I don't recall all their names, but the Maisel and Georgi were more than deserving of my *Deutschmarks* (God knows the army gave me a limited supply of these). The Gumbertus Bock was too good for a young, craven lad such as myself. I am particularly partial to dark beer, and the Germans make the best there is— apart from the Mexican darks, which of course are German in extraction.

Before getting into a brief Baedecker of German beer, let's spend a moment or two contemplating just how important beer is to the German nation. It represents 11.6 percent of the entire food industry, and trails only milk and dairy products in terms of production. The Germans lead the Common Market countries in beer consumption (total and per capita figures), with Belgium-Luxembourg, Ireland, Denmark, and Great Britain behind them in that order. Even in Germany, breweries disappear—there are 582 fewer than there were in 1960—but this leaves only 1,636 brewers to cater to the national lust affair with beer. Of this total number, 1,122 are in Bavaria and these produce 137 different beers. By *different*, we mean varieties of *hell* (pale), *dunkel* (dark), *marzen*, or *bock*—these latter two being seasonal beers. The figure also includes, of course, the special *Oktoberfest* brews made once a year when Munich goes wild and becomes one big mighty drunken city.

Löwenbräu, of course, is the brewery we think of when we think of Bavaria—or Germany, for that matter—but Hofbräu, Spatenbräu, and Hackenbräu are equally impor-

Reprinted from *Löwenbrau München* (Munich, 1969), p. 12.

tant in Munich. The oldest brewery there is Weihenste-phan, which has been pleasing the *Münchners* since 1040. Germans are intensely loyal to whatever beer they drink, and as a result of that and the peculiar development of the German nation, there are no national breweries in West Germany. Beck's, the Hamburg brewery, is the country's largest, in terms of domestic sales, and Dortmunder Union second. In our larger cities, these fine beers are usually available, along with Würzberg and Löwenbräu Dark and Light, and Holsten is also being imported in increasing quantities. I can drink any of these with nothing but plea-sure, although I find the Löwenbräu Light on the sweet side in contrast to the others. The Würzburg has what seems to be a very pleasant nutty flavor and of the darks, I definitely like Würzberg best.

Still, if you're visiting Germany you can drink the local beer with the guarantee of long local endorsement. Beck's may taste the most like an American beer, but it has more flavor than most American beers. Hamburg's Holsten would be worth experiencing if only because it's matured twelve months before bottling. The folks in Nuremberg and Stuttgart and Kulmbach all have local beers of distinc-tion which are rarely found in America, and Weihenste-phan, brewed in Freising, is one of the elite beers of the world without the word having gotten much past the city limits of that small city. Cologne, long a beer center, boasts among its thirty-two breweries the small but very highly regarded Fruh brewery, which has been in the same family for a century and a half. Fruh sells all the beer it brews, remains a strictly local proposition despite the fame of its product, and is not atypical of many small German breweries in that mode of operation.

A beer peculiar to Germany is *weissbier*, which is made from wheat. It is tart—raspberry or cherry syrup is often added to it—and is the counterpart to a dessert wine. This type of beer has its ardent partisans, of which I am singu-larly *not* one. Berliner Weisse is the most famous of the beers in this category, but Broyhan, made in Hanover, en-joys a certain fame because it looks like young wine, has a definite bouquet and somehow manages to be sweet 'n sour at one and the same time. I think it's swell that the West Berliners and Hanoverians are doing their own thing in beerdom, and if you happen to enjoy sweet wines—say, sauternes—you might care for these odd brews. Me, well, this once, at least, I'd rather go thirsty.

### FRANCE

I have deliberately violated alphabetical order in putting France after Germany because, of the various French beers I have tasted over the years, only Kronenbourg and Tigre Bock, both made in Strasbourg, give beer a good name. These, of course, are Alsatian beers and completely Ger-man in character. If you're in a French restaurant and would like a beer, try to order Kronenbourg, which is capi-tal stuff; otherwise, there must be something on the wine list you can afford.

### GREAT BRITAIN

The great ales of Scotland will be discussed later on be-cause they surely merit special comment, so here we are concentrating on English beer. A brief explanation may be helpful to you in the proper enjoyment of man's noblest ground-level achievement, the English pub.

Bitter is the generic name for the most widely sold beer, which is closer to ale than to lager, certainly. Most pubs provide two varieties of bitter—Ordinary and Special or Best. A good way to get introduced to bitter is to first try a half pint of bitter—just say "bitter, please"—and then a half pint of Best. Mild is ale, which is darker in color and fuller in flavor than the ordinary bitters—there are Pale Ales and Brown Ales (sweetish) and Strong Ales—which

# BONNE BIERRE DE MARS

Courtesy of New York Public Library, Picture Collection.

mean what they say. Porter is no longer very popular, but stout—mainly the rich, creamy Guinness Stout—is to be found in every pub in the land. The British Guinness is the same as the Irish in the bottles (and much less bitter than the Guinness exported to America), but on draft it's brewed to be served instantly—not "built" in the pint glass as in Ireland—and is simply not as tasty as the wonderful Dublin-brewed product. Barley wine is made by all the leading brewers. It's really a brew rather than a wine-beer, and is matured longer than other types of beer. It's always served in wine glasses, and the Englishman drinks it with two kinds of respect: one of affection and familiarity, the other based on its alcoholic content. A small bottle of barley wine—available only in bottle, the small split variety—is equivalent to a stiff shot of scotch. I had a barley wine once at the Whitbread Brewery in London at eleven in the morning, and it certainly set the tone for the rest of the day.

Okay, so much for basics. The really sophisticated good-

ies come a bit later on in the course. The five large English breweries excluding Guinness are Allied, Bass Charrington, Courage, Barclay & Simmons, Watney Mann, and Whitbread. Between them, Scottish & Newcastle (the large Edinburgh-Newcastle combine), Guinness, and a number of smaller breweries that supply beer to London pubs, there are around seventy different kinds of beer available in the British capital. If you are in a "tied" house, you will be limited as to choice, but not *that* limited. As noted elsewhere, the majority of pubs are owned by the brewers themselves and, apart from Guinness, found in all the pubs, they sell the brewer's products plus at least one type of lager, which is enjoying increased popularity among the young. A Watney Mann pub will provide on draft or in bottles the following brands: Red Barrel (keg), Pale Ale, Manns, Brown Ale, Special Mild, Special Bitter, Star Light, Cream Label Stout, Export Gold, and Stingo (barley wine). Bass Charrington offers these: Tavern Keg, Alton Bitter, Directors Bitter, John Courage, Courage Light Ale, Courage Brown Ale, Courage Barley Wine, Imperial Russian Stout (originally made for Catherine the Great and s-t-r-o-n-g), Tavern Export Ale, Jackpot, and Harp Lager. So it's not exactly deprivation to be in a tied house, although my own preference these days is for a free house because you get to drink more exotic British beers that way.

Before getting into these—and I wish I were right now—let's dispel the myth that British beer is flat and warm. The lack of sparkle doesn't mean the beer's flat; it means that it doesn't have any artificial carbonation. And, catering to changing tastes, British beer *is* being served at somewhat lower temperatures these days. Not cold by American standards, certainly, but at the *proper* temperature—one that enhances the taste.

I won't dwell at any length on the glorious variety of English beers because that would require a separate book, and indeed, there is a new one just published in England, entitled *The Beers of Britain*. But suffice to say that no one could fail to be intrigued by the likes of Simmons' Archangel Stout, Lovibond's Royal College Ale, Benskin's Colne Spring Ale, Old Berkshire Stout (the English stouts are sweeter, but less foamy and creamy than Guinness), Shepherd Neame's Bishop's Finger, and Meux's Extra Strong Ale. For that matter, although I would normally hesitate to recommend such a touristy London pub as the Olde Cheshire Cheese, they serve Marston's there—only one of two London pubs to do so—and this is a bitter worth braving the crowds at this folksy old pub. It is smooth and absolutely superb. Then, too, although I have just suggested you search out the free houses in London and elsewhere, I have naught but praise for the Young's and Fuller's pubs. The bitter and ales are just great there. Unfortunately, there aren't many pubs belonging to these breweries in London proper, but they're worth the trouble to find.

Beer in England, not to put it mildly, is a very good show. And I have a good friend, who's Welsh, who maintains that English beer is all right, but a poor substitute for the brews of Wales. I hope he's right. I haven't gotten to Wales yet.

## GREECE

There are two breweries in Greece. One makes Fix, the other Mark and some other brands, and this is as good a chance as any to suggest you get to know the Greek rosé roditys wines. They're dry, don't contain the resin which makes *retsina* unpalatable to many people, and are quite inexpensive.

## HUNGARY

I've not been there, but travel writer friends tell me the Kinizsi Sor (*sor* is Magyar for beer) is tasty enough, but

that the Giraffe is rather malty for the American palate. Of course, one of these guys admitted that it only bothered him after six or eight bottles.

## IRELAND

Guinness is the national drink, and if you've not cared for Guinness in the bottle or on tap in America, you're in for a grand surprise. I'm told that our Guinness is not only bottled for longer shelf life, but also for a warmer climate than Ireland's. I only use the Guinness we get here to make half-and-half. Take any American beer, no matter how undistinguished, add some Guinness, and you'll have a treat. You can vary the color, vary the taste, and in all respects behave like a child with a new toy. On the other hand, the Guinness bottled for the Continent is superb, and it would be blasphemy to do anything with it except drink it. There are other stouts in Ireland—Beamish & Crawford and Murphy's—and both are comparable to Guinness, which, I seem to recall, owns one of them.

There is a mystique, and a damned fine one, to the Irish pint. It involves the publican building a pint until it has a head that will endure through at least half the imperial pint—twenty ounces—of stout. There are clever old codgers who specialize in blowing off some of the head after a few good tugs on their pint, and then complaining about their pint, but it's a game in which both sides know the rules and abide by them. The elderly gent hasn't much money, and the publican has a regular customer; so one pint can last a rather long time that way.

Ireland isn't all stout country, of course, and Harp Lager, which is also Guinness-owned, is pretty good although not in the same league as the great world lagers. I've found Phoenix, Cherry, Time, and Macardle tolerable but just that. In any case, why bother if you have any fondness at all for Guinness? I was once treated to a lunch in the executives' dining room at the Guinness Brewery in

Another view of Dublin's The Long Hall, so called because there *is* a long hall behind the back bar wall where Irish women were expected to sit and drink by themselves. When they wanted a refill, they knocked, a panel opened, and they got a refill.

Dublin and was given both the export Guinness (to Europe) and one of the most magnificent-looking pints these beer-bleary eyes have ever seen. Asked by a friend—with the unlikely name of Billy Porter—which I preferred, I could only reply, "Don't bother me—I'm in Heaven."

## ITALY

Peroni is the big beer here, and you should try it if only for the experience. It's not bad, not good, and enough reason to get right back to Italian wine, which is much underrated.

## LUXEMBOURG

You can drive through this delightful little nation in one day, and *don't*. It's very scenic, has good food, and its citizens drink a *lot* of good beer. There are eleven breweries, but I'm only familiar with Diekirch Réserve, because my time in Luxembourg City, the nation's capital and only city of any size, was devoted to that one brew. The hangover, unfortunately, was overly familiar.

## THE NETHERLANDS

Heineken is world famous, and deserves to be although I don't much care for its Dark Beer. Amstel is also good, perhaps a little lustier in taste, and Grolsch is very smooth, dry, and refreshing. Two other Dutch beers of note: Breda and Oranjeboom, brewed since 1671 in Rotterdam. Both are lagers, and both are worthy of inspection. As in a few other nations, there are no inferior Dutch beers.

## NORWAY

Over the past decade Americans have been getting to know Norwegian beer via Ringnes, which has been introduced through supermarkets in an eleven-ounce bottle that was at first quite a good buy. It's since gone up in price, as do all things in supermarkets. Norway's Three Towns,

however, is a better beer—less sweet to my jaded taste buds—and Frydenlund is quite decent if not up to Viking standards of yore. You *can* get up and walk after imbibing a few.

## PORTUGAL

Sagres and Perola are the two biggies. *De gustibus.*

## POLAND

The Okocim Porter is an excellent one of its kind, and the Zywiec Ale is very respectable, too. A travel writer I know raves about a dark beer he drank in Warsaw, but being a lot of help in this area, he can't remember the name of it. "The first mug hits you in such a way that you have to force yourself manfully to take the second," he says, "but at the end of the week they have to drag you to your train, kicking and screaming that you want to stay so as to drink some more Polish suds."

## RUSSIA

To quote a book, a quite wonderful tome—*The Curiosities of Ale and Beer*—published a hundred years ago, "In Russia ale and beer are of universal acceptance." According to recent newspaper accounts, this is very much still the case although government production doesn't keep up with public demand. In a way, this is sort of surprising as there has been a concerted government effort to cut down the consumption of vodka. Russia, officially or unofficially, has a very serious alcoholism problem. Each year over the past decade as many as ten thousand people fall drunk outdoors and freeze to death in the Russian Republic alone. The government encourages drinkers to switch to beer, but produces a pretty dreary product—one that has been compared to cold, bitter tea. One may presume that this will change one day with Lenin Lager, Stalin Ale, and Khrushchev Extra Strong rivaling the best capitalist products from around the world. At least that will be the official Government advertising. . . .

### SCOTLAND

The Scots look down on English ales, apart from the sweetish, very strong Newcastle brews—e.g., Newcastle Strong Brown Ale. While I don't buy that chauvinistic argument, I do feel that Younger's Double Century Ale is somewhere between merely divine and pretty great. Full-bodied, tangy in taste, and nutty brown in color, this is strong beer at its sublime best. Available in bottles only, but Younger's products are available on draft in their pubs and are among the world's best. These include McEwan's ales and stout and Younger's Tartan Bitter. Another outfit, Tennent, makes very good ales, stouts and a lager, and while I haven't tried it, I hear good things about Murray's Scotch Ale. Edinburgh is one of the world's most beautiful cities, but if that isn't important to you, go there for the beer.

### SPAIN

San Miguel, the famous Philippine beer, is now brewed in Spain. I have not had the opportunity to sample it. Those Spanish beers I have tried suggest that the Spaniards would be well advised to concentrate on improving their wine.

### SWEDEN

Skal is okay, Pripps the same, but St. Erik's Jubileumsöl (ale) and Morköl (a dark beer) are better than okay. Göteborg Stout and Carnegie Stout are meritorious although hardly in the same league with Guinness. Lighter in flavor and color, and a bit too hoppy for my taste.

### SWITZERLAND

One almost hates to admit that this super-prosperous little country, whose banks own half the world, has some good beer for us common folk, because it somehow seems inexplicable. However, like most inexplicable phenomena, it's true. Lucerne's Huberstasbräu Brewery makes Dunkles Starkbier and a Helles (light) that are very good German-type beers, and another fifty-nine breweries make pretty good beer. Although Switzerland is both French and German in influence, the beer is distinctly Germanic in taste and talent. Zurich's Zürcher Löwenbräu is a good example of the very special Swiss ability to duplicate the best of all possible worlds.

### YUGOSLAVIA

The best beer in Italy, via Trieste, is Dreher's, and this is probably the best in Yugoslavia as well. I've been in Trieste, *haven't* visited Yugoslavia, but I understand the beer in general is much, much better than in Italy.

## Elsewhere

### ISRAEL

This country exports its Nesher, Abir, and Maccabee brands of beer, and surprisingly—or maybe *not* so surprisingly—these are the best beers in the Middle East.

## South America

This continent has had a lot of German settlers, including some Nazi refugees who deserve accommodation elsewhere. The continent is far too big in size and small in beers of any fame to go into detail here, especially since I've little personal acquaintance with its brews, but Club Colombia from the nation of the same name is quite a superior beer and very popular down south.

## Antarctica

There are no beers here of note, but it's all served as cold as you could possibly wish. Beer popsicles are not an impossibility here.

*"The ale-taster . . . flew not by instruments, but by the seat of his pants."*

To gentlemen and Yeomen good,
Come in and drink with Robin Hood,
If Robin Hood is not at home,
Come in and drink with Little John.

> —popular couplet declaimed at pubs where Robin and his merry men were favorite heroes

Time, gents, as they say at the end of a pub day in England, to return to Saxon England. If you remember your history, in 1066 William the Conqueror defeated King Harold II in the Battle of Hastings, and England fell under Norman rule. It became a nation divided horizontally—the Normans in their huge, strategically located castles; the former Saxon lords, who had collaborated with the victors; and most of the abbots, whose primary allegiance had always been to Rome rather than to Saxon England, all in the upper stratum of society. And the rest of the country was down below. There were no Saxon leaders left, save one—yep(!), Robin Hood himself. As John Watney points out in his book:

> The one exception was Robin Hood, believed now to have been a Saxon earl, who fled to Sherwood Forest and raised there a group of resistance fighters. It is significant that in all the tales of his deeds, he invariably robbed the rich, i.e., the conquering Normans, to give to the poor, i.e., the beaten Saxons. He was par-

ticularly hard on those abbots who had grown rich by accepting Norman rule.

To me, Robin Hood will always be Errol Flynn, not Sean Connery, and I know that Errol would have stuck to good English ale, rather than run with the Norman habit of drinking wine. Given two cultures—the Norman rulers and the fink abbots drank wine, the priests and monks, whose ties to the peasantry were far more intimate, continued to brew and drink ale just as they did before the Norman conquest—wine became the obligatory snob drink, rather than simply a mark of cultivation, and ale strictly the drink of the common folk. Church authorities, recognizing the close affinity between those clergymen below the level of Abbot and the populace, and the fact that clerics might get powerful thirsty while on the road, permitted them to step inside the nearest watering hole, provided it was out of necessity. But no going there on behalf of fun—the Archbishop Walter ordained, around 1200, that "clerks go not to taverns and drinking bouts, for from thence come quarrels, and then laymen beat clergymen, and fall under the Canon."

Dear mother, dear mother, the Church is cold;
But the Alehouse is healthy and pleasant and warm.
Besides I can tell where I am used well;
The poor parsons with wind like a blown bladder
  swell.

But if at the Church they would give us some ale,
And a pleasant fire our souls to regale,
We'd sing and we'd pray all the livelong day,
Nor ever once wish from the Church to stray.

Then the Parson might preach and drink and sing,
And we'd be as happy as birds in the spring;
And modest Dame Lurch, who is always at Church
Would not have bandy children nor fasting nor birch.

And God, like a father, rejoicing to see
His children as pleasant and happy as he,
Would have no more quarrel with the Devil or the
     barrel,
But kiss him, and give him both drink and apparel.

> —*The Little Vagabond* by William Blake, poet, painter, and mystic

In addition to their brewing duties, the monks became innkeepers as well, since hospitality and shelter was expected of them by religious pilgrims, by ordinary travelers, and, on occasion, by royal personages and their large entourage. For instance, King John was a famous—well, infamous—sponger, and once invited himself for a stay at Bury St. Edmunds "at enormous expense," moaned the prior of the abbey afterward. The king left, by way of thanks to the saint, thirteen pence sterling, this munificent sum being bestowed during the mass, when no one could in good conscience complain of His Majesty's chintziness. Partly as an act of self-preservation, therefore, the busier abbeys established separate inns—run by civilians, who had no religious qualms about the price of things—to accommodate all but the few guests they couldn't (again, in good conscience) refuse a night's lodging and refreshment.

Not so surprisingly, enter price controls. In 1188 Henry II levied the first national tax on the malt liquor trade to help finance the Crusades (a bloody tax indeed!). But his son, Henry III, looked more kindly on the consumer, equating ale with bread as daily staples and issuing the Assize of Bread and Ale to govern the retail prices of both products, these being dependent under the act on the current price of corn and malt. Since ale was considered a necessity of life, this royal act reflected the political savvy in high places that ale not be priced beyond the means of the general populace. The historic impact of this royal edict can be judged by the fact that it remained in effect for three hundred years.

> Thou oft hast made my friends my foes,
> And often made me pawn my clothes;
> But since thou art so nigh my nose,
> Come up, my friend, and down he goes,
> For 'tis O, good old ale, thou art my darling
> And my job both night and morning.

> —stanza of a poem by a dedicated, if sometimes impoverished, ale devotee; apparently he was too busy signing chits at his favorite "local" to bother signing his poem.

That this price control statute was taken seriously was particularly evident in Bristol, which issued its own Brewers' Assize in 1283 warning that any brewsters—women still brewed the folks' beer—or ale vendors who charged more than the official prices could be responsible for bringing punishment to the town itself. Another matter of official concern was what went into ale. Usually it was barley malt, but there were times when wheat was less expensive than barley, and the maltsters would offer the brewing people wheat malt. However, since wheat flour was essential to the making of bread, its use for malt was prohibited whenever a bad crop reduced the wheat supply. In any case, barley malt was—and remains—the basic raw material used in ale and beer in England. In this country, by contrast, there is a considerable reliance on corn and rice for reasons of economics and the desire to produce a bright-looking beer.

> You shall swear that you shall know of no brewer or brewster who sells . . . ale . . . otherwise than by measure sealed and full of clear ale . . . and that as soon as you shall be so required to taste any ale . . . shall be ready to do the same; and in case it be less good than it used to be before this cry, you, by assent of your Alderman, shall set a reasonable price thereon, according to your discretion . . . So God you help and the Saints.
>
> —oath taken by the aleconners of London in 1377

Now enter the ale taster: he was part of the price control board of his time and was summoned whenever an alehouse-keeper had a new supply of ale to offer for sale. This municipal post was created sometime in the mid-1300s to ensure that alehouse-keepers weren't mucking around with the price structure of ale—that it wasn't outsized-assized. The ale taster, or aleconner, as he was known in the more sophisticated confines of Londontown, made his fiscal judgments based on the official price for different qualities of ale. Hence, he first had to ascertain that the stuff was worth drinking—tasted *good*, not just okay—had the proper clarity—dark and murky would mean impurities (probably microorganisms, as we now know of beer that looks hazy)—had body to it and kept its head (as did, hopefully, the ale taster). He also had to be sure it was sufficiently strong in alcoholic strength, and since he didn't know about such modern gadgets as the

hydrometer, he flew not by instruments but by the seat of his pants. Wearing his special ale taster's leather breeches, he poured a tankard of the ale being tested on a wooden bench and then sat down on that wet portion of the bench for a half-hour or so. Whatever discomfort he may have felt, and the leather probably protected him in that regard, he assuaged with drink and talk. Then it would be time for the moment of truth: If he tried to rise and his breeches tried to stay on the bench, then the ale had too much sugar in it and was too weak. Not very precise, but not unscientific, either, for if the sugar had been properly converted into alcohol then the ale would be robust and worth drinking. Perhaps the only unfortunate aspect to the ale taster's methodology was the size of his dry-cleaning bills.

Since the ale taster couldn't check every alehouse in his district each day, and the telephone and telegraph hadn't been invented, a new use was found for the kind of pole that had been originally used to identify alehouses—that is, to distinguish them from other retail establishments. Now these poles, or alestakes as they were known, were used only when a visit from the ale taster was in order. And a new way had to be found to say that ale was available on these premises.

Other tradesmen tended to display the tools of their profession. Any form of written sign would have been quite valueless to the people, who were mostly illiterate. For some unknown reason alehouses adopted signs which bore no relation to their trade, choosing everyday things which could be easily depicted and recognized. They used the sun, moon and stars, or animals, and sometimes the coloured coat of arms of the lord of the manor.

—*A History of the English Public House,* a fine piece of social history by H. A. Monckton, published in Great Britain in 1969

Take away the TV antennae and the cars in the background, and this peaceful scene could be . . . well, a *long* time ago. A hundred years before William of Normandy conquered England, the monks of Eynesbury built a priory to venerate the relics of St. Neots. Beside the Priory and the bridge, a hostel flourished. When Henry VIII dissolved the monasteries, stones from the Priory were used to rebuild the bridge and enlarge the Bridge Hotel, an inn now owned by Whitbread Breweries.

Interestingly enough, although there was this extensive control over the price structure of ale—the position of ale taster became necessary when local authorities, being expected to enforce the Assize of Bread and Ale, found they couldn't possibly supervise the growing number of alehouses in their area—the business of alehouse hours was left strictly to local ordinance. Most places had curfews of one sort or another—9 P.M. in winter, 10 in summertime—and in London the authorities, reflecting a concern about fourteenth century crime in the streets, issued this proclamation: "Whereas misdoers, going about at night, have their resort more in taverns than elsewhere, and there seek refuge and watch their hour for misdoing, we forbid that any taverner or brewer keep the door of his tavern open after the hour of curfew. . . ."

The early alehouses in the cities were seldom buildings built for that purpose, but most likely had been somebody's house. This homey touch notwithstanding, they were pretty grim places. The buildings were close together and, being made of timber and having thatched roofs, were communal fire hazards. Outside the narrow cobble-stoned streets were dirty, and the tradespeople and residents added to the filth by throwing their garbage into the gutter located in the middle of the sloped streets. It was common practice to throw waste water into the streets as well, and this was likely to descend upon the pigs and domestic animals grubbing for food in the streets. Gadzooks, it must have been more than enough to drive a man to drink!

. . . that all alehouses be forbidden except those which shall be licensed by the Common Council of the City at Guildhall, excepting those belonging to persons who will build of stone, that the city may be secure. And that no baker or ale-wife brew by night, either with reeds or straw or stubble.

—edict by the City Council of London, a city that has known fire all too well

There was no drinking allowed on Sunday until after the High Mass was celebrated. On the other hand, in the inns—still run by the monks—you could drink anytime since inns were intended to provide a second home for their guests. If an Englishman's home was his castle, so, too, was his inn. These inns, or hostels, ranged in their civility from quite modest to absolutely glorious, being known for their food as well as accommodations. The term *pub* is derived from public house—which is how these inns later became known. But you can get a pretty good hangover-type headache trying to explain the difference between a pub and a tavern (the famous Mermaid Tavern, Shakespeare's hangout, for example) and a hotel and an inn since all served liquid cheer and all the larger ones had rooms for travelers. You can also have some fun trying to determine which is the oldest pub in the land. Ye Olde Trip to Jerusalem, a fabulous inn located in Nottingham—many of its rooms are hewn out of the solid rock on which Nottingham Castle stands—is one claimant since its name attests to the fact that in 1189 the Crusaders used to stop off there to drink to their mutual success, over several hundred tankards of ale, before setting off to the Holy Land. Another candidate: the Angel Hotel—now the Angel and Royal Hotel—in tiny Grantham, Lincolnshire, which played host to King John in 1213, thereby earning the "Royal" addition to its name. The Maid's Head in Norwich and the George in Norton St. Philip, Somerset, also date back to early medieval times, and the charming little Fighting Cocks in St. Alban, Hertfordshire, is another feisty claimant to the title. Whatever the identity of the one true oldest pub—and I think I could be coaxed into accepting a plump foundation grant to settle this burning issue once and for all time—those inns still in existence mostly date from 1400 on. After the Dissolution of the Monasteries in the 1530s, all their guesthouses came under private ownership, and the great English innkeeping tradition was underway, to be chronicled and immemorialized by English writers—Chaucer's *Canterbury Tales* is one big inn story—through the centuries.

> The World affordes not such Innes as England hath, either for good and cheape entertainment after the Guests owne pleasure, or for humble attendance on passengers.
>
> —teacher, professional traveler, and inn admirer Fynes Moryson, whose four-volume *Itinerary* (1617) established him as one of the first English-language travel writers

With the growth of gracious inns, those tacky old alestakes wouldn't do anymore. Some of them were so heavy they posed a safety problem, while others stuck out over the highway to the extent that they represented a traffic hazard, and in the late 1300s King Richard II ordered that alehouses in particular must exhibit a sign. It was a very strict law—"Whosoever shall brew in the town with intention of selling it must hang out a sign, otherwise he shall forfeit his ale." And since Richard wanted signs, he got them in profusion and in all sizes and weights. Before too long, the streets of English towns and cities were so cluttered with signs advertising ale they must have looked like some of our better highways.

> At London they are commonly very large, and jut out so far, that in some narrow streets they touch one another; nay, and run across almost quite to the other side. They are generally adorned with carving and guilding; and there are several that, with the branches of iron which support them, cost above a hundred guineas. . . . Out of London, and particularly in villages, the signs of inns are suspended in the middle of a great wooden portal, which may be looked upon as a kind of triumphal arch to the honour of Bacchus.
>
> —good reportage by a traveler from France, even though he or she got his or her gods wrong

Interestingly enough, despite the proliferation of outlets for the drinking of beer—be they alehouses, taverns, or inns—most of the beer consumed was still being brewed domestically. If you wanted an evening on the town, you could of course visit the nearest oasis for ale, and when closing time was sounded, you might still be able to buy some ale from a peculiar type of street vendor known as a huckster, usually a woman, who bought her brew from an alehouse and then resold it. The authorities did not smile on this unsupervised form of beer trade, but hucksters survived. In his book on the British pub, H. A. Monckton, who is a brewer as well as historian, surmises that the huckster's price was probably the same as that of the alehouse since the public wouldn't have tolerated an intermediary merchant raising the cost of ale. (These days, however, one would be hard pressed to find a huckster who *isn't* high priced.) "Bread is the staff of life, but beer is life itself,"—old Oxfordshire saying.

In 1437 the Brewers' Company received its first royal charter, and this City Company—the City of London granted charters for a specific trade—exercised a bit of a monopoly on commercial brewing for some years. Since their ancestors were still at home making their own beer, the great English and Scottish brewing families—the Watneys, Whitbreads, Trumans, Youngers, Barclays, and

Courages (John Courage was the son of a French Huguenot family that settled in Aberdeen, Scotland)—had yet to come upon the scene. Thus you had a marked contrast with the current situation (to be discussed elsewhere in the book) in which a handful of brewing companies descended from these families control most of the beer trade since they also own most of the nation's pubs in Great Britain. Only Guinness, which cleverly owns no pubs, can be found almost everywhere.

This is not to say, however, that none of the early British brews enjoyed any fame. In particular Burton ale from Burton-on-Trent, near Stafford in the middle of England, was revered. Some unacknowledged monk had determined that the waters of the Trent River, running over rocks of gypsum, contained a variety of minerals which helped produce an ale of brightness and clarity. This in turn led to the discovery that the best water for brewing purposes should be light on organic matter and that hard water produced a distinctly tasty beer. Despite the current Coors mystique, however—another item to be discussed in detail later on—all water used for brewing is today treated chemically, and its mineral content is probably no factor at all. Traditions are nice things, though, and it's a pleasure to report that the beers still brewed in Burton-on-Trent are still worth the high regard they enjoy.

Ne'er tell me of liquors from Spain or from France,
They may get in your heels and inspire you to dance,
But the Ale of Old Burton if mellow and right
Will get in your head and inspire you to fight.

Then let meagre Frenchmen still batten on Wine,
They ne'er will digest a good English Sirloin,
Parbleu they may caper and Vapour along,
But right Burton can make us both valiant and strong.

—old English drinking song, strongly anti-Common Market and probably written on the shores of the Trent River

Although wealthy families continued to brew their own brews, the expansion of the commercial brewing trade—there were now the Free Brewers in addition to the Brewers' Company in London, plus many small breweries throughout the country—began increasingly to account for the ale consumed by those who weren't of the gentried classes. Whatever the vagaries of the beer industry, though, there remained this one constant: only malt, yeast, and water could be used to produce ale, and any other ingredients were considered adulterants; and those found guilty of committing adultery with the integrity of their ale were severely punished.

Ancient tablet near Holborn Bridge.

Courtesy of New York Public Library, Picture Collection.

# 18/The Fight for Real Ale

(Richard Gilbert, with whom I first experimented on the possibilities of the Super Pub Crawl in Manhattan, is one of my favorite people. We have pubbed London in all directions; and if we've never managed a Super Pub Crawl because of time limitations, we've certainly managed some perfect ones. Dick first told me about CAMRA during the summer of 1973, when my family and I were spending a perfectly wonderful month in London. Since then I've been back three times, and I always inquire after the progress of CAMRA. So, rather than keep the information to myself, I've asked Dick to bring us up-to-date on this remarkable organization.)

The pound sterling may be threatened; inflation cannot be restrained; the English cricket team lost the Ashes yet again to Australia; the trains are not running on time; and there's been another record rainfall. But amid all this gloom and despondency there is one bright, if small, light shining. The fight is on to save the Englishman's pride and joy—his pint of real beer. The Campaign for Real Ale (CAMRA), founded by a handful of enthusiastic beer drinkers in 1971, now has over 30,000 members, has formed a public company to buy up pubs and breweries, publishes its own *Good Beer Guide,* and is denting the armor of the big six breweries whose taste-alike products are not recognized as real ale by the connoisseurs.

CAMRA's impact is an encouraging story for those who believe that thinking small is an essential tool for survival in this age of Goliaths. The background to their beginnings was the merger of numerous small breweries into large companies in 1969-70. The big six (who now own two-thirds of all pubs and make three-quarters of all beer drunk in Britain) are interested in quick returns on their investments, rationalization of beer production, and curtailment of the numerous brands of beer available (currently 1,500, but you have to look hard to find them) in favor of keg beer.

The real ale lovers define their favorite brew as "beer brewed from malt and hops, stored in barrels, and served by methods which do not use carbon dioxide pressure." CAMRA emphasizes that beer should leave the brewery in its natural state—still able to ferment in the cask. Keg beer, which is too often the only beer available in most pubs, is an entirely different drink. It is made with inferior ingredients like hop extracts (thus preventing the brewer from instilling individual character and flavor into his beers). It is filtered and pasteurized, which robs the beer of its taste and prevents its continuing fermentation. It is stored in kegs (thus providing the name of the concoction) or pressurized casks. When it is served, it is forced from its container by an injection of carbon dioxide pressure. Innocent drinkers believe that simply because their beer has a foaming head, it must be a good beer. In fact, the head is irrelevant to the quality of British beer since most of the head in keg beers is the result of carbon dioxide!

Many of the real ales which CAMRA supports have no head at all, but their individual taste is remarkable. These beers come from small breweries whose names are as English as the perfect pint—Boddington's of Manchester, Donnington's of Stow-on-the-Wold, Elgoods of Wisbech, Higsons of Liverpool, Ruddles of Rutland, Theakstons of Masham, and Thwaites of Blackburn. This roll call of distinguished beers is as evocative for the beer drinker as Mouton Rothschild and Montrachet are to wine lovers.

"It is an argument of choice." That is how CAMRA executive Michael Hardman sums up the campaign. "We want to persuade brewers to make available the sort of beer we want to drink. We don't want to replace keg, but we do want to see real beers on sale alongside it. A significant number of people want real ale. The brewers are ignoring them. We are providing important information for the consumer." The big brewers reply by saying that keg beer is what people want. In fact, they promote keg with enormous advertising campaigns (which add to the cost of keg) and do little to sell the lesser-known beers, which they actually own because they have taken over so many small, independent breweries.

Because of CAMRA's work, and the public's boredom with keg beer, last year's figures reveal that profits slumped among the big six, while the small breweries still making real ale boomed. For example, Fullers of West London saw the sales of their legendary Extra Special Bitter rocket by 400 percent. CAMRA's appeal has been to all age-groups and all political complexions. Britain's Minister of Defense in the Labor government, Roy Mason, launched a petition to prevent the closure of a northern brewery whose ale he liked. Just as keen a supporter of CAMRA is Conservative M.P. Nicholas Winterton. He played an important part in raising money via a stock issue for CAMRA. They expected about $200,000. The public subscribed $500,000—enough to buy up to a dozen pubs which will all serve at least three different real draught beers. The first two, in Bristol and in Cheshire, opened under CAMRA ownership and have been joined by others, including two London pubs.

The campaign concerns itself with more than the quality of real ale. It is also fighting to ensure that pubs remain public houses where beer drinkers can feel at ease. Too many city pubs are becoming glorified discotheques and dance halls. But the campaign's *Good Beer Guide* lists 2,700 pubs all over Britain where you can get good beer and a decent environment. The *Guide* sold out its first edition of 35,000 copies, and using it wisely, you can guarantee yourself an excellent pub crawl in most parts of the country. CAMRA members place great emphasis on the survival of traditional pub food like pickled onions and Scotch egg and traditional games like darts, bar billiards and shove ha'penny.

Their ninety different groups meet regularly, and they are recruiting about 2,000 new members each month. The geographical balance of membership means that CAMRA knows every brewery and the location of all the real beer in the country. Although relations with the big brewers have been sometimes unfriendly, currently CAMRA is helping them in bringing to the public's notice the threat to the survival of the smaller brewers caused by the planned new Death Duties called the Capital Transfer Tax. This could have the effect of killing off seventy small breweries and up to a thousand different beers.

CAMRA is also keeping a close watch on advertising claims put forward by the brewers of keg beers. Already they have forced one large company, Watneys, to change the wording of their advertisements on television for Watneys Special—proving that this particular keg is weaker than it used to be. The columns of CAMRA's monthly magazine, *What's Brewing*, carry regular consumer tests on different ales revealing alcohol percentage and overall strength. There is also a useful diary of CAMRA events—most of which seem to be organized pub crawls ("Meet at Foresters Arms 8 P.M.")

The grass-roots success of CAMRA is encouraging. Beer is to be enjoyed, but also it deserves to be taken seriously, just like wine. It is a sign of the times that the *Guardian* newspaper now has a beer article by a columnist once a week. Wine writers are two a penny, and the establishment of a beer correspondent in a quality paper is long overdue. The fight for real ale is on in earnest.

Postscript: Since this was written, I got a letter and some newspaper clippings from Dick about the first annual CAMRA beer bash, called the London Beer Festival. "It was a major success," writes Dick. "I spent one very beery lunch-time there sampling five or six different brews. . . . CAMRA is now thinking of an even more ambitious festival next year—something comparable to the Munich *Oktoberfest*."

According to one of the clippings he sent along, the festival, held at London's old Covent Garden flower hall, featured more than fifty different types of beer made by thirty breweries. It sounded like great fun. To quote just a bit from the article:

> Echoing to the cries of "another Old Peculiar, please," London's largest "pub" is doing a roaring trade. Queues stretching through Covent Garden streets illustrate the success of the London Beer Festival. . . . The "Old Peculiar" is a draught beer made by Theakston's brewery and is reputed to be the strongest beer available in Britain. . . . The festival is seen by CAMRA officials as a prelude to a national 10-day beer festival, which they believe could become an annual event to rival Munich's notorious festival.

Ah, brave new world of ten-day beer festivals!

An old pub, "tarted up," *(top)* as the English say, to look like an old pub. One of London's several "museum pubs," The Sherlock Holmes *(bottom)*. The great detective's drawing room is recreated inside. And there's Sherlock outside, haggling with his cocaine dealer.

FRITZ HEUSER IN ASGARD

July 1 1949

WAD

W. A. Dwiggins

# 19/Vignette: A Lecture on What to Drink Where

I am having lunch with John Segal. He is a hops sales-man and, I understand, a top one in his field. I mentioned his name to a West Coast brewmaster, and he said, "Oh, yes, a very solid, *very* good man."

We are eating in a good Japanese restaurant. I am drink-ing Kirin beer, which is made in Japan. He is drinking Schaefer, which was then made in Brooklyn, New York (the company has since moved its plant out of the state).

I find Kirin a very good beer—the third best selling beer in the world behind Budweiser and Schlitz—and I'm cur-ious why John is not drinking it as well. He can drink Schaefer any old time.

He explains that he always drinks the beer that's made locally, in this case, Schaefer. But, I argue, doesn't he think Kirin is tastier, more interesting?

He doesn't dispute this point. However, he says, he would drink Kirin if he were in Japan, but not in a Japa-nese restaurant in New York. Beer begins to deteriorate slightly from the moment it's canned or bottled, he ex-plains, and my Kirin has taken some time to get here. It traveled here by ship and then by truck or freight train, he points out, and it's hardly fresh beer anymore.

Fresh beer is important to John Segal. He can read the label on a beer bottle and tell when it was bottled. He does this, for my edification, and the beer he is drinking was bottled this same month. That's fresh, all right. It really makes a lot of sense.

We order another round of beer. He orders Schaefer. I order Kirin. I don't care. It tastes better to me. I know it would taste even better to me in Japan, but it still tastes better to me in New York. I guess I am a beer snob and didn't know it.

Still, I wonder what John Segal is drinking in New York these days, now that Schlitz, Schaefer, and Rheingold have all moved—lock, stock, and beer barrel—out of the state.

Beer and politics—an old American custom.

# 20/The Super Pub Crawl: Boston

Boston has long been one of my favorite cities. Friends and I used to go up there weekends—and occasionally weeknights—from the University of Connecticut because Boston wasn't Hartford or Bridgeport, either. Boston was a *nice* big city. Manageable. Walkable. Potentially the right place to be for a lad from a Middletown, Connecticut, USA.

I did my graduate work, after the service, in Boston, and after I learned to be adept with chopsticks, my old friends formally accepted me back as one of them. This was important because some of *them* took Chinese food more seriously than graduate school. Not me. I had my priorities down pat. The Big Five, in order of importance, were: (1) graduate school; (2) gals and/or girls (Boston is full of them, both of the town and gown sects); (3) clothes (I was building my first young man's conservative wardrobe with the help of Filene's Bargain Basement, Harvard Square clothiers, and some semisecret plain pipe rack treasures we'd collectively dug up); (4) Chinese food with the guys; and (5) Chinese food with the gals, just so long as they mastered the art of chopsticks.

By now you will have surely gathered that Boston is a great college town, probably without parallel given the number of colleges and universities in Boston, Cambridge, and outlying areas. It still is a great college town. You used to be able to tell Boston was a great college town by how quiet it got when the colleges weren't in session. It still gets that way. But Boston has a strange duality—the ultimate college town and yet a place to which you can go

home again. Boston implies permanence, tradition. More than any American city, it reminds me of London because of its parks and tree-lined streets and generations of courteous citizens.

At the same time Boston is throwing up new buildings like cities everywhere, some good ones, a few disasters, and the two reigning controversies—the new City Hall and the reflective glass John Hancock office tower, whose windows keep flying out and whose appearance and height, an architectural bonus elsewhere, intrude on the classic lines of Boston's Copley Square. Happily, Boston is also doing some fine restoration.

"This is the city's most exciting area," says my old friend, Richard Opie, as our cab moves through what used to be Scollay Square, home of hookers and nestling port for sailors. Around us are the monumentally modernistic City Hall, which I like, from the outside, new state and federal buildings, and all kinds of Boston structures being renovated or restored. It is exciting to someone who hasn't visited Boston for a few years. Opie—he is both Dick and Opie to his friends, but anyone can be a Richard or a Dick, and how many Opies do you know?—and I get out when our taxi pulls up alongside Commercial Wharf, the first (1822-24) granite wharf built on the Boston waterfront. As we enter The Wharf, which is to launch our Super Pub Crawl, he explains that both Commercial Wharf and Lewis Wharf, across the yacht basin to our left, are now highly desirable places to live because of their apartments and condominiums with harbor views, their posh shops, restaurants, and other amenities on the ground floor. "This was a dive before," he says of The Wharf as we get settled at one of the wooden telephone spool tables to the rear of the long room. "The decor was nautical overkill." Now the room can hardly be faulted. True, the new false ceiling of slatted boards painted black is designed to hide the air-conditioning ducts and the old ceiling, but this is only noticeable because it's still daytime. Later, when the light changes, the ceiling blends nicely with the other decor. On one side, there is a wall of varnished old boards, decorated only with an occasional ship captain's letter or other framed nautical document; on the other, a wall of windows looks out on the small yachts, sailing cruisers, and other vessels moored on both sides. There are tables as you enter. Opie takes pains to point out that the handle on the inside of the door is not wood but whale bone. There is a bar of unusual length and a room to the rear, all looking out on the water. The only decor on the water side is a hanging plant here and there. It's all properly understated. Why compete with the free view out there?

The draft beer is domestic Tuborg, but there's no complaint in that department. The bar is just beginning to get a little busy, and Opie points out that later on The Wharf becomes a "meat rack"—a crude term for singles bar. "They all flock in from Dorchester," Opie says, "and it really jumps here." Then he adds, "I like it best on Sunday afternoons. It's nicer, then, with a more relaxed crowd." Opie knows the three guys who own The Wharf, and I'd like to meet them and congratulate them on the tasteful bar they've created. I'd also like to enjoy the view of the water with the lights shimmering over its surface when it gets completely dark, but duty calls us all over Boston. After all, I flew up to Boston for this tour of duty.

"You could spend the entire evening just cruising this area," Opie observes as we head out for our next destination. "There are plenty of pubs to check out and interesting restaurants and all the renovation going on." He's right, of course, and in point of fact, we will be staying in the immediate area for our next two pub stops. We walk toward Durgin Park's Gaslight Pub. I am not providing precise directions because of all the construction going on, and, besides, anyone can direct you to this famous old restaurant no more than five minutes away. Opie remarks on the way that the area is this lively because it draws not only Boston area people, but flocks of tourists. Faneuil Hall over there, known to schoolkids since 1776 as "The Cradle of Liberty" because of its role in the American Revolution, is on the "Freedom Trail" through historic Boston. And Durgin Park, with its fat slices of roast beef, huge lobsters, and native desserts—Indian Pudding was a favorite in my dessert-eating days—has been the stuffing stop for generations of Bostonians, college students, and visitors. The entire block-long row of attached buildings in which Durgin Park is situated has been gutted, except for the landmark restaurant, and each building is about to undergo interior renovation. But now they look a little ghostly sitting there with their black windows and doors. As for Durgin Park itself, we don't plan to hit the restaurant this particular evening—can't let struggling with a lobster claw take away from valuable pub time—but we are going to have a beer in the downstairs Gaslight Pub. Not because of the decor, mind you—low-ceiling with a small bar in front and tables in back with the familiar red-checkered tablecloths—but because of the atmosphere engendered by the city hall types and other politicos who come here for a drink before heading homeward. You can overhear or enter into (if you're knowledgeable enough) some pretty interesting conversations, Opie informs me, and relates a few choice but uncelebrated debates he's conducted here. Still, the ambience is quite relaxed, and since there's only a service bar upstairs in the restaurant, this is the place to be. No draft beer, but the bottled selections

Reprinted from *A Seidel for Jake Wirth* (Boston, 1964), p. 33.

Jake Wirth's is a Boston institution that no amount of urban renewal can improve upon. Worth's used to provide its customers with these souvenir postcards.

Reprinted from *A Seidel for Jake Wirth*
(Boston, 1964), p. 11.

should please: Bud, Schlitz, Miller, Löwenbräu, and Heineken. Also not to be underappreciated is the excellent popcorn.

Our next pub is again just minutes away—again ask directions, for the same reason as before. It is called Clarke's, quite possibly after the popular old Third Avenue bar we visited on our East Side crawl. This Clarke's seems every bit as popular as New York's, being jammed with young government workers and singles galore, but there a distinction must be drawn. P. J. Clarke's looks the way it did the day it first opened its doors, and so, too, does this Clarke's except that it first opened its doors in July 1975 and the decor looks to be the output of an instant pub factory. It's hokey—"borrowed decor" is how the omniscient Opie put it—and an example of the axiom, "Sometimes more can be less." In fact, the restaurant room next door, with just tables and plain brick walls, at least seemed genuine and visually pleasing, even if it was opened at the same time as the barroom.

Still, there's nothing terribly wrong with the bar itself at Clarke's. It's a large, rectangular "island bar" with a lot of space around it, both nice and necessary since this is certainly one of the city's liveliest bars. To leave it off our pub crawl would be dishonest because it is so popular. The bartenders are friendly, and there's some decent brew to be had on draft. I don't recommend the Guinness, which is rarely good on draft in this country. But the Falstaff merited no complaint, and the Harp deserved very favorable mention. Next to where we were standing at the bar, a pretty young woman ordered a gin gimlet on the rocks, and you should have seen her expression of awe when it arrived in a beer stein. I'll bet she's still drinking it. So a good mark to Clarke's of Boston for its potables.

Now it's cab time, to Jake Wirth's of Boston at 31-37 Stuart Street, the city's most venerated German restaurant and bar since 1868. In that year Jacob Wirth, newly arrived from the old country, opened for business across the street at number 60. Then he moved a decade later to the present location, the red brick Greek Revival structure at number 37-39. In 1890, he doubled the size of his restaurant, appropriating numbers 35, 33, and 31 in the process.

We take a cab to Wirth's—formally the "Jacob Wirth Co. Restaurant"—not just because of the distance, but because the area surrounding nearby Washington Street, once part of the city's most popular shopping thoroughfare, is now known as the "Combat Zone" because of its prostitutes, its sailor bars, porn theaters, and bookshops. It is now considered really dangerous. By delicious contrast, Jake Wirth's has changed almost not at all over the years. The sawdust is gone from the floor—having been swept away by a city ordinance ten years or so ago—but the same magnificent mahogany bar still dominates the barroom. The medallion of the elder Jacob Wirth and his imposing mustache surveys the customers, and Jacob Wirth's motto in large medal letters—SUUM CUIQUE ("To each his own")—still glistens against the polished wood of the bar. The old bar clock (always at four o'clock) is there below the medallion and above the motto, and the three-sided cashier's cage still stands at the end of the drinking bar. But Wirth's is mostly a monument to wood; the dark mahogany of the bar, the woodwork and the tables, and a wonderful sight in this chrome and plastic age.

"You know," says Opie, who thinks he may not have been in Wirth's since the last time I was in Boston, "this was always an institution. My father was a customer all his life [his father, now in his eighties, lives in California], and so was *his* father." We decided to drink to that, this time with a large mug of the light Dawson's—both light and dark on draft—which at fifty-five cents is the best buy in New England. In the old days, Wirth's was much esteemed for the fine wines the owner imported from France and Germany and the array of beers he served. Wirth was the sole Boston agent for Anheuser-Busch beers, including Bud in the bottle and Faust on tap, the well-regarded Hell

Gate product (light and dark) from George Ehrets' New York brewery (on draft), Robert Smith's India Pale Ale from Philadelphia in bottles, and the draft beers made by Narragansett in Providence. There were also Pilsener and two German brews on draft (then "draught") and two kinds of Bass Ale and Guinness Stout in bottles. A remarkable selection, for the times.

These days, while there is just Dawson's on draft, this is hardly a cause for grousing since it's first-rate beer. No one behind the bar when we were there knew where it's brewed. The variety of German beers (light and dark) in bottles should handle anyone with a curious palate. Since I was familiar with Beck's, Wurzburger, Dinkelacker, and Augustinerbrau, I tried the Hansa Dark, which is made in Dortmund. The bartender took a bottle out of the old wooden refrigerator cabinet, poured it into a wine glass, and my knowledge of beer was soon eleven ounces superior to what it had been.

Opie and I along about this time of day decided we had better have something to eat. We didn't want to sit down to a full German meal since we might not be able to move afterward, but bratwurst and knockwurst (*mit kraut* made on the premises) are served at the bar, as is Wirth's superior rye bread and a selection of imported and domestic cheeses. We each had a bratwurst and split an order of Liederkranz, and marched out into the night fairly certain that old Jacob Wirth had winked at us from his medallion when we left his fine establishment.

You might want to take a cab to our next stop, but we definitely needed some air and exercise, and therefore proceeded across the Boston Common for a stroll around historic Beacon Hill, which deserves much better than the TV series of the same name. No trip to Boston is complete for me unless I visit Louisberg Square, which, if you could make the fancy four-wheeled vehicles disappear, would look the same as it did a century or more ago. Knowing that we had been neighbors on Louisberg Square in another life, and reinvigorated by this knowledge, the two of us then gamboled down the other side of Beacon Hill for a peek at Harvard Gardens, a bar which once had a certain seedy charm to it. Alas, now it's been fixed up, has no charm at all, and isn't worth a visit, even for nostalgic purposes. Thus, onward down Charles Street, still a handsome shopping street in back of the hill, to "The Sevens," the Colonial Cafe at 77 Charles Street, to take another chance with nostalgia. Urg! We were very disappointed. This wasn't the scruffy "Sevens" we used to know and love in our youth. Unfortunately, some cad with absolutely no sense of history whatsoever had transformed the raffish charm of "The Sevens" with its wall-to-wall artist-student-professional bohemian population, into a mock-Tudor pub. There was even a menu outside! No, let's not bother even to go in here. Best head elsewhere, to some other hostel where our illusions wouldn't be shattered by Progress.

We walked the length of Charles Street; then we hooked a right down Beacon to the Bull & Finch Pub. Once inside, we found out quickly that the place is still rather noisy. This fairly authentic (in dim light) recreation of a Tudor pub is extremely popular and deservedly so, if you can manage to ignore the din of the jukebox. A corner table, diametrically opposite the dart board area, is the best place to sit in the front room, and the back room seemed no less pleasant and somewhat more civilized as regards the noise level. We ordered a Whitbread—Pabst and Bud are also on tap—from one of the quite pretty waitresses, drank it while I gave careful scrutiny to the beamed ceilings, mullioned windows, and pretty waitresses. Then, at last, we decided to retire to more suitable (for the nounce) quarters.

The Bull & Finch is located in the basement of what once must have been someone's sumptuous house. Two flights up is the Quaffer's Club, a very handsome bar-

discotheque that someone I know has described as "the place for guys who are trying to be Boston's new young Brahmins." But you have to be a member, and Opie—nary a Brahmin streak in him—is not. So we settled for a look instead of a drink and went back downstairs. This involved no sacrifice on our part, mind you, because on the ground floor of this building is the Hampshire House, not a pub actually but one of the best-looking rooms for drinking (you can eat here, too) you may expect to find anywhere. There is a light wood bar with a large mirror as you enter and room for perhaps twelve people. If you're bored with your bar companion, you can always stare up at the giant moose head over the bar. I mention this moose head only because the rest of the room with its extremely high ceilings and comfortable couches (very welcome to weary pubcrawlers) has a quietly stated elegance in which Mr. Moose would seem like an intruder if it were not for the fact that his head is so large and his antlers so wide that he is, in his own way, rather elegant, too.

No draft beer at the Hampshire House, but the tall, blond waitress could offer Bud, Schlitz, Molson Ale, and Rolling Rock—"the Coors of the East," she said brightly. Since neither Opie nor I are that much taken with Coors in the first place, we gave Canada our vote over Latrobe, Pennsylvania, a decision we had no cause to regret.

What was beginning to concern us, however, was the passage of time. Boston bars shut their doors at 2 A.M. Since we didn't want to be shut out of our full night's explorations, we dutifully moved on to our next pit stop, the Olde London Pub & Grill in the Lennox Hotel on Boylston Street, one block down from Copley Square. This can be easily walked if one has nothing else to do. But we didn't feel that we could easily walk it, so we took a cab.

There are two pubby-type refuges in the Lennox, which, incidentally, also boasts a very good restaurant called the Budapest, but our destination was the upper bar because of its claim to be a pub constructed in England and shipped over, as a kind of reverse lend-lease in 1969. In that light—not dark, but not light, either—it was hard to tell what fixtures are authentic and what are strictly of 1969 vintage, but the place is cozy and certainly looks to the unsuspicious eye like an old English inn. We ask the friendly blond bartender about this, and she points out what she feels is genuinely old. Then she says, laughing at her dry Bostonian wit, "The sinks aren't sixteenth century, though."

There are two kinds of Britain's Whitbread on draft, which is at least as it should be, but the highlight of our visit here is a thoroughly American treat. In the small room next to the bar, occupying two booths, is the SPEBSQSA having its weekly outing. So it actually was "long ago" for a half-hour or so while the local chapter of the Society for the Preservation and Encouragement of Barbershop Quartet Singing in America, Incorporated, harmonized their way through several thousand songs of sentimental yesteryear. All this mellow melodying could give a guy the delusion that he, too, can sing, so we decided to move on before we got into the act—as did one waitress whenever she wasn't waitressing.

Left across the street and up the block—that's the route to J. C. Hillary's, Ltd., a "city tavern for ladies and gentlemen" that is a smasher. Hillary's is a model for a new "old bar." There has been no attempt at recreating a special type of decor, just a tasteful use of antique pieces and a judicious blend of brick and wallpaper. Long bars both upstairs and downstairs, but no food served upstairs. Instead, there are songs and piano music by a singer—clearly a local favorite—who immediately reminds one of Bobby Short, and not unfavorably, either. It was already late, so we could only catch his final set over a tall, chilled glass of Bud—since we'd ignored the world's leading brand all night. There are also Miller's Dark and Light on draft, but

Opie knew we could get them at out next (probably next-to-last) stop, Charlie's Eating and Drinking Saloon.

If I had to distinguish between the crowd at Hillary's and Charlie's, I'd say that Charlie's has a more sophisticated crowd of regulars because it has been in business longer. It is also friendlier, less reserved for the same reason. Up a block from Hillary's, Charlie's occupies a building that was once a stable, then a warehouse. It finally became a bar seven years ago, after the giant Prudential Center complex went up across the street. Hillary's is a far handsomer place, since Charlie's has a kitschy decor—Tiffany lamps, brick walls, a sort of strange-looking green and white checkerboard ceiling. But Charlie's really does have a very good feel to it. Opie explains that the bar is full of regulars, yet is a good place to meet new people, and thus manages the odd marriage of being at once a singles bar and a neighborhood establishment. Friendship without sex, friendship with sex—whatever your requirements for friendship.

If somehow you have managed to avoid eating thus far, do so (!) at Charlie's because the food is good, and you get a free 12-oz. mug of Miller's with your meal. Since we have eaten, and since our game plan calls for yet one more stop—at nearby Daisy Buchanan's, where Boston's Beautiful People come to gawk at or else mingle with Boston's professional athlete class—we remain at the bar talking with some friends of Opie's instead of getting a table.

Glancing at the clock, I remind Opie that our journey is not over, our trip ticket is not punched out from start to finish.

"There's sometimes a line to get into Daisy's," he reminds me. "Besides, you've been there before and thought it was kind of phoney."

He is right on both counts. Besides, I am not a Red Sox fan. Nor a Bruins fan. Nor a Celtics fan. Me, just now, I am a Charlie's fan.

Galleried inns were common in the England of yesteryear. There is now only one, alas, left in all of Londontown. It's called the George Inn, and it's quite wonderful.

# 21/A Frothy History of Suds

*"Beer was an entirely different kettle of malt, yeast and water, they pointed out. . . ."*

In the early fifteenth century, an event—a series of events, really—occurred that drastically altered British drinking history. As noted earlier, hops were being grown by Flemmish immigrants and British ale began getting bitter (now the common name for British beer, which is really still more ale than beer, by American standards) despite the previous detestation of *bierre* as a distinctly Dutch poison. Andrew Campbell is especially good on this story:

We use the words ale and beer interchangeably today, and even our most sincere consumers would find it difficult to define the difference between them. The trouble with ale was that it rapidly went sour. It had to be drunk soon after it was brewed, and the frequency with which "alegar," which was sour ale, appears in old cookery recipes, proves that every housewife had a quantity on hand, which she used as we nowadays use vinegar. Both hops and beer were imported from Holland and became popular with the Dutch community in London. Many towns in England tried to prevent the brewing of beer by forbidding the use of hops . . . but beer gradually killed ale, and in less than 100 years beer was universally liked in England; an observer of national customs could, in 1577, even refer to ale as that grand old drink of his ancestors. Probably the last real ale is brewed today at Queen's College and Merton College, Oxford, and at Trinity, Cambridge. What is interesting is that the word "ale" should have survived the drink. Whenever

a man asks for a pint of ale instead of a pint of beer, he is asking for something which has not been generally obtainable since the end of the Middle Ages.

> Hops and turkeys, carp and beer
> Came into England all in one year.
>
> Hops, Reformation, Baize and Beer,
> Came into England all in one year.
>
> —two old couplets, both authors
> unknown, on the same subject

Ale didn't disappear without a fight, however. A number of writers of considerable fame campaigned against what they felt was the tasteless intrusion of beer. For instance, the dramatist, Francis Beaumont, wrote this piece of dialogue into one of his plays: "I fear there is heresy in hops." The eminent authority on medical subjects, Andrew Boorde, in his 1542 tome, *A Dyetary of Health*, declared himself against beer in no uncertain terms: "Ale for an Englysshe man is a natural drink . . . barly malte maketh better ale than oten malte or any other corne doth: it doth ingendre grose humoures; but yet it maketh a man strong . . . bere is the naturall drynke for a Dutche man, and nowe of late dayes it is much used in Englande to the Detryment of many Englysche people . . . the drynke is a colde drynke; yet it doth make a man fat, and doth inflate the belly. . . ." Even the songwriters were heard from, as witness this angry air: "And in very deed, the hops but a

Reprinted from the *Scots Magazine*, 1806.

Robert Burns, the Scot poet, and 'Bobby' to all who regarded him as "the wonder of all the gay world," liked to hang out at an Edinburgh hostel owned by an equally free spirit, one Johnnie Dowie *(above)*. When Dowie went off to meet his fellow free spirits in the High Lands of Heaven, the place was rechristened Burns' Tavern, and became a headquarters for lovers of lyric poetry (and Youngers Ale). The dark vertical line on the left side of this lithograph by George Cattermole was a printer's error of the time, and should not detract from the vitality of his vision.

weed/Brought over 'gainst law, and here set to sale, /Would the law were removed, and no more beer brewed, /But all good men betake them to a pot of good ale."

## "DRINKE AND WELCOME
### Or The
## FAMOUS HISTORIE

of the most part of drinks in use now in the kingdomes of
Great Brittaine and Ireland, with an especiall declaration
of the potency, vertue and operation of
our English ale,
with a description of all sorts of waters, from the
ocean sea, to the teares of a woman.
As also,
the causes of all sortes of weather, faire or foule, sleet,
raine, haile, frost, snowe fogges, mists, vapours, clouds,
stormes, windes, thunder and lightning"

—title of a work celebrating English ale, one of numerous such efforts, by John Taylor, known as the "Water Poet" because he'd once been a Thames waterman. No academician he, he ran two public houses, one in Oxford and later, one in London. At the latter, he served the ale he so admired and hawked the doggerel poems he so wanted others to admire. These may be regarded as the first "live" beer commercials.

Naturally enough, this scism with regard to what was proper to go down the nation's gullet put the brewers in an awkward position. It wasn't just a matter of people's preferences, of the sweet taste of ale as opposed to the drier, sharper taste of beer. There was no question but that hops helped produce a more stable drink, and one that would last longer, and therefore, a more economical product—especially since hops were now being grown domestically. On the other hand, there was this golden tradition of ale, particularly strong outside the cities where people were less trendy and stuck to the old ways.

What to do? Well, some brewers tried to have it both ways: They brewed ale and then added hops to it, or they added beer yeast when fermenting ale. But this was a definite no-no, and offenders were fined for messing with their ale. Nonetheless, the brewers knew that sooner or later they would have to get on the beer wagon and in a suave, public relations move set out to do a complete selling job on the public. Beer was an entirely different kettle of malt, yeast, and water, they pointed out, and this distinction would be pointed out wherever beer was sold. Moreover, there would be absolutely no passing off of ale as beer. Since these moral postures won favor with the authorities the beer question, in effect, was settled out of court, and it remained only for people's tastebuds to get adjusted to the new brew.

As Campbell has pointed out, this took time as well as tolerance, but beer had found a permanent home in England and would remain there for people to enjoy and writers—Shakespeare, Dr. Johnson, Thomas Dekker, Oliver Goldsmith, Charles Dickens, the whole groggy lot—to wax eloquent over (although as often as not they still called it ale). In fact, Shakespeare, Beaumont, Dekker, Ben Johnson, and Christopher Marlowe all were regulars at the Falcon Tavern alongside the Thames, and the amount of suds they put away was no doubt equalled by the amount of froth it produced.

CLUB—An assembly of good fellows meeting under certain conditions.

—a definition from Dr. Johnson's Dictionary

Welcome to the club, all you beer drinkers of the world!

# 22/The Correct Care and Proper Service of Beer

As will be pointed out repeatedly in this book, beer is a fragile food. One brewing authority told me that beer would deteriorate in the sun faster than milk. And there is no reason, therefore, to buy a lot of it and store it away someplace. It should be kept in a cool place, certainly, and when you do put it in the refrigerator, keep the bottles upright, not on their sides, so that the least possible amount of the beer is exposed to the air in the bottle. Same goes for cans, even though there's a smaller air pocket inside them. The cans get colder, which is an American fetish, but beer lasts longer in the bottle.

Good bars and taverns get rid of their flat beer. In any case, you can surmise that the busier a place it is, the more beer is turned over, and the more likely the beer will be fresh. If you get a flat beer, or if it in any way tastes a mite peculiar, don't hesitate to send it back. The bartender knows what it's all about.

In retail outlets, the help is supposed to circulate the beer so that the oldest is always in front. This doesn't always happen, but the beer distributors are instructed by the brewers to constantly check on this and to replace beer that's too old. This is the distributor's responsibility, not the store's. But you can't complain to the distributor, so complain to the store if you get bad beer. If you don't get satisfaction, change stores or ask to speak to the manager. You don't accept spoiled milk, do you?

There is a considerable mystique about the proper pouring of beer. The head *is* important, but I've seen beers poured which ended up more head than liquid. This is fine if you like drinking foam. One fairly reliable way to produce a good-tasting glass of beer is to pour a small amount directly into the bottom of the glass, and give the foam time to rise a bit and protect the carbonation, and then gently pour the rest down the side of the glass, held in your hand at an angle. I've tried this with some handsome pewter mugs a friend gave us as a baby present—why give them to the baby?—and something about the pewter produces too much head no matter how slowly I go. Oh, well, they're very decorative beer mugs.

Glassware is important. It is not only decorative, it is there to give you the best glass of beer possible. The following advice may strike you as reeking of beer snobbery, but I don't mind. If you're paying for it, and you enjoy it, you ought to treat it right. Beer deserves no less love in this department than wine, though it seldom receives it, I have to admit.

Use the beer glasses only for beer. This may seem slightly indulgent, but glasses used for milk or iced tea or coffee or soda may have residues of fat or some other substance on the inside, no matter how clean you think you've washed them. This foreign matter interferes with the head and may bother the taste of the beer as well.

Don't wash your beer glasses with soap of any kind. You may be ultra-conscientious about your dishwashing, and your dishwasher may be a marvel of a machine, but the soap often manages to adhere to the inside of the glass. I know, I know, the guys at the corner bar do it that way, dipping the glasses into soapy water and then clean

Two stone bottles, usually filled with mineral water but sometimes used for beer. Two beer bottles—one dating from 1886 and the other from about the same time probably. Two mineral water bottles—one a sample of the famous Codd bottle with the marble in the neck and the other with the swinging top replaceable stopper.

water—which rapidly gets soapy—and then letting the glasses drain, but they're in the business of mass producing customers, and you aren't.

Believe it or not, plain cold water is fine. Wash the glasses, if possible, immediately after they have been used—well, don't grab them out of your guests' hands, but don't let them linger unwashed overnight. Then you'll have to go the soap and hot water route.

Don't dry the glasses with anything. Particles of lint or other foreign matter get left inside. If you do have to use soap and hot water, rinse the glass out vigorously with cold water as it's more likely to get rid of the soap. Hot water makes more soap bubbles than cold water, remember?

When you're serving beer, it's not a bad idea to rinse the glasses out in cold water to get rid of any uninvited guests inside. Also the wetness helps prevent friction, which causes the head to evaporate more quickly.

Now, to glassware. As I've said, pewter mugs look great, they keep the beer cold, they even cause tiny globules of condensation on the outside. But they also turn color, the head's harder to control, and they may taste slightly metallic against your lips.

On the other hand, there are all kinds of nifty glasses for beer: the standard straight-up shell glasses; sham pilsner glasses which curve out a bit at the top; footed pilsner glasses—you know, the ones with a base, that look like an inverted cone; hourglasses, which are usually twelve-ouncers that fit nicely in the hand; goblets, which look grand but can be heavy to pick up and hold; and mugs in all sizes and designs, including some elegantly modern affairs.

Beer looks classier in some glasses than others because the color of the beer can be very attractive to behold. Dark beers and stouts look as fine as wine does in short round burgundy glasses, for instance, so fool around a bit and see what pleases your eye as well as your palate.

Two final "Don'ts":

Never shake the beer. Take it out of the fridge as though it were an old friend. You don't like to see your friends all-shook-up, do you?

Don't serve the beer at Arctic temperatures. The idea is to taste the flavor, not the efficiency of your refrigerator. In the case of dark beers, stouts and even ales, this is tantamount to ruining their flavor. If you know you're serving beer, take it out of the refrigerator a few minutes before it's intended to be drunk. This sounds like heresy to most Americans, but you'll be glad you've done it. In fact, your guests may be so dazzled they'll think they're drinking imported beer. And how's that for beer snobbery!

Reprinted from Bill Wannan's *Folklore of the Australian Pub* (Sydney: Macmillan Co., 1972).

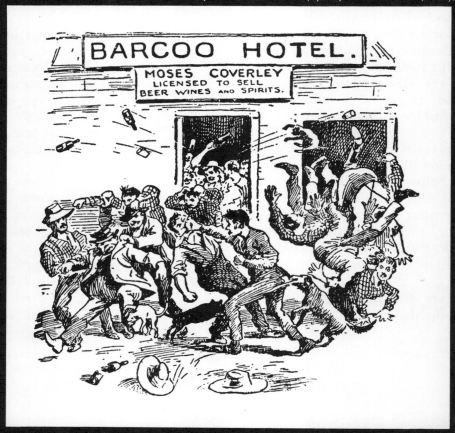

Now, *that's* no way to run a pub crawl!

# 23/Beer Down Under

(Who better to write about beer in Australia than an Australian? Craig McGregor, of course.)

Beer is more than just a drink in Australia: it is one of the great symbols of Australian identity, a habit, a cult, a ritual, one of the ways in which the typical man identifies himself as an Australian. It is at the center of a great deal of Australian popular culture, and the pub is the focus for a great deal of Australian life—from betting on the horses (strictly illegal in pubs, but popular nonetheless) to meeting mates, to having a dance with the wife or girlfriend. When Cyril Pearl, the author, set out to write a book on the subject he began flatly and succinctly with the statement: "Beer is a religion in Australia." And he's not far wrong. It is *the* local drink, downed by everyone from the company director to the "garbo man."

Over the years the consumption of wine (curtly known as *plonk*) has risen to well over a gallon a person per year, and the consumption of spirits has shot up quite a lot. But beer! For many years Australians were the heaviest beer drinkers in the world, and it is only recently that they have been edged into third place by the Czechs (who have nothing else to do) and the West Germans (who should know better). Even so, the average Aussie dumps over 22 gallons of beer down his throat each year. And in Darwin, in the tropical north of the continent, he has set an unbeatable record of 62.4 U.S. gallons per person! *The Guinness Book of World Records* reports soberly that a society for the prevention of alcoholism in Darwin had to disband in June 1966 for lack of support. No wonder. I mean, even the Czechs only manage 40.3 U.S. gallons a year, and that was a *big* increase for them. In a recent survey in Australia, it was found that the younger the age group, the bigger the proportion of drinkers. The Czechs had better watch out.

Like American beer, Australian beers are basically lagers. They are light, effervescent, and served very cold. But there the similarity ends. They have more flavor to them than American brews, they are not so sweet, and some brews—notably Resch's Pilsener—are quite close in taste to the European Pilseners. And they are notably more alcoholic: the average strength is 4.02 percent alcohol by weight, but in Sydney and Melbourne they go to 4.3 percent and higher. Australian beer gained a great reputation for its kick among American troops during World War II, and R & R servicemen from Vietnam have more recently confirmed it—so much so that Australians who have never swallowed a gulp of American beer can refer to it scathingly as "cat's piss." They're helped in their patriotism by such American businessmen as the one who told me he always traveled Quantas because it served Australian beer. "Best beer in the world!" he told me affectionately—and you could hardly find an Australian who would disagree.

In New South Wales there used to be fierce loyalties among drinkers between two brews, "old" and "new," put out by Tooth's Brewery; but new won the battle and is now the standard draft Tooth's beer—except in some die-hard country areas, where devotion to the old brew is still an article of drinking faith.

Toohey's, Resch's, and Miller's are the other New South Wales brands. Resch's is one of the best draft beers in Australia, and its bottled Pilsener is one of the best bottled lagers—Resch's DA (Dinner Ale) is noticeably sweeter. Victoria is the home of Victoria Bitter, Foster's, and Courage; Foster's is probably the best known beer overseas. You can buy it almost anywhere from New York to London, but many Aussie drinkers prefer the other local brands. Swan, from Perth in Western Australia, is another light, sweet beer. The closest to a hoppy English ale is Cooper's, a cloudy and full-bodied beer brewed in South Australia alone. Queensland brews Castlemaine and Bulimba, and Tasmania is the home of Cascade.

And that's just about it. There used to be scores of small local breweries in Australia, each brewing its own distinctive product, but over the years most of them have been taken over by the big city breweries in Sydney, Melbourne, and Brisbane. Mac's beer, brewed in the Queensland coastal town of Rockhampton, and Grafton, named after the New South Wales country town where it is brewed, are among the last to hold out.

The major breweries put out a range of beers, and most of them brew stout as well. In the last couple of years there has been a rush to package premium beers, which are more expensive (and allegedly more alcoholic) than the standard brews. But virtually all of them are light, strong lager beers still; if you want something *really* different, you have to brew your own.

Although Australian beers may be among the world's best, Australian pubs are among the world's worst. Many of them are anachronistic hangovers from the Twenties and Thirties, closer to those buckets of blood in the north of England than anything else, and even the more modern ones tend to be strictly utilitarian places designed for hard drinking and nothing else. The typical bar has a long, slops-wet counter where the men drink standing up, no chairs or tables, lavatory tile walls and floors which can be hosed down when the drinkers empty out for the night, a decrepit radio for listening to the races, maybe a TV set stuck high up in one corner, and if you're really lucky you might get a dartboard and a chalk-and-blackboard counter lunch menu thrown in as well. It's divided into two main sections: a large public bar for the ordinary drinkers and a small saloon bar for the more fastidious. Stuck somewhere out the back is a tiny ladies lounge where women are tolerated but little more. Australian bars are like Irish pubs in being predominantly male domains, citadels of masculinity where the ordinary bloke can go and have a few drinks with his mates after work before wending his way home to the wife and kids, and where he can escape to again on Saturday afternoon to "yarn" and listen to the races. With a few exceptions women are kept out of hotel bars, and if a woman fronts up to a bar in an ordinary hotel, she's likely to be refused a drink or regarded as a Women's Lib freak. The typical hotel scene is a crowded, incredibly busy bar with men standing around in groups swilling beer, talking at the top of their voices, laughing, swearing, "shouting" each other drinks, the roar of it all blasting out through the windows and doors onto the footpath outside. James Morris, the travel writer, concluded that Australian bars exuded a "frightening sense of male collusion," but for Australians that's just part of the boisterous bonhomie which is part of the good life.

The Aussie beer culture has its sidelights. Broken beer bottles litter many a park, highway, and beauty spot. Upended beer bottles are a popular garden border in many a working class suburban home. And the passion for taking a dozen or so "tubes" with you wherever you go, from beach to picnic to football match, has made a small fortune for a local company that manufactures portable iceboxes called *Eskys* (short for Eskimos). It also led to a great new spectator sport called beer-can throwing, in which spectators on the world-famous Hill at Sydney Cricket Ground would pelt each other with empty cans whenever the game got slow or some drongo was stupid enough to stand up in front. "DOWN IN FRONT!" the cry goes, followed by a barrage of tin missiles. After a while, the cops step in and spoil the fun. . . .

These days the stereotype has begun to break up a little. The pubs are improving: some of them have dance floors, sit-down lounges, cabaret shows, talent quests, and a few have even begun to model themselves upon English pubs (complete with lampshades and carpeted floors) and the cosier American bars. For a long time it was impossible for a bar to exist simply as a bar, American-style, unless it was part of a hotel offering accommodation, but that's changing. Most pubs close religiously at 10 P.M. each night, but a few stay open later—as long as you pay a cover charge and have something to eat. Even the great Australian beer monopolies, whereby a handful of giant companies have long dominated the national market, have been challenged: A few years ago an English company, the aforementioned Courage, set up a brewery in Melbourne and forced the local brewers to extend their range of beers and improve their pubs. But beer and the roaring corner pub are still close to the heart of Australian popular culture, and it will be a long time before Australians move closer to what happens overseas. I mean, why should they?

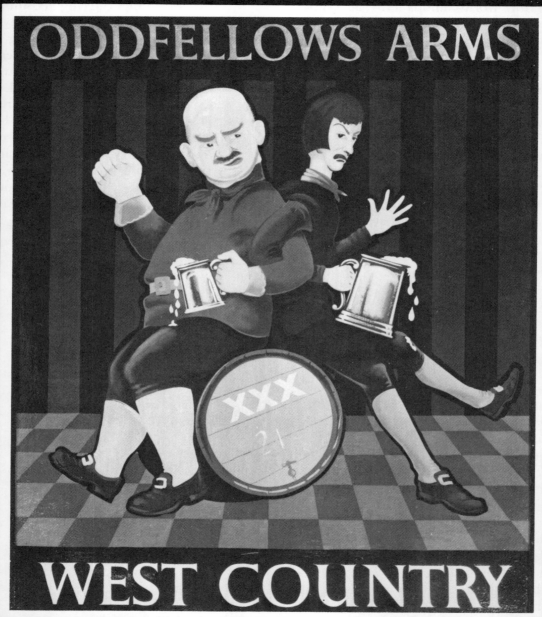

# 24/The Super Pub Crawl: Chicago

(Your host and mine this time out is Jay Robert Nash, author, mover of men, pub crawler to the seventh power, and great good friend. I first met Jay when he was the leader of a band of Chicago writers who called themselves "The Rejected Generation"—Ray Puechner, elsewhere represented in this book, was another member. But they were really the Dead End Kids of literature. They wrote, and they wrote, and New York publishers kept rejecting what they wrote. So they, in turn, rejected New York publishers, via erudite—at the same time recondite—letters, with carbon copies to T. S. Eliot, Hemingway, and other great men. And when they weren't being literary, they were being feisty beyond eastern belief, offering to throw cream pies in the faces of those haughty New York word czars, especially Bennett Cerf, who kept sending back their stuff. At one point the postage bills for their reverse rejection activities must surely have exceeded any income from writing, but these were good men and nowhere as crazy as those cats in Manhattan thought them to be. They kept on writing and started getting published, even if they had to produce their own lit'ry magazines and newspapers to do so. And eventually the writers from the Windy City calmed down, because the day was theirs. Publishers finally published them, and none of the "Rejected Generation" has been so much published as Jay Robert Nash. His *Bloodletters and Badmen* was a considerable success two years ago—it's now out in three separate paperback volumes—and this year [1976] he will publish over 2,000,000 words in the form of three books, each one fatter than the other.

These tomes are: *Hustlers and Con Men, Sins of the Cities,* and *Darkest Hours.* Cut it out, Jay! Leave room for the rest of us.)

The serious pub crawler in Chicago has three pedestrian and several ethnic routes to travel, all north of the Loop and within blocks of the lake. The Rush Street Route, which, with the exception of Pat Herrin's, serves strictly domestic beers (but the atmosphere is comfortable, the chatter pleasant), is tired and predictable; the hoods and flesh-flabbed dancers are all too glad to glom the sucker money, and a stein of beer can cost you a buck and up—it's the "entertainment," you see.

These Rush Street hangouts for such columnists as Kup (Chicago *Sun-Times*) and Aaron Gold (Chicago *Tribune*) are as passé as the wide-brimmed fedora without the snarl beneath its shadow. Next to the girl watching, it's dull, dull, dull, punctured now and then by a fistfight or an occasional shooting by a would-be swain plugging an unresponsive single girl as was once the case at Butch McGuire's. This is properly called the Lower Route.

Diversey Street north up Broadway to Belmont is the Upper Route (or Root Canal), a massive jumble of new "out" bars for the ultra-young hippies-with-money crowd. These bars are forged in the style of early Old Town, with a lot of exposed brick, rough-hewn wooden beams, stained glass, and pseudoartifactual facades smacking loudly of plastic antiquity. Almost all the beer to be found along the Upper Route is purely domestic and unimaginative.

It is the Middle Route that the serious pub crawler and beer aficionado must follow for authenticity in atmosphere and people, plus the availability of beer variety.

This area begins roughly at North Avenue (1600 north) and runs up Clark Street to about Fullerton (2400 north). This is the original area of Old Town when there were but three bars amidst the cheaply rented apartments and broken sidewalks. The bars have all disappeared in their original form, albeit they have nostalgically found their way into several Chicago novels. The bars were Moody's Pub, once slightly south of North Avenue on Wells Street (now replaced by a hideous plastic palace, having been removed to the far, far North Side), The Dram Shop on the north side of North Avenue (its site disfigured by the permanent rubble of urban renewal), and The Ale House. Only the latter—relocated—remains, a stubborn haven for the beer drinker.

But we are turning things around. We do not begin at the Ale House, we end there.

The practiced beer drinker in Chicago (or any other kind of intelligent drinker, for that matter) never begins his crawl on an empty stomach, unless his perverse desire is to slosh out early.

Food. It's important—not too much, but enough. A good place to begin is much farther south than Old Town. Riccardo's. You'll probably be staggering out of the Loop after shopping, seeing, and snooping, and Ric's place, as it's known in the trade (it is now owned by Nick de Angelos, a super-genial host), is like a warm fire for tired winter feet. Situated just off the underpass beneath Michigan Avenue (437 Rush St.), Riccardo's has a palette-shaped bar, the only recognized sidewalk cafe in summer, and some of the most astounding murals of the Lively Arts to be seen in *any* Chicago saloon (pardon me, it's currently against the law in Chicago to call any bar a saloon). The paintings alone make the trip to Riccardo's worthwhile.

They were done by the Albright brothers, Malvin and Ivan (Ivan's sinister portrait of the Devil has since been sold off and replaced), Vincent D'Agostino, John Foote, William Schwartz, Rudolph Weisenborn, Sherman Henry Linton, and Ric Riccardo, Sr., in the depression-ripped Thirties when the elder Riccardo almost wholly supported these artists (legend has it that they not only ate free at the restaurant but slept there at times when pressed).

The art aside (if possible), Riccardo's food is superb, both Italian cuisine and regular—or should I say super regular? The cooking is North Italian with butter base, which enhances any of the mouth-drooling pasta dishes. Believe me, Mr. Ripley, Riccardo's is also one of the best spots in town for steak. A delightful singing duo, Roberto Rossi on accordion (there for more than 25 years) and guitarist Marvin Berkman entertain at the booths in the bar section.

But the beer, the beer. Take it easy. You are eating. If you can't wait, the imported beers available at Riccardo's are Löwenbräu, Heineken, and Carta Blanca (all at $1.25 a bottle). Domestic brew consists of Bud, Schlitz, Miller's, and Old Chicago at 80¢ per, and can be had at the nod of a head. Careful not to nod too far lest you brush the uplifted glass of columnist Will Leonard of the Chicago *Tribune* or political cartoonists Bill Mauldin of the Chicago *Sun-Times* and John Fischetti of the Chicago *Daily News*. Riccardo's, you will discover either to your delight or your spiritual mortification—if your conversation doesn't hold more than branch water—is the nightery hub (beginning about 4 P.M.) for many of the city's journalists and writers, with a sprinkling of advertising types, and it buzzes, hums, sings, shouts (but not too often), electric with personality and eclectic in style.

Types, types everywhere. One habitué is the rasping, energetic, gnome-like Studs Terkel, editor of the bestselling interview books *Hard Times* and *Division Street*,

*America.* His mentor, the vindictive and talented author Nelson Algren, wouldn't be seen *morte* in Riccardo's (his recent move to New Jersey, as all wise fools know, is but transitory; he'll be back, folks) but ofttimes novelists Harry Mark Petrakis (*A Dream of Kings*) and Curt Johnson (*Hobbledeboy's Hero, Nobody's Perfect*) will stroll through the imbibing mass sans malacca cane and white wombat skin gloves.

Riccardo's is as good a place as any to begin this "night of nights," as Rod La Rocque was wont to say fifteen thousand evenings ago. Leaving Riccardo's with the lyrical strains of "Back to Sorrento" tickling your earlobes, it might be intriguing to waddle to your left, turn the corner and walk a block east to the Billy Goat Tavern just beneath the Michigan Avenue underpass (440 N. Michigan). It's a walk-down beer joint with Spartan tables and chairs. Guzzling steins of Schlitz on draught at 35¢ a crack are the lowly but gifted reporters of all three Chicago newspapers and the burly, grease-smeared, newspaper-capped workers who man their presses. Sam Sianis, a smiling, good natured host, has adorned his raggedly quaint hostelry with blow-ups of memorable newspaper accounts dealing with the flamboyant history of his famous tavern, along with photos of his literary clientele—Mike Royko, Terry Schaeffer, Bill Granger, Paul McGrath.

Not much variety at the Goat's, but the price is right: Miller's, Schlitz, and Old Style in bottles for 50¢ each. For the continental types there is Heineken's at 75¢ a bottle, a public order of which evokes loud uggery from those noble worker ants of the Fourth Estate. Wing it, pal, you are with the most real people of the night.

Before leaving the push of Rush, you might like to saunter back around the corner and walk a block north of Riccardo's to the quiet little Corona bar on Rush. Not much action and only domestic beers available here, but it may give you a respite from the din of the Goat's. If you are not yet satiated with the gossamer and glory crowd, then the imposing swank of Arnie's, several blocks north at 1030 N. State, should do it for you. Plenty of prancing glamor queens and crown princes strutting here in flashy elegance, with domestic brew and Heineken. Of course, Mr. First-Nighter, you will pay through the nose or hose or wherever you lug it.

Oglers and gapers might hit one other spot, Eugene's at 1255 N. State, across the street from the Ambassador. It's quieter than Arnie's but is also a fancy-dan eatery; if you plan on dining at either place, make your reservations a couple of million years in advance. Again, domestic beer and Heineken. These soft-light spas are really mixed drink spots, so if you're ordering up a brew, don't mind the bartender's arched eyebrow (or a bent wallet).

Now, by cab, car, bus, El, you must cross the Near North rim of Chicago to the John Barleycorn Pub at Belden and Lincoln streets, one block south of Fullerton. It is a cool and sprawling place with a gigantic bar. Its modest redecoration does not destroy the basic 1930s bar it once was—which is typical of the Barleycorn Pub's former owner, Van Gelder, a bearded and shrewd businessman who began the Ale House in 1958 (also resurrected from the remains of a neighborhood bar).

There is a large L-shaped seating area in Barleycorn so there is always (except Saturday nights) plenty of room. No TV here, but classical music and continuously shown four-color slides of classical art playing upon a specially rigged screen (its position does not distract from conversation).

If you *still* haven't eaten, do it now or forever hold your stomach. Barleycorn's food fare is light but tasty. The bar features especially: a huge hamburger with delicious accouterments and a monster Roquefortburger with same.

Affable bartenders will handily serve up a sizable stein of imported beer on tap—Guinness stout, Henninger, and

Proof that the Bowery—now New York's skid row—has seen better days, this sumptuous beer garden certainly played host to the whole family. So *that's* what people did before radio and television.

Bass Ale. The imported bottle beer is impressive: MacE-wan's (three varieties), Heineken, Harp, Whitbread (English light and dark ale), Peroni, Carlsberg (Danish light and dark), and the one far-out brew, Fix from Greece, a grumpy light beer.

Take note of the dozens of sailing ship miniatures lining the narrow, elevated platforms that run about the walls of Barleycorn like a frieze. The models are exquisite, and no, Van Gelder did not build a one of them; they're imported from Spain at about $300 a crack. It's the Van Gelder touch.

By cab (it is impossible to walk from Barleycorn to our next destination, unless you're a long-distance runner), we now journey to the thoroughly German Zum Deutschen Eck at 2924 North Southport Ave. Zum is *always* packed on weekends and is a giant family restaurant with a mammoth bar. If you haven't eaten yet, you rascal, you might want to try a plate of knackwurst or Thueringer Bratwurst here; it's tasty, and the hot German potato salad is something special.

Zum offers the beer drinker a fair shake. Available in one, half-, or one-fourth-liter steins on draught are Becks, Dortmunder Dab, Hofbrau (dark), and Pschorr Brau (light). Pschorr Brau and Bavarian Weiss is offered in bottles. Domestic on tap is Blue Ribbon and in bottles Hamm's, Bud, and Schlitz.

You can have a lot of fun at Zum. On weekends Hans and his Bavarian band (consisting of Hans Rager and a musical assistant) conduct hefty sing-alongs. You *will* sing number thirty-nine!

Cutting back to the Lincoln Avenue strip—yes, most certainly by cab—we alight not far from John Barleycorn's at *Oxford's Pub* (2261½ N. Lincoln), operated by Marty Sinclair. A cavernous place about as bright as your average coal bin, Oxford's is gathering place for the apprentice drinkers and the just-old-enoughs. It is not an "in" spot, although the regulars lining the unending bar think it is.

It is, quite simply, an en route curiosity with a lot of acting going on, mostly by bad actors, but the beer is surprisingly varied.

Oxford's will serve you Carling Black Label on draught at 70¢ a stein and such imported delights as Becks (light) at 90¢ a stein and $1 a pint. A stein of Bass or Guinness will cost you $1, a pint $1.25. In bottles you can order Pilsner Urquell at $1.30 each. To round out this above-average beer menu, Oxford's has Australian Foster Lager in 25 oz. cans at $2 each, which is a bit stiff, but it's the only game along Lincoln Avenue, pal.

Okay, you've had your few at Oxford's and have received the usual insults, big stares, and shoulder-knocking. Out. There are plenty of cruising cabs along Lincoln, so grab one and tell the driver to take you to the finest old-style German restaurant and bar in Chicago, The Golden Ox at 1578 N. Clybourn (imperative you cab to and from the Ox, since it's in a tough neighborhood).

Old-world Bavarian decor with three large, charming rooms, and a delightful rathskeller with an inlaid stone floor await you. This bit of history has been in Chicago since 1921 and offers, far and away, the best German cuisine in the city. So if you haven't eaten *yet*, consider yourself fortunate, and order Fritz's wiener schnitzel or sauerbraten with all the spaetzles, dumplings, and red cabbage—supreme stuff.

The beer will also delight you, for owner Fritz Sinn is strict in keeping the coils cleaned and the gauges on the barrels at 44°. Believe me, you may get the same beer elsewhere, but it will *taste* better at the Ox. Available in varied stein sizes are Pilsner Urquell from Czechoslovakia, Dortmunder Dab, and Pschorr (dark). You might even want to try the two local beers of interest: Augsburger and Old Chicago. The Ox is a great place to eat, drink, talk, be merry, and even serenaded, if you're in the Siegfried Room (so-called because of murals depicting "Der Ring der Nibelungen," scenes of German mythology incorporated

"Belly up to the bar, boys," the photographer ordered, and everyone did just that. This 1898 photo is all that remains, thanks be to Progress, of this handsome home-away-from-home for the lads.

with bombast and gusto into the works of Richard Wagner). The Fountain Room is so named after a six-foot-tall solid bronze fountain showing Aesop's "Fox and the Grapes," along with one of the largest beer steins in the U.S.

It's time to do some nightcapping. After giving the Ox's doorman a reasonable tip for getting you a cab, put in an order for O'Rourke's Pub at 319 West North Avenue. Operated by Jay Kovar, Jeanette Sullivan, and Jim Lundberg, O'Rourke's is Irish to the marrow, with Old Sod music crammed into its jukebox and massive potato-face photo blowups of Yeats, Behan, Shaw, and Joyce mounted on the walls.

The bartenders—for the most part a taciturn, aloof bunch who bless from afar—will serve you Bass Ale in steins (70¢ each) and pints ($1), and Guinness from the tap (stein, 80¢, pint, $1.10). Also on tap is Pschorr Brau (70¢ a stein, $1 a pint). Domestic beer consists of bottled Bud and Special Export with Stroh's on tap.

O'Rourke's is colorful enough but rough at times. On Thursday and Friday nights it brims with literary drunks, racetrack touts, and millionaires striking phony intellectual poses. There are some genuine people, but it's difficult to sort them out without what Hemingway once termed "a built-in shit detector."

In the dimly lit wooden booths you might catch a glimpse of our local Bartleby, Mike Royko of *Boss* fame—lean faced, churlish, hunched before his mixed drink (perish the Watney's)—or Pulitzer Prize columnist and book writer Tom Fitzpatrick. There are painters and sculptors and wonderful ne'er-do-wells here. Film reviewer (and screenwriter of *Beyond the Valley of the Dolls*) Roger Ebert is a nightly specter.

There's a dart game and a lot of wild chatter (threats abounding) in this curious, unkempt, mottled, wholly charming a la Quasimodo bar. Since it's on the fringe of a fast becoming rough-and-wreckage area, O'Rourke's is a good place for the next-to-nightcapper, particularly if you crave action.

East of O'Rourke's and one block west of Wells Street at 219 W. North Avenue we find the Old Town Ale House (or it finds us). The original building was gutted by a fire in February, 1971, but the intrepid owners moved lock, stock, and beer barrel across the street and reestablished.

It's a small saloon now with two bars, but it's congenial and colorful. One of its sagging walls is coated with water color portraits of its regular patrons (customer insurance). The music from its unholy jukebox alternates between classical to wail rock. No food here except some lip-smacking deviled eggs, but you should be far beyond that now. The bartenders and owners are talkative and funny. Jim Small and Art Klug were Figaro (on Rush) characters until they moved north.

Art (von) Klug turns his head with a sneaking smile if you mention his grandfather, Field Marshal Guenther von Klug, Hitler's elite commander of the Eastern Front during World War II. (Art, however, was born in Rangoon, Burma, and claims total repatriation to humanity.)

These boys are movie mania nuts, and when there is a lull in the conversation they will barrage you with questions on the flicks—"Name the seven of the *Magnificent Seven*. Who played the school teacher in *Back to Bataan*?" Woe to the man who can't remember Beulah Bondi.

The Ale House is the last bastion, save for O'Rourke's, of the disoriented, disenchanted, getting-on artists, film-makers, and writers in Chicago. Tom Buckley and Bob Connelly, novelist Marc Davis, poet Jim Agnew, actor Tom Erhardt (once "the voice of Schlitz"), painter Eddie Balchowsky, Channel Eleven newspeople consort at its bar and tables. Sometimes the Ale House will show movies free for its nostalgia-bent patrons (Bogart/Cagney/Ford, etc.) There will be some questions on those, too.

The beer at the Ale House is well-rounded. On tap is Miller's light, dark, and a half and half, all at 60¢ a stein; Löwenbräu at 90¢ a stein; Guinness Stout at $1.10 per pint, 60¢ a stein; Watney's Ale, 90¢ per stein, $1.20 per pint. The bar's black and tan (half stout, half ale) sells for $1.20 per pint. Domestic brews consist of Special Export and Bud at 70¢ per bottle.

The Ale House is a novel hovel and your evening could interestingly enough wind up here. It should.

Take a cab. Sit back. Remember. You may be five pounds heavier from all that beer, but you are also fat with knowledge and taste. In Chicago it's called "The Good Girth."

Goodnight, chum.

The Salisbury.

# 25/A Frothy History of Suds

"As he brews, so shall he drink," wrote Ben Jonson in *Every Man in His Humour,* and with the Englishman all hopped up about his new beer, all was right in the nation. It was now the Elizabethan Age, a time of new fame and glory for the English nation, and the queen—who must be reckoned a ruler of considerable talents to have had an entire age named after her—of course, bowed to no man, even when it came to quaffing beer. Among her many accomplishments was the ability to outdrink most of her kingdom, and she and her maids of honor began the day with pieces of toast floating in quarts of her favorite suds. Whenever she traveled, part of her retinue was a taster of proven palate, who foraged ahead to make sure that any local brew offered Her Majesty would be, quite literally, to the royal taste. Another of Elizabeth's accomplishments, you may recall, was the beheading of Mary, Queen of Scots, and possibly the only thing the two women had in common, apart from great ambition and mutual antipathy, was their fondness for beer. Mary had been weaned on beer as a wee one, and when she was imprisoned in Tutbury Castle, one of her first concerns was the availability of good beer. If nothing else, her stay in prison was mellowed by the presence of the finest beer around those parts since good old Burton-on-Trent was nearby.

There is not one drop of good drink here for her. We were fain to send to London and Kenilworth, and divers other places where ale was; her own bere was so strong as there was no man able to drink it.

—letter from Robert Dudley, Earl of Leicester, a favorite of "Good Queen Bess," to William Cecil, Lord Burleigh, the Lord High Treasurer and chief architect of Elizabethan policy. The queen, who has been described as "unpleasantly masculine and weakly feminine," cared deeply for Leicester, a handsome, but dissolute, fellow who was one of the more discernible cads of his time, but Cecil remonstrated against any permanent alliance. Leicester died in 1588 of poisoning, a fate said to have been intended for his third wife.

The Elizabethan Age was perhaps the high point in the nation's total affection for the noble brew. In the seventeenth century, during the protectorate of Oliver Cromwell, the royalists who had backed Charles I and lost—in Charles's case, the loss included his head—now turned their backs on beer because the Puritans, ironically enough, continued to hold it in high esteem. Wine became the only fashionable alcoholic beverage among the elite, and a brand new liquid fad (tea) began to appear on well-appointed dinner tables as the beverage of that meal. Then, as English sea trade around the world continued to

Courtesy of New York Public Library, Picture Collection.

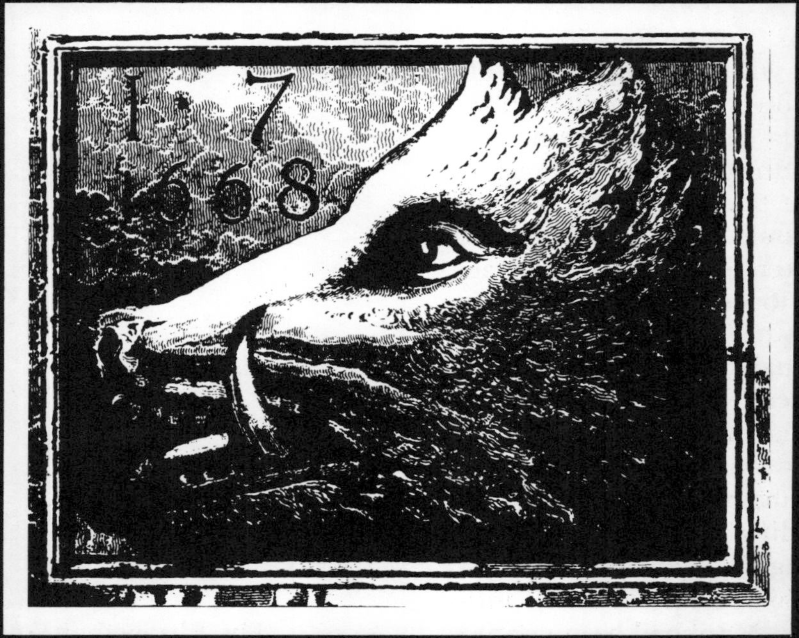

expand, coffee joined tea as a popular mealtime beverage, making further inroads into the consumption of beer. Given this fall from social grace, beer was rapidly becoming a lower-class drink.

## THE HIGH AND MIGHTIE COMMENDATION OF THE VERTUE OF A POT OF GOOD ALE.

Full of wit without offence, of mirth without obscenities, of pleasure without scurrelitie and of good content without distaste

>—in defense of beer (ale), this amusing title page introduced a late seventeenth century poem by that famous Yorkshire poet, Bard Anonymous

At first glance, it might seem as though England was becoming a more sober nation, but such was not the case. At the close of the 1600s, James II, the monarch who ascended the throne at the time of the Restoration, was driven from the country in the wake of much religious upheaval, and William of Orange arrived from the Netherlands in 1689 to take over the throne and restore order. With him came a complete palace load of Dutch courtiers, a very large shipment of brandy and gin, and a considerable fondness of both. The English did not drink much hard spirits, and William set out to change this, almost immediately getting an act through Parliament to encourage the distilling trade.

Few experiments in the making of public policy have worked so dramatically and to such public detriment. While the wealthy and sophisticated types rapidly accepted brandy as a logical—and, indeed, estimable—gastronomic addition to their claim to connoisseurship, at the same time continuing to nurture that terribly British snobbery about wines, the bulk of the populace switched from beer to gin because it was stronger, cheaper and everywhere available because of a population explosion of stills throughout the land. The brewers, ever an adaptable lot, became overnight distillers and in London, one out of every four establishments selling beer switched to the juniper juice. And you could get juiced on gin for the princely sum of one penny.

>Not only were there in London and Westminster six or seven thousand dram shops, but cheap gin was given by masters to their workpeople instead of wages, sold by barbers and tobacconists, hawked about the streets on barrows by men and women, openly exposed for sale on every market stall, forced on the maid-servants and other purchasers at the chandler's shop, distributed by watermen on the Thames, vended by pedlars in the suburban lanes, and freely offered in every house of ill-fame until as one contemporary writer (Theophilus, *Gentlemen's Magazine* Feb., 1733) put it, "One half of this town seems set up to furnish poison to the other half."
>
>—*The History of Liquor Licensing in England* by Sidney and Beatrice Webb

The government, seeing the country going to the dregs, tried a variety of legislative acts to stem the tide of gin drinking and the deaths resulting from it. Gin could no longer be sold in the streets, and it became more costly to buy because of government levies on it and the creation of expensive licenses for the retailers. This produced, not less gin drinking but gin riots. Moreover, new retail shop outlets for gin—"chemist shops" selling "Cholick water"—soon appeared and in pubs and taverns, sometimes now known as "gin palaces," gin was colored and sold as wine or given fanciful labels—"Ladies' Delight" was one winner. And so the government passed new legislation in 1751 forbidding any distiller to sell gin either directly or to a retailer without a license and again raising the tax on this lethal stuff. This measure proved more effective than the earlier ones, and when the government also made drinking debts irrecoverable at law, that finally got to people where they lived. The struggle between gin and beer was over—gin never really supplanting beer in the countryside—more for economic reasons than the more important life-or-death ones.

In the aftermath of these gin-soaked years, beer was accorded new regard as a wholesome drink for cityslicker and countrysider alike, and the brewers responded to this by doing some economical thinking of their own. A new product, called pale ale and brewed from the choicest barley malts, was introduced to lure the fast crowd back to beer, and a more heavily hopped brown ale was produced for those who had tired of the same old brown ale. Since these two new products were more expensive, the brewers proved they hadn't forgotten the working classes by introducing another brew, first known as *entire*, which was darker in color and stronger in alcoholic content than other beers in that price range. It became so popular with the porters in the London markets that it became known as *porter,* but its popularity was soon evident throughout the country. Anyway you sliced it, cheap beer with a belt to it had proved to be the answer to cheap booze with a belt to it.

> Poor John Scott lies buried here;
> Tho' once he was both *hale* and *stout,*
> Death stretched him on his bitter bier:
> In another world he *hops* about.
>
> —punning epitaph, surely for a lively fellow, found in an old graveyard in England's West Country

*"William Penn was quite likely the first brewer in the Pennsylvania Colony. . . ."*

Before setting off for Plymouth Rock, we may as well ask ourselves if the Indians in America drank any form of beer. There is no evidence that they did so, and this is probably attributable to their migratory, not agricultural, way of life.

On the other hand, it does seem a bit strange because other primitive cultures had their versions of beer.

In addition to archaeologists and their shovels, we owe much of our first knowledge about the beer habits of earlier civilizations to intrepid Western explorers—many of whom were not loath to conquer whatever they explored. The Spanish conquistadors, who accompanied Cortes to Mexico in 1518 and then moved north to Navajo country and south through Central America to the Incas of Peru, found the natives enjoying *chica*, a beer produced from maize. Later expeditions southward into the jungle valleys of the Orinoco and the Amazon encountered a form of beer made from cassava root. Captain James Cook, the famous English navigator, who did more than any other man to add to our knowledge of the Pacific and southern oceans, found Polynesians drinking a very exotic form of beer, called *kava*, that was fermented from a variety of pepper. Cook failed to note if this was the origin of the expression, "crying in your beer."

Before the white man came, America was a garden of peace and prudence, with respect to drink. Reading from north to south, the population was divided into the following groups:

1. Nondrinkers
2. Reformed hard drinkers
3. Light-wine-and-beer drinkers

> —from *Drinking in America*, an "unfinished history" published posthumously in the excellent collection, *The World of John Lardner*. Preface by Walt Kelly. Edited, with an epilogue by Roger Kahn.

In his 1502 travels, Columbus found the Indians of Central America drinking a beerlike concoction—"a sort of wine, made of maize, resembling English beer," reported the great explorer. But it is believed that the first brewers of beer on the North American continent were probably the forlorn colonists on Roanoke Island, who settled there under the leadership of Sir Walter Raleigh in 1585. According to one of those settlers, among the few pleasures they had was drinking homemade beer: "Wee made of the same in the countrey some mault, whereof was brued as good ale as was to be desired."

Those hardier folk, the Pilgrims, were themselves headed south, for Virginia, when a shortage of provisions forced them to land at the tip of Cape Cod, at what is today Provincetown, Massachusetts, where they founded the colony of Plymouth. Much has been made of their shortage of beer in particular. While as Puritans they would have had a circumspect but habitual fondness for their brew, it's necessary to point out that beer was also taken along on the Mayflower because it kept better than water. Still, a resident diarist on the ship did write, "Our victuals are being much spente, expecially our beere," and so thanks should be given for the beer they were able to have when they were having more than one. And thanks were surely given by Priscilla Mullins for the presence of one John Alden, a cooper who had been brought along to make and repair beer barrels for the colony and stayed to make Priscilla Mrs. Alden.

During the earliest days of America's colonization, it's unlikely there were many more than a handful of commercial breweries (known as "public" or "common" breweries). One of the first—quite possibly *the* first—was erected in 1612 by two Dutchmen, Adrian Block and Hans Christiansen, in a log structure on the southern tip of Manhattan Island, site of the colony of New Amsterdam. The first child born in New Amsterdam, a 1614 arrival named Jean Vigue, would later himself become a brewer and an official of the colony. Around a decade later, Peter Minuit, Director-General of New Amsterdam, erected a municipal brewery on the *Marckvelt* (market field,) and this continued in business until 1638, when competition from the private "public brewers" proved too much. That there should even be much competition in the beer trade says something about the drinking habits of these Dutchmen since the population numbered but a few hundred people.

### High Mighty Sirs:

Here arrived yesterday the ship The Arms of Amsterdam which sailed from New Netherland out of the Mauritius (Hudson) River on September 23; they report that our people there are of good courage and live peaceably. Their women also, have borne children there, they have bought the island Manhattes from the wild men for the value of sixty guilders, is 11,000 morgens in extent. They sowed all their grain in the middle of May, and harvested it the middle of August. Thereof being samples of summer grain such as wheat, rye, barley, oats, buckwheat, canary seed, small beans, and flax.

—part of a letter dated November 5, 1626, from Pieter Jansen Schagen of Holland to the States-General (Dutch Parliament) in session at The Hague. The letter, now in the General Government Archives, The Hague, is believed to be the only authenticated record of the purchase of Manhattan Island.

Quite apart from its historical content, Schagen's letter provides evidence that not only were the Dutch brewing beer in New Amsterdam, but they were also growing the grains needed to produce a beer that was, by local estimate, "as good as that brewed in the fatherland." One of the first streets outside the original New Amsterdam settlement, more fort than settlement, was *Brouwer Straat*, or Brewers' Street, which later became Stone Street since it was one of the first New Amsterdam thoroughfares to be paved with stone. The name change infers no loss in prestige, as those former Brewers' Street residents were not only among the most prominent members of the city, but their family names exist to this day as place-names in New York City—e.g., Van Cortlandt Parkway, Beekman Terrace, Vanderbilt Avenue, and Kip's Bay.

It would be nearly two centuries before one could say that a sizable brewing industry existed in America (129 commercial breweries by the 1820s), but this doesn't mean that the industry wasn't already in the fermentation stage. A letter dated June 27, 1632, from Kiliaen van Rensselaer (a director of the West India Company and founder of a famous Dutch-American family—his son, Stephen, founded Rensselaer Polytechnical Institute) to a business associate in Leyden, Holland, confirms this: ". . . As soon as there is a supply of grain on hand, I intend to erect a brewery to provide all New Netherland with beer, for which purpose there is already a brew kettle there. . . ." In 1633 a tract of land was granted Van Rensselaer to establish a brewery in upstate New Netherland where the state capital of Albany now stands. He apparently ran quite a decent brewery for some years, despite (to beer purists) his malt being primarily derived from wheat.

Upward reverse mobility in old New York: early in 1642 the West India Company, which ran the province of New Amsterdam completed "a fine inn built of stone" not for the needs of the local imbibers, but "in order to accommodate the English who daily pass through with their vessels from New England to Virginia." Eleven years later, the *Stadts Herberg* (City Tavern) became the *Stadt Huys* (City Hall). History doesn't explain this sudden transfer in purpose, but perhaps the polite, eminently practical-minded Dutch had tired of there being no room (for them) at the inn.

1633—John Josselyn, an English tourist, went into a tavern in Boston to refresh himself. After he'd had a few drinks, a stranger who was sitting nearby told the landlord not to give him anymore. Josselyn said, "You take care of yourself, friend, and I'll take care of Josselyn," but his supply was cut off just the same. What Josselyn had run up against was Boston's human drunkometer, by which drinkers at that time were protected against themselves by grog sleuths, or public eyes.

—more from *Drinking in America,* among the promising works unfinished at the time of John Lardner's death in 1960 at age 47

During this shakedown period in American life, there was considerable indecision as to who should be allowed to sell beer. For example, before 1637 in the colony of Massachusetts, taverns and alehouses brewed their own beer, but in that year one Captain Segwick was granted the exclusive right to brew beer—a monopoly he was to enjoy but a short time since two years later brewing rights were also restored to the taverns. Rhode Island licensed a brewery (1638) before it did taverns, but at the same time Connecticut a few miles to the west had no shortage of taverns for the corn-based beer being produced. New Hampshire, going its flinty way even then, declined to license anyone to brew beer until 1670.

Oh we can make liquor to sweeten our lips
Of pumpkins, of parsnips, of walnut-tree chips.

—early New England song indicating what a grab bag home-brewing was

In later years New England would produce sufficient malt to be able to send it to other outposts in the New World. But most of the colonies had to import their malt from England, and much of it was used for distilling hard liquor. The colonials also had to import hops, although they grew wild in some sections of the country, and experienced brewers—who just didn't grow in the wild.

Beare is indeed in some places constantly drunken, in other some nothing but Water or Milk or Beverige; and that is where the good-wives (if I may so call them) are negligent and idle; for it is not want of Corn to make Malt with, for the country affords enough, but because they are slothful and careless; and I hope this item will shame them out of these humours; that they be adjudged by their drinke, what kind of Housewives they are.

—*Leah and Rachel,* by John Hammond, a 1656 author who either didn't know how to make his own beer or else felt that a woman's place is in the brew-house

All the problems notwithstanding, brewing was encouraged in New England, and elsewhere, as a kind of economic leverage, with a moral bias, against the production and consumption of the harder stuff. Yet, here, too, inconsistency was the rule. For instance, at one point during this period in New England, imported malt was kept out in order to stimulate the domestic malt industry. Not too long thereafter, it became illegal to malt domestic wheat, rye, or barley because these cereal grains (used as food also) were in short supply. On another occasion, a punitive fine was placed on brewers using wheat because New England wanted to export wheat. Still later on, even though New England wanted its people to knock off drinking the demon rum, it also wanted to expand its trade with the West Indies, in which rum had become a chief medium of barter. The response, not a little schizophrenic, was to compete fiercely with the other colonies for the West Indian trade, despite the barter trade requirements, and at the same time encourage local distilling interests. As history shows, New England didn't succumb to rum, it didn't

become a distilling center, and it also lost the leadership it might have had, given its grain supplies, in the brewing trade.

It's a moot question whether or not New Yorkers are as independent and self-contained as the rest of the country (and world) pictures them to be, but around this time a gentleman named Francois de Bruyn gave an early lift to the tradition. Found guilty of insulting and striking a court messenger, he was fined two hundred guilders. He refused to pay, stating he would rather suffer prison for the rest of his days. Fortunately for De Bruyn, New York hadn't gotten around to building any prisons as yet, and the usual imprisonment was a kind of house arrest. "Prison fare," however, was mandatory—bread and milk, or homemade beer. Given De Bruyn's audacity, he was sentenced to a "respectable tavern" and a better punishment.

. . . cans of buttermilk or good beer, brewed perhaps by the patroon, washed down this breakfast of suppawn and ryebread and grated cheese and sausage or head-cheese; beer there was in plenty, in ankers, even in tuns in every household . . . of the drinking habits of the Dutch colonies I can say that they were those of all the colonies—excessive. Tempered in their tastes somewhat by the universal brewing and drinking of beer, they did not use as much rum as the Puritans of New England, nor drink as deeply as the Virginia planters; but the use of liquor was universal.

—confirmation that our ancestors were "wet" from dawn past dusk, as contained in *Colonial Days in Old New York* by Alice Morse Earle

William Penn was quite likely the first brewer in the Pennsylvania Colony. Even though he brewed only for his family and guests at the estate he built in Pennsbury, the size of the vats in which he brewed his beer were so huge that they caused the Philadelphia *Evening Bulletin* to comment: "Certainly the householders thought highly of beer as a thirst quencher, if one judges by the size of those vats." At the other end of the home-brewing spectrum was the housewife brewer, whose beer caused comment only when she used some new weird ingredient in brewing it. Just about anything that grew was a likely candidate, but laws against backyard ingredients would be impossible to enforce. So in 1677 Massachusetts passed a law aimed at the most common manufactured ingredient—vile molasses—being used in those parts. This was also impossible to enforce, but it did have the effect of ensuring that the "strong beer" produced by commercial brewers would be an all-malt product. The homemade brews were known as "small beer." They were not to exceed 2.5 percent alcohol, were not subject to taxation, and were not to be marketed. They were not marketed, they were not taxed, but they often did exceed that alcohol level—but two-out-of-three isn't bad.

The richer sort generally brew their small beer with malt that they have from England, though they have as good barley as any in the world; but for want of the convenience of malt-houses the inhabitants take no care to sow it. The poorer sort brew their beer from molasses and bran, with Indian corn malted and drying; with persimmons dried in cakes and baked; with potatoes; with the green stalks of Indian corn, cut small and bruised; with pompions, squashes and pumpkins and with the *batates canadensis,* or Jerusalem artichokes, which some people plant purposely for that use, but this is the least esteemed of all such before mentioned.

—*History of the Present State of Virginia,* written by Rogers Beverly and published in London in 1705

Courtesy of New York Public Library, Picture Collection.

Doc Fisher's Saloon in the wilds of the Bronx sure had no shortage of regulars in the 1880s. Written in pencil on the back of this photograph was the following caption: "Bill Morris and His Billy Goat, Lewis Coombs on Bicycle and Judge Hauptman in the doorway."

# 27/Report from Minneapolis: A Choice Beer-Taster's Choices

(Brian Richard Boylan, excellent friend, night owl, author of several books, and author of this report on beer in the Twin Cities, filed the latter under duress, the duress being that he can't wait for me to start my next book, for which he is the editor. I regard this as the sincerest form of bribery.)

## Olympia

Although long-popular on the West Coast, this Washington State beer has appeared in the Midwest during the past two years, and it is exceptional. Olympia has taken over the Hamm's Brewery in St. Paul, and is reportedly negotiating to put up a new plant in Wisconsin. It is a full-bodied American brew yet without the medicinal flavor frequently found in European beers. It is less watery in texture than Coors, but stronger in flavor than most local beers. It certainly is superior to Budweiser, Pabst, Miller's, Ballantine, or Falstaff.

Olympia now controls one of the more remarkable beers distributed in Minnesota and Wisconsin—Hamm's Preferred Stock. According to local merchants, this particular product of Hamm's is a rice beer, which supposedly was widely brewed during World War II. It is lighter and more thirst-quenching than the regular Hamm's and, for that matter, most other domestic beers. Its development, sales figures, and future should be checked out, because it is an excellent beer. It's a brew that I particularly enjoy in the hot summer, for it does not leave a beery aftertaste and does not seem to be bloating.

## Schell's

Originating in New Ulm, Minnesota (the site of the last major Indian Uprising), Schell's comes in light, dark, and bock. In bottles and cans, it tends to be lighter than Budweiser or Schlitz; yet it leaves a distinctive aftertaste. Schell Bock is a joy, surpassed only by Grain Belt Bock in flavor. Schell and Grain Belt bocks are the closest in flavor and winelike mellowness since the decease of Rheingold Golden Bock back in the mid-sixties. The winey characteristic is my chief criterion for a good bock, and both Schell's and Grain Belt have it.

## Huber

Brewed in Monroe, Wisconsin, this has become something of a cult beer on the east coast. The regular beer is excellent, but the bock tends to be rather watery. The regular Huber has a slight bite and a hint of body, which makes it go down smoothly.

## Leinenkugel

Brewed by Jacob Leinenkugel Brewing Company, of Chippewa Falls, Wisconsin, this is one of my favorites. It has a distinctive flavor without an after-bite. This is a beer to be consumed for several hours on end, for it leaves no acidity or flavor backlash. It's a beer I would serve at a party, confident that its subtle flavor would be appreciated by beer connoisseurs. Its smoothness and lack of pungency are traits that I treasure in a beer. Guests and friends consistently rate it among the top three beers they have tasted.

## Anchor

This San Francisco product, better known as Steam Beer, has been available in Minneapolis only recently, on a trial basis. Selling at $4.05 a six-pack, it consistently sells out all available stock. Unlike Coors, which has been a snob beer, Steam Beer is almost totally unknown outside of San Francisco. Less than a year ago, the brewery started an experiment in Minneapolis, and it has succeeded wildly, according to Twin Cities retailers. Steam Beer is amber in color and winey in consistency. Like other beers I have mentioned, it avoids the European medicinal flavor. The closest comparison I can make is with Watney's Red Barrel Ale. It leaves a nutty aftertaste and can be guzzled for hours without loss of taste.

Anchor also puts out a porter which, to my taste, is superior to any American porter since I drank Utica Beer mixed half-and-half with Utica Porter at New York's White Horse Tavern in 1964.

## Cold Spring

This beer comes from, of all places, Cold Spring, Minnesota. It is light and pleasant, but not nearly as clean-flavored as Leinenkugel. One or two glasses are enjoyable, but any more leaves an almost imperceptible aftertaste, one that is unpleasant.

## Schmidt's

Another beer brewed in the Twin Cities, this is similar to Schlitz and Pabst in taste—neither memorable nor sickening. It apparently sells well, perhaps to the beer drinkers who don't really care what they're drinking so long as it is beer.

## Grain Belt

This Minneapolis beer is consistent in its lightness and taste. The Grain Belt Bock is magnificent, winey without being tart. A relatively small batch of bock is brewed each year, resulting in a scarcity. I understand that Grain Belt is now owned by the large brewer, G. Heileman Brewing Company of La Crosse, Wisconsin, and I hope that the move doesn't result in Grain Belt shriveling up and blowing away.

# 28/Tommy's Joynt: What's in a Name, Anyway?

I will forgive Tommy's Joynt, Van Ness at Geary, in San Francisco for its cute name.

I will forgive all that crap on the ceiling that looks like someone's junkyard, the mass-produced captain's chairs, the red-flowered carpet that looks like it came out of some defunct movie house in the Bronx, and the exterior that is a decorator's regurgitation. Yes, I will forgive Tommy's Joynt for being as visually appealing as the backside of a water buffalo—the place serves something surely odious called a "Buffalo Burger"—and the fact that the beer list badly needs to be copyedited.

I *have* to be this magnanimous because Tommy's has an extraordinary number of bottled beers to offer the public. If the beer list means what it says, there are over sixty-five kinds of bottled beer to be sampled there, plus Anchor Steam Beer, Bud, Guinness, Michelob, and Löwenbräu on tap.

We needn't concern ourselves with the foreign beers we'd expect to find in any place which features a large number of imported beers, but even so, there are many surprises at Tommy's. For instance, Castlemaine from Australia and Zealandia Half and Half from New Zealand. The beer list says Mon-Lei is Chinese, but it's brewed in Hong Kong. Singapore is represented by Tiger, and the Philippines by San Miguel Light and Dark.

From Europe there are some beers I've just never seen in New York. Okocim Porter and Ziwiec Ale from Poland and Moldau Brau from Czechoslovakia. Pripps from Sweden and Fryden from Norway. Puntigam from Austria and Feldschloesschen from Switzerland. Germany sends the expected famous brews, but there are also Monchshof Light and Dark and Kulmbacher Light and Dark.

I would expect Mexican beer in a California pub. There are seven kinds here, and I'd never had Tecate before. For that matter, although it wasn't on the beer list, Tommy's was featuring Belgium's Stella Artois when I was there, and I was glad to have that for the first time in a long time.

Tommy's also has British cider (the alcoholic kind), all kinds of coffee with booze in it, and cheese plates. They make beer crepes, which don't sound too inviting, but are quite a treat.

Just don't ask me to have a Buffalo Burger. I'm sure there are excess buffalos these days, but I don't plan to help a once almost extinct species get that way again.

# 29/A Frothy History of Beer

*"... The men who created and led the American Revolution were not unknown in the taverns ... that revolutionary fire was fueled by 'strong beer.'"*

A geographical brew: according to one listing of the important commercial breweries started in the New World before the American Revolution, all but one were in the thirteen original colonies. The first one, in New Amsterdam, was followed by Kilian Van Rensselaer's establishment in Albany, then by breweries in Boston, New Haven and Watertown, Massachusetts. Then none of record for three decades. Portsmouth, New Hampshire, was the next brewing outpost, then two were built in Philadelphia. Then another long hiatus. Then breweries in Baltimore and Philadelphia, plus one in Christian's Springs, Northampton, Pennsylvania—a colony of Moravians (religious group from Czechoslovakia) erected this one—and one in Reading, Pennsylvania. The first one outside the colonies, in the French territory of Cacasquias, Illinois, a man named Beauvais began a brewery at what was then a Jesuit post.

Although this is surely an interesting list, it is almost certainly incomplete because not only are a number of the original colonies unrepresented, but the important brewers were men of substance and esteem in their communities and not likely to be unknown to the populace. Indeed, as pointed out in the scholarly tome, *History of the Brewing Industry and Brewing Science in America,* published by Dr. John E. Seibel and Anton Schwarz in 1933: "Brewers and tavern-keepers in those days enjoyed the highest respect of their fellow-citizens. In days when the church dominated all public affairs, only voters and church members of exemplary character were able to obtain licenses to conduct taverns and breweries and were held responsible for the proper conduct of their guests." The authors further point out that many of the men who created and led the American Revolution were not unknown in the taverns, either, precisely because these were the meeting places for patriotic activity and surely some of that revolutionary fire was fueled by "strong beer."

... the character and standing of the business ... derived additional lustre from the character and standing of the men engaged in it, for it is an indisputable historical fact that many brewers and taverners not only occupied prominent civil and military positions, but became influential leaders, distinguished alike by valor in the field and wisdom in council, and transmitting to their off-springs (by heredity, perhaps, no less than by the formative power of example), that spirit of patriotism which gave birth to our Nation.... Nearly every liberty-pole in revolutionary and pre-revolutionary days stood before a tavern, the head-quarters of the Sons of Liberty; and not infrequently the tavern-keeper was the leader of the band.

If the British considered the taverns as the hot-beds of sedition, as in fact they did, the Patriots with equal justice regarded them as the nurseries of liberty; and it is not at all unlikely that in the tavern of his father-in-law, where he so often made himself useful as a tapster, Patrick Henry imbibed the ideas which culminated in his soul-stirring utterance, "Give me liberty or give me death."

From the Museum of the City of New York.

The Old Brewery at Five Points. Pen and ink sketch by R. E. Trebes, 1852.

—*AMERICAN BEER Glimpses of Its History and Description of Its Manufacture*, catalog for an exhibit mounted in 1909 by the United States Brewers Association

Samuel Adams, "father of the revolution," was the son of a brewer and a brewer himself. Thomas Chitenden, the leading political figure in Virginia and its first governor, was both a brewer and tavern-keeper. Generals Putnam, Weedon and Sumner were brewers. George Washington had a brewhouse on his estate at Mount Vernon, and he left his recipe for "small beer" to posterity. It's on display at the New York Public Library, but it's against library rules to brew beer there. In any case, his handwriting leaves something to be desired.

It is to be hoped that the Gentlemen of the Town will endeavor to bring our own OCTOBER BEER [old or "strong beer"] into Fashion again, by that most prevailing Motive, EXAMPLE, so that we may no longer be beholden to *Foreigners* for a *Credible Liquor*, which may be as successfully manufactured in this country.

—newspaper advertisement for Samuel Adams' "OLD MALT" that combined patriotism with self-interest

In retaliation for edicts issued in 1767 by the British Parliament not only levying new duties and local payment for the king's troops stationed in America, but also requiring the colonials to supply them with beer, American merchants drew up an agreement, signed by Washington, Patrick Henry, and others, vowing not to import a number of British products, including "beer, ale, porter, malt." The

Philadelphia merchants, especially the brewers, were as good as their word, but Rhode Island and then New York both received merchandise from abroad. By 1770 the movement had pretty much broken down, but it was an idea (nonimportation) whose time was just beginning. By the time of the First Continental Congress in 1774, the Americans had suffered the East India Company's tea monopoly and had responded by the Boston Tea Party and the closing of the port of Boston. Any members of the Congress who would not go along with the embargo against British goods were regarded as un-American, finks, and worse.

How important, really, was their daily brew to the revolutionary Americans? Well, so important that the Continental Congress decreed that every American soldier fighting in the war should be supplied with the daily ration of a quart of beer, and that was an imperial quart—forty ounces. During the bitter days at Germantown in 1777, when supplies of everything were short, Washington wrote Congress that the troops sorely missed their daily beer ration.

> We have already been too long subject to British prejudice. I use no porter or cheese in my family, but such as is made in America: both these articles may now be purchased of an excellent quality.
>
> —George Washington, the new President, to the Marquis de Lafayette on January 29, 1789

Again that recognized importance: when the war was over, states began to encourage the fledgling beer industry by exempting commercial brewers from taxation. The federal government followed suit for a few years, with similar exemptions and by placing duties on imported brews. Beer was regarded as a class beverage and, more to the point, the "beverage of moderation."

> Whereas the manufacture of strong beer, ale and other malt liquors will promote the purposes of husbandry and commerce by encouraging the growth of such materials as are peculiarly congenial to our soil and climate, and by procuring a valuable article for exportation, and
>
> Whereas the wholesome qualities of malt liquors greatly recommend them for general use as an important means of preserving the health of the citizens of this commonwealth. . . .
>
> —tax-exemption measure passed by the Massachusetts State Legislature in 1789

During the administrations of Washington and his immediate successors, brewing was advanced in this moral direction. There was, somewhat briefly, a scheme for a national brewery—the creation of one Joseph Coppinger, the author of a book on brewing. Coppinger, sounding either like a hustler or a visionary, wrote Jefferson, then president, because he knew of the great man's interest in perfecting the brewing done on his own estate at Monticello, which included collecting all the books available on the subject. Jefferson never brewed for profit, however, although he constantly sought to improve his knowledge of brewing among a myriad of subjects. His vast library, including the books on brewing, form the nucleus for the Library of Congress. In any case, although Coppinger wooed Jefferson again when Madison was president, there never was any national brewery formed then for the same reason that there is antitrust legislation today. "One Beer, One Nation," might be a terrific slogan, but we'd all hate to drink under it.

Jefferson, of course, was a Virginian, and the southern states, whatever their sincere interest in brewing, had found that their warm climate and the refrigeration problems with beer (no refrigeration, no problem, really) made tobacco a more moral—and potentially profitable—growth industry. Not so Pennsylvania. The Pennsylvanians had for some time regarded their beer as the best in the colonies, and officially said so in a postwar proclamation urging brewers "to bring their beer and ale to the goodness and perfection which the same was formerly brought to, and so the reputation which then was obtained, and is since lost, may be retrieved." Presumably this nobility of liquid purpose was not lost upon the citizenry, but by the 1790s there also were an estimated five thousand stills in operation in the state. A scholar has determined that this breaks down to one still per every eighty-six Pennsylvanians, including kiddies.

However, this did not mean that the call for better beer had been lost upon the brewers themselves. Indeed, Philadelphia-brewed beer would once again become a standard for excellence through the colonies. Beer or booze, the Pennsylvanians liked to drink. So much for eternal verities.

> Beer was brewed in Philadelphia for several years before the revolutionary war, and soon after peace the more substantial porter was made by Robert Hare. Until within three or four years (1810) the consumption of that article had greatly increased and is now the common table drink of every family in easy circumstances. The quality of it is truly excellent: to say that it is equal to any of London, the usual standard for excellence, would undervalue it, because as regards either wholesome qualities or palatableness it is much superior; no other ingredient entering into the composition than malt, hops and pure water. . . . Within a few years pale ale of the finest quality is brewed and justly esteemed, being light, sprightly and free from that bitterness which distinguishes porter. . . . Great quantities of beer are exported to other States. The hops are almost entirely brought from New England; much of the barley comes from Rhode Island.

> —*Picture of Philadelphia,* written in 1810 by a gentleman named Mease

The struggling young government, to raise revenue and promote the domestic brewing industry, put stiff import duties on distilled spirits and imposed a federal tax structure on spirits produced in this country, but this was far from well received by all members of the First Congress. Speaking for the southern regions, Florida's Jackson complained that his constituency had "no breweries or orchards to furnish a substitute for spiritous liquors." Parker of Virginia objected to the internal revenue tax on different grounds: "It will convulse the Government, it will let loose a swarm of harpies who under the denomination of revenue officers will range through the country, prying into every man's house and affairs, and like a Macedonian phalanx bear down all before them." Prophesies and rhetoric aside, what *did* happen is that in Pennsylvania, where a man's moonshine was both physically near and spiritually dear to him, the four western countries rebelled against a new federal levy of eight cents per gallon on beer, ale, and porter *and* against a higher excise tax on home distilled spirits. The citizens of these counties regarded this new tax as "unjust in itself and oppressive to the poor" and declared themselves in open revolt against the government. Only swift military action by the federal government prevented the Whiskey Insurrection from spreading into our first civil war. However, it proved easier to extinguish the fires of insurrection than to put out the fires underneath all those stills or to collect the taxes on the liquor produced therein, and in 1802 the government gave up the war as not being worth the battle. American citizens displayed at least as much verve and resourcefulness in evading the tax men as they had in fighting the British.

Reprinted from *Löwenbräu München* (Munich, 1969), p. 12.

Reprinted from Bill Wannan's *Folklore of the Australian Pub* (Sydney: Macmillan Co., 1972).

# 30/The Great Australian Beer-Bust through America

*or Running Away from Milwaukee in All Directions*

(Craig McGregor, who introduced you to the possibilities of home brewing earlier in the book, here introduces you to the impossibility of traveling through America and avoiding representatives of the kingdom of Milwaukee. Remember the commercial that asked, *"Who is the Ale Man?"* Craig McGregor is the Ale Man, *that's* who! A bloody Australian is the Ale Man. . . .)

Drink your way around America in 99 days?

Well, it's an idea. You see the country, you drink its beer. So we set off from New York, two portable coolers in the trunk of the car, and headed south. The aim: to drive from East Coast to West Coast and back again without ever emptying the coolers of ice—or alcohol. Could it be done?

New York stretches a long way south. For the first hundred miles or so it's the familiar Empire City beers you find in the bars and the supermarkets: Schaefer, Ballantine, Rheingold. You might as well be back in Greenwich Village. It isn't until you hit the Appalachians that the scene changes. Not to moonshine whisky, either. Or to romantic local beers, though no doubt there's a lot of home brewing going on in those high mountains. Like most of America, the gateway to the South has been annexed by Milwaukee and St. Louis, and the signs outside the bars are those which we were to find again and again right across the United States: Budweiser, Schlitz, Pabst, Miller. Virginia has only two breweries (and one is Anheuser-Busch), West Virginia has none and South Carolina none. The only brewery in North Carolina is Schlitz. So right down the

East Coast the same smiling, blonde, All-American guy with a glass of the stuff that made Milwaukee famous leers from the illuminated signs.

"You got any local brews around here?" I asked a guy in Asheville, North Carolina. "No, but there's a drive-in liquor store down the road—they got most everything," he said. And so they did: rows and rows of six-packs of the same premium beers. But I noticed there were a lot of malt liquors in among the usual beers, and the deeper you get into the South the more popular the malt liquors become. In Tennessee and Alabama the supermarket shelves are stuffed with Country Club, a heavy but somewhat sweet malt liquor that tastes great the first can, cloys a little on the second, and becomes hard to drink on the third. "Some beers are for just one or two," said one of the travel-stained sampling party. "This is one of them." Everyone agreed. Maybe in the South it's just drunk as a whiskey chaser.

Mississippi. I call around to the ice factory just off the main street of Fayette, the tiny township that at one time had Charles Evers as one of America's first black mayors. A young black guy is slamming blocks out of the ice chute and sliding them along the slippery wooden floor. I collect some ice for the coolers. I'm hot, sweat dribbling down the side of my face. "Hey, what do you all drink around here to keep cool?" I ask. The ice man grins. "Schlitz."

It's not until you get right down to New Orleans, the old Crescent City itself, that Milwaukee starts to fade away. Of course, the tourist bars serve national brands of beer to the holiday makers who have traveled three thou-

# Chowning's Tavern

I TAKE this Means of acquainting the Publick that I have opened Tavern under my Name and Sign in the *Market Square*, near the *Court House*, in *Williamſburg*. All who pleaſe to favour me with their Cuſtom may depend upon the beſt of Refreſhment, at reaſonable Rates. A courteous Reception will await ſuch as wiſh to inſpect the Premiſes.

## —JOSIAH CHOWNING

N. B. A Lot in the Rear is ſet apart for the Vehicles of Lady and Gentlemen Travellers.

sand miles just so they can get exactly the same taste as they do at the li'l neighborhood bar at home. All along Bourbon Street the jazz floats up into the summer air, the sightseers stumble along the narrow pavements, and Lake Michigan gushes from the beer pumps. Al Hirt's, would you believe, serves Miller's (hell, it's even got a Miller's sign outside).

But New Orleans has been brewing its own beer for a long time, and you only have to penetrate the tourist haze to find what the locals drink: Dixie and Jax. Along the Mississippi waterfront, in the taverns where jazz began three-quarters of a century ago, that's what the black stevedores and seamen drink. Dixie is the sweeter of the two. It's made by the Dixie Brewing Company on Tulane Avenue here in New Orleans. Until recently, its main competitor was another local brewer, the Jackson Brewing Company—which also gave its name to one of New Orleans's best rock groups—but now Jax has to be brought in from Texas. Falstaff has a brewery here, too, but it's harder to find in the local bars.

We turned west, across Louisiana, and began the long thirsty trek across Texas. Four of the big premium beer manufacturers have breweries in Texas, but the most interesting beers are made in the dry, desert-gripped, half-Mexican city of San Antonio. There are two of them: Lone Star and Pearl. We found them available right across the southwestern corner of the country. They are mild lager beers that need chilling to really taste good, but since everyone in Texas seems to drink their beer near freezing point, that doesn't seem to matter. We drank them day after day, and by the time we left Texas we'd decided that Pearl was the better of the two. In a cafe in San Antonio not far from where the battle of the Alamo was fought, everyone was eating tacos, enchiladas, Mexican chili beans, and drinking Pearl or Coke.

New Mexico. Heading north on Interstate 25, from El Paso towards Santa Fe, the country is even more barren than in Texas: hot, shimmering rocks blistering in the sun, tumbleweed blowing across the bitumen, roadsigns warning against the dangerous sidewinds which can come blasting out of those pressure-cooked gulches. We pull into a gas station at Truth or Consequences, a tiny bizarre township named after the TV show and notice that clouds have begun massing overhead.

"Look like rain?" I ask the gas station manager.

"Well, it hasn't rained all year," he says laconically. It is now June. "Clouds been coming up like that for the last month, but ain't nothin' ever happened."

We stop for a drink and discover, right there in the center of Truth or Consequences, one of the best selections of beer we will find on the whole trip. It's a liquor store, run by Frank Vomack.

"Most popular beer around here? Coors," says Mr. Vomack. "It's the most popular beer right through the southwest. It only operates in eleven states, but I think it's fifth in sales in the entire nation. It's a Colorado beer and it's brewed with Rocky Mountain spring water. I think that probably sells it more than anything else. No sir, that's not just a gimmick; it's located right in the mountains there, in Golden, Colorado, and that's the reason. It doesn't have a brewery anywhere else.

"Why is it so popular? Well, it's a good beer. And they do a tremendous amount of advertising. Yes sir, they really buy it in lots of parts of Texas. I had a man here from Chicago not long ago, he was just visiting here, and before he went back he bought ten cases to haul back to Chicago. They can't get it there, either.

"Of course, we have the premium beers such as Budweiser, Schlitz, Hamm's. They sell pretty well, generally to tourists. But this Coors is really something. It's a light beer, and it's just as popular with men as women—they both buy it."

Any local beers? "No, we don't brew any beer here in New Mexico," says Mr. Vomack. "But there's a brewer in

Phoenix, Arizona, whose beer we sell here as A-1. Then over in Texas there's a beer called Pearl—it's a very good seller in these parts. . . ."

Frank Vomack comes from Iowa; he used to work with the State Liquor Commission there, and maybe that's the reason he has such a fine selection of beers: Löwenbräu and Dortmunder from Germany, Asahi from Japan, San Miguel from the Philippines, among others. "There's a certain class of people who buy imported beer," he explains. "Your professional people, those who have a little more money, they feel they can splurge a little more for a better quality beer. Löwenbräu, there, that's an excellent beer we have. And the Japanese beer is very good. Yes sir, there's plenty of demand for beer around here."

We got back into the car, the desert air hot and sticky, Interstate 25 slashing like a ribbon across those dry sun-blasted hills and gulches. And as we left Truth or Consequences the first heavy, warm drops of rain splattered the township.

West Coast. Apple wine and beer ads vie with each other on the AM radio. Coors is the name you hear most of the time, and the billboards are plastered with lurid paintings of Rocky Mountains spring water. But Olympia is a popular beer, too: It's in all the supermarkets from Los Angeles to San Jose to Oakland. You can buy it in tiny cans about half the size of the normal one, but I wouldn't advise it: I bought a dozen, and found they were undrinkable. Beer deteriorates if it's left for months in the can, and maybe these had been hanging around too long. In San Francisco, along Broadway and around the North Beach (the old Beat hangout), you can buy just about any beer in the world; in fact, some of the bars and tourist cafes specialize in imported brands. Down near the waterfront the Steam Beer Brewery is still making the original steam beer which everyone in California drank a century ago; a lot of people still do.

Further up the West Coast the scene changes again.

Oregon has only one brewery, Blitz-Weinhard. But Washington State is the home of some well-known beers: Olympia, in Olympia; Carling, in Tacoma; and Rainier, in Seattle. This last brewery makes an ale that is sold all over the Northwest; it's one of the few distinctive brews you can recognize immediately: Its deeper, richer color, for a start. But even in a blindfold test you can usually pick the pungent, hop-flavored taste of Rainier Ale.

Time to head home. We turned east, cutting down through Yellowstone Park and into the long, rolling slopes of Wyoming. The Colorado beers were the first we noticed: especially Colorado Gold Label, brewed by Walter Brewing in Pueblo. Like Coors, it's a light beer and advertises itself as being brewed with SPARKLING MOUNTAIN WATER. The can itself is plastered with glittering mountain streams and snowy peaks.

As we hit the real Midwest, however, the brands changed. First came Storz, an inoffensive beer from Omaha. Then North Star, a light beer with a sweet aftertaste that is brewed by Jacob Schmidt in St. Paul, Minnesota, and has that familiar XXX on the can (when I was a boy the newspaper cartoonists always used to draw drunks with an X for each eye). And then another Minnesota beer, Grain Belt, which seemed popular right through the great American heartland. In Deadwood, in what used to be the Dakota Territory, the bar where Wild Bill Hickock was shot dead—Bar No. 10—serves Grain Belt as draft; so does just about every second bar from Rapid City on east. It's a pleasant, somewhat fruity beer . . . or is that just the taste of the grain which we drove through for mile after unending mile, across the prairies of the Midwest?

(Sorry to interrupt Craig's narrative, but according to *Brewer's Digest's* 1976 *Brewery Directory*, published by Siebel Publishing Company in Chicago, Colorado Gold Label and Storz have now become products of the past, victims of the sweep of the national brewers across the land.—B. A.)

It wasn't until we reached Minnesota itself that the other famous Great Lakes beers, such as Hamm's, began to come into their own. Finally, the brewing capital of America: Milwaukee, on the shores of Lake Michigan, which produces more of the amber liquid than any other city in the world. They say that you can tell which beer in America is selling best by simply sniffing the air over Milwaukee, and certainly the list of major brewers is impressive: Schlitz, Pabst, and Miller. Most of the breweries give visitors conducted tours of their factories, plus free samples of their beer. It's one way to get drunk cheaply. But all good things have to come to an end, and it wasn't long before we were on the turnpikes heading back towards the east coast. In Indiana we met a college student who swore by a beer we never did manage to track down, called "Old Timers." At last we asked him why he liked it so much. "Well," he explained, "I used to get it free—I had a friend who knew the brewmaster really well!" In Ohio we sampled Hudepohl, Schoenling, Carling, Burger, Top Hat, and Fehr—they tasted slightly different than the Milwaukee brews, with less of that pungent aftertaste which you sometimes get with Wisconsin beers. Hudepohl was one of the best: no kick at all. Pennsylvania has thirteen breweries, more than any other state, but none of those we tasted seemed outstanding. "That tasted like it was made in the steel mills," said one of the sampling party of a brand which had better remain nameless.

Maybe we were getting tired. We drove straight through the last night on the road, hit the George Washington Bridge, made it back to our neighborhood bar. It has illuminated palm trees on the outside, sort of like Miami or San Diego: very exotic. And a familiar sign in the window.

"Glad to see you back," said the guy behind the bar. We told him about our trip.

"Wow, you sure must've tried a lotta beers. What'll you have?"

"Gimme a Rainier Ale," I said, grinning.

"All we got is Ballantine," he said, a bit defensively.

As though I didn't know.

Courtesy of New York Public Library, Picture Collection.

During the War of 1812, we were fighting the British again and a huge American flag was sewn by Mrs. Mary Young Pickersgill of Baltimore to fly over Fort McHenry in anticipation of a British naval attack. The flag was so enormous that she had to borrow space in a Baltimore brewery. With Mrs. Pickersgill sewing up a storm, the flag was completed and flying over the fort when the British attacked, and it was there the next morning, April 14, 1814. The sight of it inspired Francis Scott Key to write you-know-what hard-to-sing song, and he retired to the Fountain Inn, a venerable Baltimore hostel, with the rough draft of his creation in his pocket. Needing something to fuel the continuation of his labors, he ordered a beer. When the beer was done, so was the song. One may only speculate that it might have had been a better tune if he'd had a couple more. . . .

When the war was over, the nation could get back to its domestic concerns, among which was the two-edged sword of serious drinking and illegal distilling. President Madison publicly expressed the desire of the government to see the influence of brewing fruitfully extended to every state in the union and Jefferson, now our most distinguished elder statesman, put it even more fervently: "No nation is sober when the dearness of fermented drinks substitutes ardent spirits as a common beverage." But to no avail. Brewing grew all right, New York and Pennsylvania being the centers of the trade, but illegal distilling grew like a forest fire. By the 1820s there were an estimated 14,000-plus distilleries in operation in this country, and the moon-shine industry still flourishes today, still illegally, in parts of the South and is both a federal and state concern.

As for the beer industry, it remained free of federal excise taxes until the Civil War, when the brewers willingly agreed to the new taxes levied in 1862 to help underwrite the mounting costs of the war. Brewers in the New York area met in Pythagoras Hall on August 22 to discuss the need for banding together to support the government in these dark hours and from that meeting the United States Brewers Association was born. Eschewing the more familiar business stance as regards new taxation, the brewers endorsed "a uniform, faithful and conscientious obedience to the new law throughout the whole land." Later that year the organization expanded on a national basis and three years later sent a delegation abroad to study European internal tax systems. Would that there had been as much unity between the states themselves.

By the time of the formation of the USBA, as it is known in the trade, the brewing industry had left the eastern seaboard and moved westward with the rest of the country, toward the Mississippi and beyond. Cincinnati and Chicago became important brewing cities, and then Detroit, Cleveland, St. Louis, and, of course, Milwaukee.

It is general knowledge that Milwaukee makes more beer than any other city, which is true; that its citizens drink more beer per capita than those of any other large American city, which is true; and that brewing is Milwaukee's major industry, which is false.

It is difficult to believe now, but there was a time when hardly anyone drank beer in Milwaukee and if they did they had to haul it in from out of town. The city's first brewery was not opened until 1840 and then—I hesitate to mention this, but it's so—the proprietors were not German but Welsh. They were versatile fellows, too. They made ale, white beer, porter and what they claimed was scotch whiskey.

Within a few months, thank heavens, things improved. Herman Reuthlisberger, who was certainly not Welsh and had never developed a taste for scotch, made the first lager ever produced in Milwaukee. Since then there have been bad times, but no one there has ever gone thirsty.

> —*This is Milwaukee* by Robert W. Wells, a most engaging portrait of the city whose citizens aged twenty-one or over consume an average of 46.75 gallons of beer each annum. And lots of brandy, too!

That the great expansion of the brewing industry would have happened even without the advent of lager beer in America is at best arguable, but it is uncontestable that the rate of expansion and the extent to which beer may be said to be our national drink both attest to the importance of lager in America. Before its arrival on these shores, the ales, stout, and porter we drank were all British (or Irish, in the case of stout) in inspiration, but lager provided a light (in color and taste), hoppy, sparkling beer that was in considerable contrast to the stronger, malty, but flat, British brews. Lager was the creation of some unknown German brewers who stored (*lagern* means "to store") their beers in cool cellars. Part of the secret was in the storing of this beer in cellars or cool places during the winter months, so that it would be just right to drink come springtime, and part of it lay, quite literally, with the yeast used. Instead of ale or top-fermentation yeast, which rises to the top at the end of the fermentation process, this mysterious bubble maker from Bavaria (naturally) sank to the bottom, causing the fermentation, and with it the laughing bubbles, to work upward. And it was on the strength of these bubbles that lager beer foamed from coast to coast.

No one knows when the lager yeast first fermented in America. It was only with the arrival of the fast Baltimore clipper ships that the yeast regularly survived the sea journey, down from months to three weeks' time. A German brewer named John Wagner was definitely producing lager in Philadelphia in 1840. He had managed to bring the yeast over from a Bavarian brewery where he was brewmaster, and made his beer in a small shanty behind his house in the outskirts of Philadelphia and stored it in his cellar. That his yeast was much coveted goes without saying, and Charles C. Wolf in his *One Hundred Years of Brewing* reports that Wagner's brother-in-law was "tempted beyond his strength and stole, or at least took without leave, about a pint of it." That the authorities regarded this as a theft, or else a leave-taking, of serious consequence, is evidenced by the stiff two-year prison sentence given the brother-in-law after his prompt arrest and conviction.

In any event, Wagner's lager proved a great hit with the German-Americans of Philadelphia and his own employees, smelling a good thing (lager was more aromatic, too, than ale) went out on their own. And why not? The market was there. The first Germans had emigrated to this country for religious freedom, but now the tides of Germans coming here were doing so for economic and political (to avoid the draft) reasons. Still others came here after the 1848 uprisings in Germany. From Brooklyn to St. Louis to Texas, they liked their lager, their beer gardens

"Roll out the barrel . . . ."

and each other, and "Germantowns" became a factor in the local economy and sociopolitical structure across the country.

Contrary to the popular notion, beer did not appear suddenly in this country around 1850 when German-born brewers began to introduce a specific type well known in their homeland, *lager*. . . . But there is no contesting the fact that the homesick German brewers and their *lager bier*, once established, to all intents and purposes took over the American brewing industry and have ever since been dominant. Only the ale we drink today, and—in special localities—the stout and porter, can in any way be identified with the English brewing tradition that preceded the German. . . . The modern lager, with its emphasis on lightness, dryness and sparkle, is an American adaptation of the original German brew and may be considered in both its character and its method of production, as an indigenous creation.

—Introduction to *Brewed in America,* by Stanley Baron, published in 1962

By 1880, lager production had risen from the eight-gallon capacities of Wagner's tiny brewery to an annual figure of 13,500,000 barrels. And in the next decade, it would double. The Schaffer brothers, Frederick and Maximilian, were enjoying a huge success in the New York area with what is today called "America's oldest lager beer," and their prosperity was being emulated in other parts of the nation by Joseph Schlitz and Theodor Hamm and Eberhard Anheuser and Adolphus Busch and Frederick Miller and Frederick Pabst and Adolph Coors. There had been 431 breweries in 1850 and there would be an all-time high of 4,131 in 1873, that figure to drop under 3,000 two years later as a result of business failures, consolidations, and takeovers, plus the first serious work of Prohibitionists. As we know, their ultimate triumph would be almost half a century in the making, but they were hard at work even back then. In the early days of the movement, their primary freneticism was directed at hard liquor and the consumption of spirits did undergo a decrease in the second half of the nineteenth century, whereas per capita consumption of beer rose from 1.36 gallons in 1840, the first year for which we have these figures, to 3.22 gallons in 1860 and 16.06 gallons at the turn of the century. In 1910 per capita beer consumption hit its highest level before Prohibition—19.77 gallons. The brewers were doing their number, and so were the beer drinkers.

Milwaukee was founded in 1835 and received a city charter in 1846. Its growth has been rapid, especially in the last 10 years.

The chief articles of its extensive commerce are grain, flour, and lumber. Its flour-mills are very large, and its grain-elevators have a capacity of 6 million bushels. Milwaukee beer (Pabst, Schlitz, Blatz, etc.) is known all over the United States, and in 1892 was produced to the amount of 2¼ million barrels.

—*Baedecker's United States,* 1893 edition

# 32/Serious Drinkers of the World, Stand Up and Be Counted!

Every year I look forward to the new edition of the *Guinness Book of World Records*—which probably outsells the Bible these days, in its various cloth, paperback, English-language, and foreign editions—to see who's leading the world in beer drinking these days. I don't mean those wild Australians in the humid northern part of the country whose annual statistics (62.4 gallons) in this department boggle the imagination as well as the mind (theirs, surely) or our own heavy guzzlers in Milwaukee. I mean a complete nation. Which country leads the world in per capita beer consumption?

In the 1968 edition, the Czechs were in front with 28.4 gallons downed per person, and in the 1970 edition they were still in front, with 34.1 gallons per person (that's counting the kiddies and the teetotalers, you know) per annum. In the 1973 edition, however, the West Germans had taken the lead with a new record high of 36.7 gallons. Two years later, they were still in the lead, but the per capita figure had slipped to 31.9 gallons. What had happened to the West Germans, I wondered. This wasn't rhetorical wonderment, however; I really didn't have the answer to the question.

Now comes the 1976 edition of the book, which gets fatter with each passing year—more expensive, too, alas—and the West Germans are up to 38.4 gallons. Good. I was worried about them for a year or two.

However, the *Guinness Book of World Records* is not the only source for this kind of information. I know the people who publish the book, but I've never thought to ask them where they get their information in this exotic area. I do know that every year a Dutch organization considered very reliable in such matters—the *Produktschap voor Gedistilleerde Dranken*—collects this kind of information from government sources and their ranking for 1974 beer consumption. (Incidentally, the figures in the latest *Guinness* were for *1973* beer consumption.) The Dutch publication showed Czechoslovakia leading the world with a 40.3 gallons per capita figure. Belgium, according to these records, had been first in 1973, but was now fourth. Second was West Germany, and Australia third.

It may be that the current regime in Czechoslovakia has led the citizens to drink more and more, but this is only supposition. In any case, they are *not* among the world's leading drinkers, in terms of absolute alcohol consumption—that is, alcohol from whatever kind of beverage. Even the Germans, who consume oceans of their great beer, plus schnapps, plus lots of wine, are far from leading the world in this department. According to an interesting book published in 1975 by Tom Burnam, *The Dictionary of Misinformation*, (Thomas Y. Crowell, $9.95), West Germany was fourth among twenty countries during the 1960s in its use of hard spirits, fifth in its enjoyment of wine, and trailed, among others, Australia as a hard drinking (all departments) nation. The Australians drink a lot of their own wine, and according to a high executive of John Haig and Company, may be the world's largest per capita consumers of scotch whisky. In the Uni-

ted Kingdom, where scotch is produced, it's simply too damned expensive for most people to drink on a regular basis, and England was lowest among the nations surveyed in Mr. Burham's book in terms of spirits consumption.

At the head of the class, with livers to show for it, are the French. It has been said that a Frenchman's bad liver is a mark of social distinction—presumably he can afford to drink as much as, and *whatever*, he cares to imbibe. But it's still a mite shocking to learn that the French drink three times as much as we do in terms of absolute alcohol consumption. Another surprise: The French don't drink the most wine per capita—the Italians do. But France leads the world in spirits consumption, relishing their own classic brandies, cognac, armagnac, and others, and probably represents the world's second-largest market, after the U.S. for Scotland's most famous gift to the world. Since Americans are second only to the French in their use of spirits, and the French drink about half as much beer as we do, it's their staggering (woops) intake of wine—25.2 gallons per capita in 1974 as compared to 1.7 gallons here—that accounts for the three-to-one ratio in absolute alcohol consumption.

The Italians, not commonly thought of as big boozers, happen to be second only to the French, and primarily it's their world class consumption of wine—29.2 gallons per capita in 1974, which was *down* from 30.6 gallons in 1968!—which accounts for their position. The Italian *lira* may be a soft currency, but all the cheap *vino* must help ease the pain.

During the decade of the Sixties, according to Mr. Burnam's research, the Swiss were third in per capita wine consumption and the Japanese sake drinkers fourth. However, 1974 wine consumption figures show the Swiss sixth and the Japanese not among the top ten per capita consumers. As listed by the *Produktschap voor Gedistillteerde Dranken*, the top ten wine-consuming nations, after Italy and France, on a per capita basis, were as follows: Portugal, Argentina, Spain, Switzerland, Luxembourg, Chile, Hungary, and Austria. Then, to show you how statistics can confuse, although the U.S. is sixth among the nations of the world in wine production, trailing France, Italy, Spain, Russia (surprise?), and Argentina, we rank thirty-first among the world's nations in wine consumption. So all the talk about California's good jug wines and equal-to-Europe's-best varietals hasn't reached the average American household.

Of course, we far and away lead the world in beer production, brewing twice as much as West Germany, nearly three times the annual barrelage of England, more than three times as much as Russia, and over five times as much as Japan—to rank the Big Five beer-producing nations. Using the United States Brewers Association's 1974 figures, the rest of the world's major producers line up as follows: Czechoslovakia, France, Canada, Mexico, East Germany, Australia, Brazil, Spain, Belgium, Poland, Netherlands, Yugoslavia, Columbia, Denmark, Italy, and Austria. What's intriguing here is how some of the world's most famous beer-producing nations have achieved part of that fame not only on the basis of how good their beer is to drink, but on the number of countries to which it is exported.

Here are some Serious Drinkers, taking time off to chase after some small animals.

# 33/A Frothy History of Suds

*" 'Hurricane Carrie Nation' was building in force...."*

There can be no doubt that the Noble Experiment was the most significant event affecting brewing and beer drinking since the introduction of lager, but before entering that tangle of good motives and bad politics, let us briefly consider several technical advances that were of signal importance both to the industry and the consumer. According to a lengthy report issued in 1969 by the American Can Company, entitled *A History of Packaged Beer and Its Market in America*:

> Modern brewing began in 1876 when Louis Pasteur and later the Danish scientist, Emile Hansen, published papers that paved the way to more uniform yeast fermentations. Later, development of mechanical refrigeration by a German engineer, Linde, made brewing independent of the seasons. Pasteurization, quality control and precision bottling were additional factors contributing to the industry as it is known today.

Frederick Birmingham adds the wry supposition that Pasteur was influenced more by patriotic motives than scientific or philanthropic ones "in turning directly to the study of beer to apply his theories." Perhaps Pasteur was chiefly motivated, Birmingham wonders, "by a desire to make the French beer at least as good as the German, following the Franco-Prussian debacle on the battlefield that proved Teutons were very much the masters in the arts of war." If so, Pasteur seriously missed the mark since French beer is still pretty blah, the exceptions being the beers of Alsace-Lorraine, the region annexed by Germany in 1871 and recovered by France in 1919. But that's still German beer on French soil. "A true German can't endure a Frenchman, but he likes their wine." —J. W. Goethe.

Given the technological and scientific advances afforded their industry, the larger American brewers were thinking of going national, and they began widening their distribution and constructing plants in other areas of the country. They also indulged in price cutting to drive out the small, local breweries and backed up these moves with strong merchandising and advertising campaigns. What began to happen, as it always does, is that fewer companies were producing more and more beer. Pabst, having absorbed another Milwaukee brewery, hit the million-barrel sales level in 1893, and both Schlitz and Anheuser-Busch, which produces Budweiser and other beers, were selling a million barrels annually around the turn of the century. The beer business was so lucrative that British financial syndicates moved in and tried to buy the largest brewers. Failing on this level, they tried to buy out some of the smaller brewers and succeeded. Well, in a way.

> In most cases the former owners had sold under the most favorable circumstances, although it cannot be said that they have deceived the Englishmen. Still they took advantage of the English craze for buying and demanded high prices which, in many cases, they secured without much ado.
>
> —*American Brewer*, 1895

At first the new British invasion must have seemed to them like sound fiscal politics because these were palmy days in America and beer consumption was continually on the rise. Some of the German-Americans, still feeling more German than American, began importing their favorite old brews, and the American brewers responded by introducing premium beers of a superior nature, generally richer tasting than the other domestic beers and obviously fresher than the imported brands—which is very important, since beer, *despite* all the advances in brewing, packaging, and shipping techniques, was then and remains a fragile food. This didn't destroy the imported beer trade, however, nor did it have to since even today imported beers represent only a small percentage of the market. Nor did it really matter. There was plenty of business for anyone with a competitive product.

Lüchow's [the New York restaurant] became the American agent for Würzburger beer in 1885, and for Pilsner soon after. August [August Lüchow, founder of the restaurant] was not the first man to serve these fine imported beers in America, but he was the first to make them popular, a fact attested by the popular classic Harry von Tilzer wrote to honor August and his restaurant, *Down Where the Würzburger Flows. . . .* The song traveled from Fourteenth Street to the beer gardens of Cincinnati, St. Louis, Chicago, Milwaukee and far beyond, and attained such popularity that August declared in some bewilderment: "I feel like a kind of beer Columbus!"

Of the trenchermen who ate and drank at Lüchow's, the Baron Ferdinand Sinzig, of the House of Steinway, established a record which still stands by downing thirty-six seidels of Wurzburger—without rising. Envious competitors observed that he was a native of Cologne, and therefore presumably without kidneys.

*—Lüchow's German Cookbook*
by Jan Mitchell

The reference made earlier to the prescience of the British interests in making large investments in American brewing was not so much predicated on the financial size of those investments, but on the fact that in many cases they would be relatively short lived. Hurricane Carrie Nation was building in force, and the brewing industry, because it owned so many saloons, would find itself directly in the eye of that force. Emulating the British and Germans, the American brewers had begun buying up corner saloons, beer gardens, restaurants, taverns, and even hotels as a means of ensuring that their product was sold in those outlets. For a few decades, this seemed like very sound business practice although only the larger brewers could really afford a heavy investment in this area. Looking back on the corner saloon industry in 1950, *Fortune* magazine agreed that it seemed a fine idea at the time: "Few will deny that the saloon deal laid the foundation for most of the great brewing fortunes in America. A brewer simply went out and captured as many corner locations as he could, then rented or deputized the premises to a saloonkeeper who sold the owner-brewer's beer exclusively." One doesn't know if this *tied-house* (the British expression for brewery-owned pubs) system would not eventually have offended beer drinkers who felt they deserve some choice in what they're offered, but the question is academic since Carrie Nation, her followers, their moral indignation, and—most destructive—their hatchets were on their way into the American saloon.

There is a kind of awful irony in this because beer had always been *the* temperance drink in this country, but the extraordinary success of lager gave such a boost to the industry and caused such a change in American drinking habits that beer could no longer be exempted from the fury

of the prohibitionists. As William Iverson points out in his excellent article:

> Militant prohibitionists no longer discriminated between beer and ardent spirits. They were antisaloon, and since beer had built the American saloon, they were out to ban beer. Through the agitation of feminist reformers, Prohibition was emotionally linked with the fight for woman suffrage. The clergy and large corporations joined the crusade to stamp out "the curse of drink," and when the Kaiser overran "little Belgium" in 1914, American indignation was directed against beer as a German beverage. No one thought to point out that the Belgian victims were themselves the world's leading beer drinkers, with a per-capita capacity almost twice that of the German invaders. . . .

Barley Water: 1. Pick clean, and wash well a handful of common barley, then simmer gently in three pints of water with a bit of lemon-peel. Prepared thus, it does not nauseate like pearl-barley water. 2. Take two ounces and a half of pearl-barley: wash well, then add half a pint of water, and boil for a little time, throw away the liquor, pour four imperial pints of boiling water on the barley, boil down to two pints, strain flavour with sugar, and lemon-peel, if wished.

—*Practical Housewife*, 1860, collected in a delightful book entitled *Early American Beverages*, by John Hull Brown, published some years ago and now, unfortunately, out-of-print

Looking back at that highly charged era, it's not so difficult to see how the work of the Anti-Saloon League and the rest of the Prohibition movement could have been so successful in shutting down American drink (at least in public), but it is hard to understand why Prohibition lasted so damned long when it was obviously both economically stupid and impossible to enforce. Despite all the clamor, beer had been given a token respite, brewers being allowed to produce a beer of no more than one-half of one percent alcoholic content, and some brewers did try to stay in business by brewing this "near-beer," which was so dreadful that it prompted one observer to quip that whoever had called it "near-beer" was an extremely poor judge of distance. The brewers also tried to get away with 2.75 percent beer, their argument being that no normal human had a stomach large enough to drink enough to get drunk on it, but the authorities wouldn't buy it, and so the public never got a chance to do so. Some brewers shut their doors never to open them again, while others—particularly the large ones—turned their hand to other products. Anheuser-Busch brought out a nonalcoholic drink called "Bevo"; Schlitz made candy; Blatz manufactured industrial alcohol, which *was* legal, though one may presume that not all of it was eventually put to industrial use; other breweries tried to keep their malting equipment in use by producing malt syrup and malt extract. Others made money making ice cream, and one brewery—Fortune Brothers in Chicago—switched fields by becoming a spaghetti and macaroni factory. In despair, another brewer—David Stevenson in New York—tried to make economic ends meet by renting part of its plant for fur storage. When the war was over, America leaped into the "Roaring Twenties," but the brewers remained fairly miserable, the only roaring to be heard from those who were crying in their near-beer. "A Prohibitionist is the sort of man one wouldn't care to drink with—even if he drank."—H. L. Mencken.

If the Great Dry Spell was hard on brewers, imagine what it did to saloons and taverns. Some sold food, many more just padlocked their doors. At that Mecca for beer lovers in New York, the famous Lüchow's, only food and tradition were served during the years of Prohibition, and during the last few years of that period, the restaurant didn't even bother to open on New Year's Eve, even though customers had shown themselves more than willing to bring their own "holidaze" cheer in a flask. In May 1933, when the noble experiment was officially closed down, Lüchow's hosted a thousand people at dinner, who consumed the equivalent of a thousand seidels of the Würzburger beer readied for the occasion. Things were hardly back to normal, however. In pre-Prohibition days, the normal daily consumption of German beer at Lüchow's was 24,000 seidels.

Elsewhere on that momentous occasion, in those states which weren't dry, the brewers rushed out their beer and Americans rushed out to drink a million barrels during the first twenty-four hours of the new era, with the only folks remaining dry being the brewers themselves—who ran out of beer. But it wasn't a simple case of "happy days are here again." This was the Great Depression, and there was now very strong competition from the soft drink industry. By June 1933 there were 33 brewers back in operation, and the next year at this time there were 756, but brewers now knew that they were competing with a giant young industry whose worth in 1931 was reported by the United States Department of Commerce at $175,000,000. Yes, their previous response to soft drinks had been along the lines of this supposedly droll comment published in *Brewer and Maltster* in 1917: "Aside from wholesomeness, which is equally desireable in tooth-paste, teething rings and everything else that enters the mouth, the qualities which are essential in food are not particularly required in these drinks." But in 1933 the brewers had to compete with

these products not only in retail outlets but also in the home. The new beer advertising, therefore, had to show consumers quaffing beer not in saloons or taverns, but at home and at ordinary social events. Canned beer was introduced, which helped keep the brews chilled, and took the church key out of the church, and some years later, when the self-opening cans were introduced, they provided a generation of comedians with bad gags like these: "Have you tried those self-opening cans, or don't you like the taste of blood?" and "There's a rumor going around that Alcoholics Anonymous is working on self-closing cans."

It took the industry until 1940 to attain the sales volume it had enjoyed in pre-Prohibition days, but by that time the number of brewers was down to less than half their numbers in 1910. And that trend has continued, a subject we will explore in some depth elsewhere in the book. So, too, has the trend of drinking beer at home rather than at taverns and bars, with television being the greatest reason for Americans becoming drink-at-homes. In more recent years, the marketing developments of most significance have been the introduction of malt liquors and beers for waist watchers. Malt liquor enjoys a steady, but small, market, and the beers for dieters may be the wave of the future, with both Miller and Schlitz having a major go in this direction. Americans want to grow lighter, and the brewing industry will gladly help them in that direction so long as the direction of beer consumption continues upward. We are now drinking more beer than ever— 145,464,143 barrels in 1974—and our per capita consumption has reached at least the highest pre-Prohibition levels. But perhaps the most dramatic figures are these: Any one of the top twelve brewing companies in America produces more beer today than did the entire industry a century ago. Obviously, beer pleases some of the people a lot of the time. But then, you never can please some people a lot of the time, as witness the snobby antisudser quoted below:

Cartoon by Bill Murphy.

" . . . I'll have a beer, and . . . uh . . . a white crème de menthe frappé with an avocado peel for the lady."

. . . we may as well concede that beer is a low-brow drink. Once in a way it is admitted to high society. . . . There are, however, high low-brows who stand loyal to beer and honestly prefer it above all drinks for certain specified occasions. These like to remind us that even Kings have condescended, with relish, and that time was when certain monarchs of minor principalities (notably in Germany) demanded their tribute in hogshead of fine beer.

The trouble with beer devotees is that, for the most part, they have failed to hedge it around with the nicer etiquette. Indeed, there is a marked disposition to regard the fellow who can drink the most beer and remain above the table as the best connoisseur. This is to be deplored.

—*BACCHUS BEHAVE! The Lost Art of Polite Drinking,* by Alma Whitaker, published in 1933 and, with good reason, long out-of-print

Still, if you see Alma, and I hope she's still alive and kicking about beer, invite her over. Perhaps by now she has changed her mind. Well, why not at least drink to that. *Prosit! Skaal! Slainthe!* Down the hatch! Bottoms up! And most of all, cheers!

# 34/Steam Beer: Our Only Native Brew

An absolutely unique American beer, in fact probably the only native American beer, is steam beer.

It's brewed in San Francisco, in almost exactly the same way it was back in the Gold Rush days. At that time nearly all the breweries on the West Coast made steam beer: San Francisco alone had twenty-seven steam brewers. It was before the great influx of German brewers—many of whom came here after the 1848 revolution—had swung America toward the lager beers they brought from their own country. In some old San Francisco bars you can still see steam beer advertised on the patterned glass transoms. Today only one small brewery, the Anchor Steam Beer Brewing Company tucked way behind some warehouses near the San Francisco Bay waterfront, still makes steam beer. But it has been making the brew since 1851, and the beer it produces is the real thing.

Just what is steam beer?

That's a tough question. Basically it's somewhere between a lager and an ale: it's made with a bottom-fermenting yeast, like lager, but it tastes and looks more like ale. One of the reasons for this is that it is fermented at a higher temperature than lager—from sixty to seventy-five degrees Fahrenheit. Lager needs to be chilled while it is fermenting, but in the Gold Rush days, ice was almost as scarce as women and local miners had to work out a way of making beer without it. They succeeded. "When steam beer is cleanly and properly brewed from good material, it is a pretty fair drink," said the *Western Brewer* in 1898.

It still is. To look at, it's something like a good British ale: rich amber in color, foaming head, perhaps a bit more effervescent. It has a rich, full flavor as well, tasting more of hops than the average American lager. You can even smell the hops before you drink it. And because it's often served warmer than lager (ideally, at about forty-six degrees, compared to in the high thirties for lager), the flavor isn't chilled out of it.

In fact, it probably tastes better now than it did in the old days. "I'm sure that, a hundred years ago, it was foul most of the time," says Fritz Maytag, who owns the Anchor Brewery and is the brewmaster as well. He is a well-built, forthright man of strong opinions, especially about beer.

> There was a good risk of most things tasting foul in those days—that's why you always tasted a bottle of wine. And I know how easy it is to spoil beer. They had no refrigeration in those days; they only had ice, and that was expensive even when it was available. Also, the breweries tended to go on making steam beer in the old way even after refrigeration came in—they'd make it, take it down to the bars on Market Street, sell it as soon as they could . . . and undoubtedly the quality was sometimes very low.

That's one of the reasons the steam breweries gradually faded away. Also, it was regarded as a working man's beer, and not so "high class" as lager. But the main reason, ac-

cording to Fritz Maytag, was that people's tastes changed. "Lager swept steam beer off its feet," he says. "Americans began to go for a lighter, thinner, blander product, just as they do today." The Anchor Brewery held out; it was run by the one family and the one man, Joe Allen, from Prohibition until just a few years ago, when Maytag came in to help rescue it, too, from closing. "The only reason it survived was because it was so small, nobody thought it worthwhile to bump it off," he says. "But now it's beginning to come back in popularity. We have about fifty outlets in the Bay Area, plus literally thousands of outlets for the bottled beer in the western United States. We're selling beer in eight states in the west plus, on an experimental basis, in Minneapolis and in New Jersey."

Maytag also points out that Anchor is the first steam beer to be bottled since Prohibition. "People used to think you couldn't bottle it—you know, they *still* think of it as a wild and wooly beer," he says. "But it's not especially difficult to bottle—the process is similar to bottling champagne. Of course, Joe Allen, when anyone asked him why he didn't bottle it, he would say, 'Ah, you can't bottle a beer like *this*, this is a different breed of beer altogether.' " Maytag laughs. "Of course, it *is*, but it can be bottled."

Just what is it that makes steam beer so different from the usual American beer? Fritz Maytag answers:

Well, when people ask you that, they usually want a very simple, unique explanation—for instance, like it's made out of artichokes or something. But like any other beer, you can vary it by using different malts, different hops, and so on. I have in my mind what I consider a good beer to be, and I try to brew it. I want a beer which is not an extreme beer, but which definitely has a malty flavor, a hop aroma, and pronounced bitterness—which is anathema to the American lager brewer. In Germany lagers are hopped: They smell like hops, and they taste like hops. So we are after something between a good German lager and an English ale, if that makes any sense!

The point is, a hundred years ago steam beer wouldn't have tasted so remarkably different from American lager beer. But we haven't changed very much, and the lager beers have. They're now using corn and rice for malt; only about half their grain is barley malt. But we use only barley malt, which gives the beer more flavor. They're brewing it purposely to be very light, they're using maybe a fourth of the hops they used to use. But we use much more hops—close to a pound of hops to every barrel of beer. Whereas the average in this country now is a little under a quarter of a pound per barrel. You put your nose in the average American beer, you can't smell any hops; but you can in ours.

Hops give it bitterness, too. Did you know there is even an international unit called IBU, International Bitterness Unit, that measures bitterness? And there are different types of bitterness: there's a bitterness you feel on your tongue when you first start to drink, which is good; and then there's an aftertaste of bitterness, which is not so good, and you try to avoid that.

We use a mashing system which is a rather crude one. Our mashing temperatures are significant in that they are designed to produce a beer with a good head, a good flavor, plenty of body, but in the process we lose physical stability: The beer will haze up when you chill it. We also use a very shallow fermenter; it's unique. The beer is maybe only twelve inches deep during fermentation; nobody else uses one so shallow. Other brewers say we're crazy to use such a thing, but—well—it's traditional. And the temperatures in that fermenter are much warmer than they are for lager beer.

And our beer is one hundred percent krausened, which is a natural method of carbonation—it's a method of secondary fermentation by which you add newly fermented, highly charged beer to the original brew. There's no carbonation in our beer other than that which comes from the krausening. And I think that's unique; other brewers may krausen some beer, but they blend it out among their various brews. Some brewers inject $CO_2$ into their beer. Krausening's important, which is why you're beginning to see it in beer ads. It gives you more flavorful, more interesting beer with more head to it, more foam.

Fritz Maytag doesn't have much enthusiasm for the flavor of American beers; he finds them "too light, too bland, too thin." He has respect for the brewers who are able to turn out such "incredibly bland beer" in large quantities: "I know for a fact that a number of them take great care over their product," he says, "they know what they're doing. But it's not for me." He continues:

> It tastes like water. Honestly, I'm just not interested in lager beers of the type that're brewed here in the United States. They all have as little flavor as possible, and they all taste exactly the same. That's intentional, of course. I hear it from the horse's mouth, from brewmasters of other breweries, every day. Any brewer with any sense is trying to make a beer that's just as bland as everybody else's.
> I know that many brewers model their beer as closely as they can to the top seller. Coors is the one that's selling big in the West now; well over a third of all beer sold in California is Coors. And so some of the other beers copy it.
> Budweiser. Coors. They both have distinctive flavors. I think you could probably tell the difference between the two brands in a blindfold test. . . . Ballantine Ale, that's different again. It's dry-hopped, with a particular brewers' hops. You open a can of Ballantine in a room, and I can smell it right away. But the others . . . you'd find it hard to say which is which. In general, I think American beers vary more within the brand than they do between each other. Beers are very fragile food. And the flavor deteriorates with time and temperature. So *all* American breweries are concerned with having their beer sold as fresh as possible; they take back old beer, at a cost to the distributor, whose job it is to make sure that supermarkets and other retail outlets don't let a particular brewer's beer get shoved to the rear, and not get bought as fresh as possible.

Another of Maytag's observations—or complaints, if you will—is that American beers are usually served far too cold, which tends to diminish what flavor they do have.

> In a hot climate people insist on a cold beer, and there's something to be said for that. But people do everything they can to make it even colder than it need be. We had a bar owner who called up once and said our beer was no good, it wouldn't pull, so we went out and checked it and found his lines were frozen. His beer must have been twenty-eight degrees Fahrenheit or something. What can you do with someone like that? We'd like our beer to be served warmer than any other brewer would want, because it brings the flavor out. Sometimes we have people come here to the brewery and have a glass and say, "Gee, that tastes better than it did in my local bar last night." That's because it's warmer. But unfortunately we can't control what the bars do.

How did steam beer come to get its name? There are some nice old stories about that. One of them has it that a man called Harlie Steam invented the brew. Another calls him Pete Steam.

The more likely reason is that while steam beer is going through its secondary fermentation it builds up pressure like a steam engine, until it reaches fifty or sixty pounds per square inch. "In those days most beers were in the English tradition, they were flat," says Maytag. "It was before lager beers swept America; but steam beer was unique, it was carbonated. The brewer would put the krausen, the green beer, into the wooden barrel, put the bung in, and wait for the pressure to build up! And then when it came out, it foamed. I mean, someone would say 'Give me a glass of steam' and it would come foaming out of the barrel. I think that's how it got its name. That's what one of the local brewmasters here wrote, anyhow."

Fritz Maytag first got interested in steam beer by drinking it. He was a student at Stanford at the time, and had a glass of steam at a local bar called The Oasis. He liked it, became more and more interested, and finally joined the Anchor Brewery in 1965. The beer is still popular with students at places like Stanford, and at San Francisco tourist spots like the Old Spaghetti Factory, and Tommy's Joynt, and several places in Ghirardelli Square. And you can get it in quite a few of the old-style neighborhood taverns.

But Maytag thinks the market for premium beer should probably always be limited to the major metropolitan areas and college towns, which is where most of the imported beers are sold today. "We will never go national in the sense that our beer would be available everywhere," he says. "We don't have any delusions of ever becoming a major brand in any market." Anchor refrigerates all of its bottled beer, as *soon* as it's bottled, and the wholesaler and the retailer are absolutely required to keep it refrigerated. "I often say that a pure beer is like homemade cookies—they are absolutely delicious when they're fresh, but unless you treat them chemically, they have a short life," he observes. "You also have to treat beer very carefully . . . so there's not a bottle of Anchor beer *anywhere* that's not cold at this moment."

German beers, he points out, have very strict limitations on what can be used in their manufacture. However, with the Common Market expanding and becoming more entrenched, he wonders how long that will last. "What are the Germans going to do?" he asks. "Maybe it won't be too long before their beers, too, are full of foaming agents, and preservatives, and antioxidants, and soya beans. . . ."

He likes English beer best of all, but admires the top European brews as well. "There're some very interesting beers in Europe, which are as different from each other as steam beer is from the usual American lager," he says. "We don't have that tradition of diverse beers anymore. For instance, there's a beer that's traditional around the Berlin area that's a top fermented, krausened beer made with wheat. And there's another one in Belgium which I understand is just incredibly foul to the non-Belgium taste—extremely sour, and tart, and fermented for more than a year, I believe. It's a weird folk beer."

Fritz Maytag pauses, smiles, a brewmaster brewing some thoughts. "Maybe that's what steam beer is: a weird folk beer. It's the only beer in America that's a native type of beer; it came about in San Francisco, and only here. That's pretty nice."

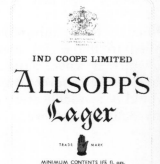

# 35/The Super Pub Crawl: San Francisco

(I once suggested to Bill Ryan that he submit his resume to the Smithsonian Institution. He laughed and took the idea under advisement. I don't know about all of Bill's careers, but when we first met, he was running a beautiful "little magazine" called *Contact* from a houseboat in Sausalito. Angel Island Publications also got into books—good ones, too—which proved to be a more artistic than economic move. Exit Angel Island Publications, at some loss to the printer but with considerable loss to the culture of the Bay Area.

Since then Bill—William H. Ryan on his résumé—has been New York Bureau Chief for Magnum Photos, the famous photographers' cooperative; Advertising Director of Random House; toiler in network television; publisher of the San Francisco *Fault*, sort of a west coast combination of the *Village Voice* and the *New York Review of Books*; editor at *Esquire*; editor-in-chief of *Swank* and a new and very interesting position he'd rather I not mention lest it go poof(!) in the night, and those things sometimes do. I hope not . . . I need friends in high places.

Bill has a vast knowledge of the San Francisco area, and this interview with him was taped over two evenings. I'd say his pub crawl belongs in the *Guinness Book of World Records*.)

BA: Bill, the purpose of the Super Pub Crawl is not just to go out and get drunk, which is not a bad idea, but it's also designed to provide a good taste of a city. So where would we start off in San Francisco?

BR: Now if you have a fairly well-to-do and action-oriented friend, who is a member of the Merchants Exchange Club, that's a good place to start . . . Friday, about 12:30 when the market closes. You can drink there, very good drinks, solid drinks, and you can play a fast game of dominoes if you happen to like dominoes. I happen to like dominoes, and while I'm fairly sober, I can play dominoes with some very fast guys. These are the gamesters from the stock market who come here, the dealers, the floormen, and fast brokers, and they play dominoes the same way they operate in the stock market.

BA: Well, do they go there at lunch time?

BR: Oh, yeah, because the market in San Francisco closes at 12:30; it also opens at 6:30 A.M., so by this time these guys are ready to roar. Anyway, I would play with these guys until they're about to shuffle on home on the 3:00 ferry. Then you take a walk with them down to the ferry building and see them off on their ferry. Then get in a cab, and since you're starving by now, you go down to Fifteenth and Mission to a place called the Deer Inn, which is, I think, the restaurant I enjoy most in San Francisco. Also it has a bar I enjoy a great deal. It's a bar that is generally full of mailmen and truck mechanics because it's way down in the industrial section of the Mission. The Deer Inn's an Italian place, and why it's called the Deer Inn, I have no idea. It's been in the same family for about twenty-nine years, and they serve the greatest Italian meals in a very, very Italian restaurant-oriented town—three or four-course luncheons, really marvelous stuff and very, very pleasant people. A lot of the sheriff's deputies and investigators in the DA's office also hang out there. A good lively place . . . In other words I go places where the *people* are and in San Francisco I happen to know where the people I want to talk to are.

BA:   Sure, that's the purpose of a good pub crawl.

BR:   At the Merchants Exchange it's the high end of the business community, and when you go to the Deer Inn straight out of the Merchants Exchange club, you simply go from one extreme to another. You have a great lunch, a few beers, whatever you want, all made good by Harry or Joe. There are three brothers who run the place—they alternate cooking, and they are all equally good. It was the hangout of the dear old San Francisco *Fault* when there was such a thing and the place where we took our guest celebrities for lunch, etc. I've yet to meet one who didn't have a hell of a good time there.

BA:   Has the place any decor of note?

BR:   Oh, sure—the graffiti on the walls. There are twenty-seven years of graffiti on the walls, so you can imagine what it's like.

BA:   Would you care to be a little more eloquent on the subject of this graffiti?

BR:   I mean beer promotions and everything from pretty girls to *Oui* kinkers, but it's the strangest combination of girls, profanity, obscenity, everything else, in a very, very politically—conservative-cum-reactionary—situation. So it gives a lot of flavor. I've always had a lot of fun talking there because I never agreed with anyone. I don't recommend that for everybody, but——

BA:   Did that ever result in any interesting violent-type experiences?

BR:   Actually I never had a fight at the Deer Inn, but I had some pretty good arguments. This is really in the Mission District just before you get into the real Chicano Brown Buffalo section. And there are a lot of pensioners who frequent the Deer Inn, and I like old drinkers. They come in and buy their bottle of port and sit there all day and drink it. Across the street, if it happens to be your bag, there is a very extreme leather and brass belt thing called The Three Spurs, or something, with a huge leather curtain to a rather active back room—doesn't happen to be my deal, though.

BA:   So I guess we'll skip that. However reluctantly.

BR:   Yeah, let's pass. By this time it's about 4:30, right? Still Friday afternoon. . . .

BA:   We've started earlier than any pub crawl in recorded history.

BR:   Well, we've gotten a hell of a good meal in us, and so we are pretty well stabilized for an evening of wandering around. Let's see . . . hell, let's make it 4:00 because the time to visit North Beach is mid- to late afternoon rather than into the evening when the topless and strip joints start, which doesn't interest me very much.

BA:   That's something I'm curious about, because this is an area I always find fascinating when I visit San Francisco. Somehow I always have the feeling that the "real people" are at certain places at certain times, and they're trying to avoid the tourists. Don't the tourists know about *those* places?

BR:   Well, the tourists know about certain places; certainly many of the ones I go to are semitourist places, but they're not the strip joints. The strip joints are rip-offs. Plus the fact the poor girls just depress me so, staggering around up there with nothing on but a speed rush. The only strip operation on Broadway that I get a kick out of are the belly dancers. They are really tremendously exciting, and they make all the strippers and the topless look like nothing. Across the street, of course, there's what used to be Barnaby Conrad's The Condor, which is still a good jazz spot and quite an intimate room, but that's not where you go towards the late afternoon.

BA:   I don't know about you, but I'm still back at the

Deer Inn.

BR: Don't worry, I won't leave you stranded. About this time, we can go to Vesuvio's, which is up near City Lights, around Columbus and Broadway—right on the alley there. Vesuvio used to be run by Trader Henry. He sold the place, but he still hangs around a lot, and he'll tell you grand tales about the bohemian days in San Francisco. It's a good, comfortable, kinda intimate, kinda crazy place, where the bohemians still hang out a lot. I would say to have a drink or two there and then go up Grant Avenue, the great street of the beat generation days, and there are still a couple of places worth hitting. There's one Irish place, Mooney's—it's a great swinging Irish bar, almost the last bar as you go up Grant Avenue.

BA: That's literally about a five-minute walk.

BR: Right. Then there is the old Coffee Gallery, which is still kind of good but a little bit too hysterical, for my taste. Everyone there is on the make for something and usually they're all excited about things. I don't like to go to bars where people are excited. I go *away* from excitement to bars, kind of bring the pressure down.

BA: Gee, Bill, if you're going to do an honest pub crawl, you have to include bars whether you like them or not.

BR: Well, I don't know what's an honest pub crawl . . . a pub crawl is a pub crawl. This one is mine; it isn't anyone else's.

BA: Gotcha.

BR: Anyway, there are a couple of other bars in that upper Grant neighborhood, none of which are any good, most of them tourist rip-offs because people still come looking for beatniks around there. There's a bar around the corner—on Green Street, I think—where Charlie McCabe has his eye-openers in the morning. He's the wise-ass columnist of the *Chronicle*. The place is kind of fun, and you can play a lot of pool. And some nice people hang out, but it tends toward the violent types. There are a couple of other bars in North Beach that tend to be for the real whackos, which can be fun if you're looking for action.

BA: Action? Sir, are you implying . . . ?

BR: I think you get my drift. . . . In any case, these places are to be avoided. People freak out there occasionally, and I don't really care for *that* kind of action, certainly. Still, we've been to a couple of places, and around this time the folks are assembled at Enrico's Coffee House on Broadway.

BA: Good place. I remember we met you there once, and your car got towed away while we were sitting there having a fine time.

BR: I remember that, too. Painfully. Anyway, Enrico's *is* a fine spot. Open air tables out on the sidewalk. You can watch the strippers hurrying on their way to work. And the crowd is interesting there. Glenn Dorenbush, who's a publicist, Blair Fuller, Herb Gold, Don Carpenter, this is a bit of a literary trip that goes on there occasionally, a kind of Lion's Head West. Evan Connell is often there. Anyway, you can have a drink there, find a friend, and have a pleasant time. It's pleasant also to sit there about 5:00, relaxing over a Marguerita or something on the sidewalk, and watch everyone scurry for the Bay Bridge or scurry in the other direction for the Golden Gate Bridge, and you ain't scurrying nowhere. *You* just sitting there having a good goddamn time. Maybe a little bit of the exhaust fumes get to you, but that's okay—until one of those big diesels go through. Then, maybe it's time to move on to new sights and smells. Across the street, there's a place—it's changed hands recently, and I don't know what it's called now—but anyway, it's directly across from Vesuvio's. And by this time you're probably ready for a little bit of a slowdown, so have a coffee royale at this marvelous place. Sit with your coffee royale, which are beautiful there—and there are several variations because they also specialize in espresso—and there's opera on the juke box, which is nice, too. And you sit and cogitate, because by this time it's about 6:00 or later, and North Beach is beginning to fill up with people who come to North Beach on Friday night. So your next move is to get out of there, unless, of course, you want some Friday night action. . . .

BA: Is that sort of thing all right for a respectable pub crawl?

BR: Well, I mean, if you do want some body action, you'd be better advised to walk down a couple of blocks to California Street and take a cable car up to Hyde, transfer at Hyde and go down to the bottom of the Hyde Street cable car run to the Buena Vista. The Buena Vista on Friday evening at 6 or 7 is really something else. It's loaded with people who are trying to get loaded, but it's also lots of nice people. Mainly there's the advertising and art directing and the commercial and creative crowd, and also a lot of very nice chicks around. It's a good place to make a connection if you want to do that on a Friday night and some people do.

So anyway—we're in the midst of getting off on a very nice little pub crawl. And the Buena Vista is really lovely. I used to go there in 1952, when there was no one there but me and a gal and a beautiful big bowl of chowder and a few beers and a bartender and the whole San Francisco Bay looking at you. It was an absolutely remarkable place.

Anyway, from there you might as well get a little more action and that means that you should probably go over to Union Street, which has a lot of good different bars—kind of pseudopubs, a lot of them highly decorated operations with all kinds of fancy effete names. And you can start at one end, at Van Ness, and work your way up to the other, about Fillmore—if that's your choice, and I happen to like to do that sometimes. I heard that one night they eighty-sixed Charles McCabe at one place. He'd called it a "body shop," or something in his column. But it's a beautifully managed and beautifully run place. Good bartenders; it gets very crowded later on Friday, but it's plenty crowded

by 6:00. And it *is* a body shop. There are an awful lot of chicks there; and there are an awful lot of guys; and everyone is looking for action.

BA: Have we named this bar?

BR: Perry's. Glenn Dorenbush is kind of host-in-residence there. He's always sitting up in the end of the bar and is usually surrounded by the local sportswriters and the celebrities-cum-celebrities, pseudocelebrities such as myself, etc. It's a place where I always find someone who's good to see and fun to talk to.

BA: As an aside, one of the things I'd like to get into about San Francisco is that it's my perception that the cocktail hour there. . . . Well, on my first trip to San Francisco, oh god, at least fifteen years ago, I was astonished at the—well, to put a negative cast on it, the freneticism, and to put a positive cast on it, the amount of good-looking women in one place—so that the cocktail hour is really a major phenomenon in San Francisco. In a way that it wasn't—maybe *now* it is, with all the singles bars—in New York.

BR: That's right. Well, you see in San Francisco there's never been much to do except drink, talk, and chase ladies. I mean, those are the three major occupations, and I do mean occupations or obsessions. By the way, the Buena Vista is credited by the Irish whisky people as having introduced Irish whisky to America, and this is where Howard Gossage got a hold of it and began the whole Irish whisky campaign, which introduced it all around. Buena Vista is where it really started.

BA: My experience in San Francisco is that you go to the Buena Vista to have an Irish coffee. At least that's the fame of the place.

BR: Absolutely, and we'll get to that on Sunday morning because there is a ritual of brunch and Irish coffee at the Buena Vista. I mean that *has* to be a stop. Howard Gossage was not a pub crawler himself, but he knew a good thing when he saw one, as we saw in many of his advertising campaigns. Anyway, getting back to Union Street, there's a place out there called Hudson's Bay, which I like. There's one . . . with a lot of stained glass that I also like. These bars are quite intimate places. There are a couple of live music places, but most of them are strictly drinking bars. Perry's serves a pretty decent piece of food, and some of them serve some steaks. But mainly it's drinking that is done on Union Street. Drinking and . . . meetings, shall we say.

BA: Out of all these Tristan and Isolde situations, where would you recommend a stranger go?

BR: To see it at its crest or its ninth wave, it alway seems—the ninth wave always seems to come in at Perry's, but that's very late on Friday. . . . There is always action up and down Union on Friday, and you can get tired of that after a while. At which time, I recommend your going somewhere else. There are a lot of little neighborhood bars out in what they call the Sunset District, which I happen to like, but I don't know if I would recommend them in terms of a pub crawl. Maybe it's time to catch your big cab or to hitch a ride with someone who is going—and there probably *is* someone who's going—out to Sausalito. Say by now it is 9:30 or 10:00.

BA: This has *got* to be the first Super Pub Crawl to become a tale of two cities.

BR: Yeah, we dream big, baby. And maybe by now we're even ready for a little dinner. If you want to spend a lot of money, the only place to go, the only real place to go is Ondine's Restaurant, which is out on a pier, of course, on the bay in Sausalito, run by one of the most colorful and interesting gentlemen, not only in that bar, but in town, George Gutekuntz. George is the flamboyant host there, and it is frequented by everyone from John Houston to Steve McQueen and all the rest of them. It is very much a celebrity place for dinner—very expensive, very good food, marvelous chef and an unbelievable view of the entire San Francisco skyline. Instead of being in San Francisco at the top of the Mark or the top of this or the top of that, I think it is much more charming to go to Sausalito to a couple of bars there where you can look back at San Francisco. San Francisco is much more interesting to look at than Sausalito.

BA: I have to agree, because we went there and used your name——

BR: Oh, oh. . . .

BA: Well, it worked. We got a table by a window, and you're right, it's about one of the most enchanting views of the world from a restaurant.

BR: Very often there are all kinds . . . well, if there is nobody else crazy to talk to there, there's George. If he likes you, he's never too busy to sit down and talk and buy you a drink.

BA: He was marvelous, I mentioned your name and——

BR: I must have paid my bill—but it is the kind of place for when you want something special. You're on vacation, or it's somebody's birthday or someone's anniversary, this is the place to go. Downstairs, of course, is the super-hippie establishment that I know of on the West Coast—the Trident, which I believe is still owned by the Kingston Trio. It's gone through several different kinds of management and development, but now it has become a health food bar, would you believe. It's a hell of a bar where people do a lot of drinking, a lot of wine drinking, basically, and good wines, but the menu is a health food menu—basically, not completely.

BA: They do serve beer?

BR: Oh, sure, they serve beer, wine, and booze.

BA: You know, we've been violating my rules of the Super Pub Crawl where I list all the beers in various places. It's not terribly important, though—I mean it's not *really* terribly—

BR: You like Anchor Steam Beer? The first place in Sausalito that had it on tap in those days was the No

Name Bar when we opened up, but I'll get to that in a moment. I have never liked steam beer, it always gave me a headache. It is naturally fermented like champagne—and champagne also gives me a headache. The beers I like if I'm going ape are Würzberger light or a combination of Australian ale and Guinness, half-and-half, I am sorry to say.

BA:  Wait a minute—Australian, you mean Foster's?

BR:  Foster's, yes.

BA:  Foster's and Guinness? You are a very strange animal.

BR:  It's marvelous, marvelous. Foster's and Guinness, it is the greatest, I think, there is. But generally speaking, in beer I like Michelob wherever I go—it's just a good light American beer with a little bit of oomph to it. I prefer draft beer when I can get it. Würzberger on draft is the best beer I know of, but I'm not a connoisseur. I drink anything—Bud, Schlitz, Miller's. . . .

BA:  Okay, your beer credentials have been accepted. Back to our safari now.

BR:  Well, let's say you do have your dinner at Ondine's since it *is* a special occasion, and you take whatever George wants to give you. I mean, if you have any sense at all, you'll do that because he'll give you the best thing in the house, and he'll charge you for it—unless you're a gourmet, and you think you know what you're doing (which I'm not and I don't). So I usually take George's word for what I should have, and I always enjoy it. And it's always as expensive as hell, but we always have a good time. Then you go downstairs for an after-dinner drink at the Trident—the view's as good, only twenty feet lower—and quite often they have some live music. It used to be a great place for jazz, but I don't think it is anymore; it's more kind of quiet folk music. In any case, you dig the Trident, and then you stagger on up through Sausalito on Bridgeway——

BA:  Speak for yourself, fella, my pub crawlers don't stagger.

BR:  Oh, they don't?

BA:  Nope. And another thing—we didn't miss any good places in San Francisco, did we?

BR:  Undoubtedly, but this is still Friday night. Anyway, so we are not staggering, we are strolling down Bridgeway going north now, and we go by a couple of cute little joints. But we're not stopping just now because up the street a ways is a new bar run by Bill Patterson, who is just a hell of a pub master. He is a Scotsman, a very nice young guy who's taken over a grand old bar in Sausalito called the Plaza, where we used to have a lot of fun, and it is one of the few cases where someone has taken an old bar you loved dearly and has completely changed it, and you still like it.

BA:  That's very rare.

BR:  Yes, well, I like Bill Patterson, who started out as a bartender at the No Name and came back to be the biggest competitor to the No Name. But, anyway, Patterson's is a very tastily done place with a nice big fireplace and Watney's Ale on tap and good people. Good booze, comfortable chairs, comfortable tables, and a great juke box, which by this time of night becomes important to me. Good jazz. Probably at the other places we stopped at, I heard about enough of the rock, etc., that I want to hear for one evening. Although I'll probably get some more of it before we're through. Anyway, Patterson's is a great place. Bill Patterson is a fine guy, and he hires good bartenders so that the guys there are very nice. It's a place where the Sausalito regulars now go. They used to go to the No Name, which we will get to after a brief station break for a commercial for the Tides Book Store, in which I used to be a partner.

BA:  Ah, another Ryan career I didn't know about.

BR:  Yes, well, those were fun days in Sausalito. Anyway, I went one night into this bar which is near the Tides—I think it was early '59—and it was empty except for the proprietor, an elderly gent named Herb. The bar was called Herb's Place, and we talked away the night. You know how I love deserted bars. I got the distinct impression that Herb, who was about seventy-three at the time, wanted to retire, but this didn't prompt any original thinking on my part until my bladder, as one's bladder does, called on me, and I went back to what I thought was the men's room. This wasn't a bar I'd very often frequented, and I steppd out instead into a really quite large court in back, which is very strange because the hill comes right down into the back of these buildings. And yet there was this beautiful little garden back there. When I went back and sat down, it occurred to me that this could be a tremendous bar if you would tear out a lot of stuff and open up the back, which in the course of things is what happened.

BA: Were you actually involved in taking over the bar?

BR: No, I dearly wanted to be, but the old cash flow wasn't there. But six friends, or else people I knew, got involved, and they took it over and completely redecorated it and had good KJAZ jazz playing all day on the hi-fi and——

BA: Did everything except name it?

BR: Well, among the people involved were Herb Beckman, my partner at the Tides, and Pat Castle, who worked there, and Mort Hertzstein, our attorney; so my voice could be heard on the matter of naming the bar, and I wanted to call it Wolf House after Jack London's place up in the Valley of the Moon. But nobody else would go tor that. And with six partners involved, they couldn't agree on anything, and the place opened, finally—without a name. And that's the only reason it's the No Name Bar. It became then very, very chic to say I'll meet you at that place that doesn't have a name, it's down there near the Tides, or wherever they happened to say it was, and so it became rather quickly famous as the bar with no name.

Partially because of its style and its location, right across from the yacht harbor in Sausalito. And, again because of the very good bartenders and nice people around, and it became the headquarters, in effect, after-hours for Calvin Kentfield, Kenneth Lamott, and myself and a lot of the people who were involved in the magazine.

BA: You mean *Contact* magazine.

BR: *Contact*, yeah, but that's way back. When the visiting celebrities would come in those days, we would take them to the No Name and get juiced up. We had a lot of fun there. It was a great place. Very congenial, very quiet and kind of cool except when we were raising a little harmless hell. And, of course, we were so identified with the bar. For example, in the men's room, the wallpaper was all covers from the magazine and that kind of thing— we felt at home there. . . . I frankly don't care for the No Name anymore. After about six months, my six associates were bought out one by one by another fine guy by the name of Neal Davis, who I understand has now sold out, and the place has become a kind of gathering and wandering place for hippies-come-lately. The music is bad, so I go to Patterson's. Still, since this is a pub crawl, I'd probably fall by the No Name and see if Connell is playing chess there, which he very often does. But that's because he has no other interests; he's not Irish. Then I'd go back to Patterson's, which, as I said, usually has a nice big fire going because by this time of the evening in Sausalito, it is usually pretty chilly and damp, and there are usually some nice people I've known a long time sitting around, and we sit and drink.

Patterson's is very comfortable, I like it. You like the places where you feel comfortable and you know a lot of people. A lot of people like the Lion's Head, and whether you or I like it, doesn't make any difference. The reason a lot of people like it is because they will be recognized or recognize someone there or feel comfortable there. I go to the Lion's Head, and Mike the bartender there used to be one of the bartenders in Sausalito at the Owl and the Two Turtles. I know Mike from Sausalito, and I feel comfortable going to the Lion's head.

BA: I don't think there's any place in America where you wouldn't feel comfortable.

BR: So anyway, let us say we put an end to Friday either at the No Name or at Patterson's, or we can go back up to Ondine's and close Ondine's with Gutekuntz, which I really recommend. But you have to be a close friend to do that because that's quite a ceremony, if he's drinking. If he isn't drinking, forget it. . . . On Saturday morning, let's say it's about 11:00, you arise, and you find yourself in Sausalito. . . . And you look out the window, and you see the bay, and Sausalito is a very lovely place to wake up in, with or without a hangover.

We then go down to the cheapest bar in Sausalito, which is not on Bridgeway, it's a block off the waterfront. It's called Smitty's, where we can have a bit more beer to welcome the day.

BA: Ryan, I have to remind you this is a serious pub crawl.

BR: Who's not serious? At Smitty's you can also play shuffleboard, pool, and some other highly skilled games to kind of get your heart started and the blood flowing. Particularly in Smitty's, which is not one of the chic places in Sausalito. It's where the fishermen and the workingmen go, it's a great place—a big long bar run by a great old lady, whose name I forget right now, and a bartender by the name of George who's been there forever. Anyway, by about 12:30 or so you're getting hungry for a little food, so jump in the car—with someone who's sober and who can drive, of course—or you can call a cab. I would call a cab. And you cab over to Tiberon, which is a ways, to Sam's Cafe. Sam's is right on the bay facing the city, although it's further from the city than Sausalito. But again, there's a spectacular view of . . . Alcatraz and a gorgeous long-range view of San Francisco. You can have . . . Sam's spe-cial brunch.

At Sam's at this time of day, it's gorgeous, with seagulls soaring all around you and with boats sailing all around you. The San Francisco Yacht Club is right next door. Not too expensive. The bar inside is good if you happen to be an indoorsman, but outside on the deck it's great. But we'll stay at Sam's and have a very lengthy, highly conversational brunch which, say, lasts until about 2:00. . . . But now it's time to return to the city with your chauffeur, taxi, or whatever. No, actually from Tiberon you take the ferry, which is down a couple of doors from Sam's. You take the ferry across San Francisco Bay back to the ferry building.

Now that you are back in San Francisco, you go up two blocks to the right to Club 19, which is actually Pier 19, where there is another great bar where you can sit outside. This time you can look at Oakland and the other bridge for a while—until late afternoon when it's time, really to begin calling this pub crawl to a halt. And the way I do that, since we don't believe in drinking and driving, is to walk back and get on a streetcar on Market Street—because you're at the bottom of Market Street at the ferry building—and go up to Fifteenth Street and Market to a place called the Cafe du Nord which is a Norwegian place, really a marvelous place, run by a guy named Ernst, who is both a great cook and manager. The bar's also great, and there are lots of polkas on the juke box—jazz and polkas are my bag—and you end up there with beer and schnapps until either you or they or somebody turns out the lights. Is this a serious enough pub crawl for you? Anyway, that's the way I do it.

BA: Are we done—or done in?

BR: Well, you can get up in the morning and go to the Buena Vista for brunch only you're really among the walking wounded by now . . . a bloody mary or an Irish coffee for your health's sake, but you should begin to taper off at 1:00 or 2:00 Sunday afternoon. . . .

"It's priced like champagne." This, from a high executive in the beer industry who was commenting to me on the price of a six-pack of Coors beer in his area in Virginia. Coors costs $3.50 for six cans there. It costs $5.50 in the Harrisburg, Pennsylvania, area. It costs as much as $1.40 a can in other areas of the country. Therefore the "champagne" label.

"I thought it was good at first, but then I got tired of it." This, from a friend who loves beer—he drinks nothing else—and who first tried Coors in California and soon found it too mild-tasting and uninteresting to bother with anymore.

The beer that is the subject of discussion among beer connoisseurs in many areas of the country is officially sold by the Colorado company only in a twelve-state area in the West—Montana was recently added and distributorships are now being opened, to considerable demand, in Texas. But the beer has been bootlegged into the East in recent years and now can legally be sold there, just so long as it goes through normal wholesaler channels. In February 1975 the Federal Trade Commission ruled that Coors cannot restrict the marketing of its beer to that twelve-state area, although Coors cannot be forced to sell to eastern wholesalers. Coors appealed that FTC decision to the Supreme Court, arguing that the quality of its beer would suffer if distribution got out of the company's control, but the high court didn't buy that argument.

Part of the Coors mystique, you see, is that the beer contains no additives (stabilizers or preservatives), is not pasteurized (a process which takes away some of the flavor), and is taken from the brewery to the consumer in refrigerated trucks. The average can of Coors is said to travel 960 miles in one of these refrigerated trucks and the average time span between brewer and consumer is about a month. In other words, the Coors devotee is guzzling this light, dry, mild beer around one-third sooner than the average drinker of most other beers brewed by the large nationally ranked companies. Then, too, Coors's brewing process takes eighty days, which is more than four times as long as some other brewers—which seems admirable, but has also prompted one cynic to remark that it shouldn't take that long to brew a beer with so little taste.

He is, of course, *not* one of the people who drink Coors as though it were the beer equivalent of the finest chateau wine made in America. To these aficionados, Coors is the best there is, regardless of price. It's said that Paul Newman won't drink any other brand on screen. Air Force cargo planes have provided the White House mess, under President Ford at least, with Coors to accompany the Thursday "Mexican Food Day" lunches at the executive mansion. President Ford himself was frequently described as a "confirmed Coors man," and such other Washington names as Ethel Kennedy have often been linked to romantic attachments to the beer. On the other end of celebrity in this country, the entire Miami Dolphins team has been said to be addicted to Coors as its favorite beverage of refreshment (except, of course, on the night before the big game).

Moreover, this has been just the tip of the iceberg. Advertising executives in New York like to brandish their supply of Coors in the executive refrigerator to clients worth impressing after normal business hours. Easterners who've been skiing in Colorado would schlepp back six-packs of Coors as either a trophy of sorts or to prove they'd gone skiing at Aspen or wherever. It really has gotten pretty damn silly. I know one publishing executive who drinks Coors and hot tea in his office late in the afternoon. I mean, how "ying-and-yang" can you get!

It goes without saying, I trust, that part of the Coors mystique has been predicated on the fact that the beer is unavailable in the East through normal supermarket and liquor store channels. This may change as the beer is trucked west to east in increasing amounts. It may also change as more people get to taste the beer and experience *it* rather than the mystique.

In the fall of 1975 the food editor of the Philadelphia *Inquirer* decided to give Coors a real welcome to the City of Brotherly Love by inviting six of the paper's staff—both editors and reporters—to come drink some Coors for a taste test. Bill Collins, whose little party this was, invited only beer drinkers who'd expressed a fondness for the beer—in fact, two were recent arrivals from California, which was "Coors Country," they declared. The beers to be sampled were nine in number, of which four were imported brews—Becks, Kirin, Heineken, and San Miguel. The domestic brands, besides Coors, were Piel's, Rolling Rock, Schmidt's (the Philadelphia Schmidt's), and Miller High Life.

Now it must be said that taste tests are treacherous things, even if you go by the rules—a little taste of beer, then spit out, then some bread to neutralize the taste of what you've just had. But Schmidt's, the local beer, was not only mistaken for Coors by three of the panelists, it came in leading the field in terms of "perfect purity, body, and flavor." Coors came in fifth in the rankings, which were done in those three categories on a scale of one-to-ten. To quote Collins: "The California contingent complained that the subtleties of Coors had been hidden because it was served following the heavier, full-bodied Kirin. Other Coors apologists have suggested that perhaps the beer, like some fine wines, doesn't travel well."

All this proves is that taste tests are fun for those whose existing opinions are confirmed, and that Schmidt's had lucked into a terrific gimmick for a new advertising campaign.

Meanwhile the head of Coors, fifty-nine-year-old William K. Coors, son of the founder of the firm, says things like this: "By 1990 there will be only three major companies left, and we intend to be one of them."

# 37/Some Notes on Drinking in Los Angeles

When the author was asked if he were going to conduct a Super Pub Crawl through Los Angeles, he explained that since driving and drinking are taboo, it didn't make sense to attempt anything of the sort. Oh, sure, you do have the bars along "The Strip," but that's not super pub crawling. Or you could take cabs all over the place, but that's inviting an evening's expenses rivaling the national debt. No, Los Angeles is just too spread out—a bunch of places under the guise of being one city.

There are a few saloons I've visited and found worth the visit, though, and would like to mention them. The Oar House in Santa Monica has sawdust on the floor and every piece of junk ever created on the ceiling and crude wooden booths. It's an honest-to-goodness mess, complete with lots of peanuts on the tables and shells on the floor. It doesn't seem to really belong within the confines of quite respectable Santa Monica, but then its spirit is more akin to neighboring Venice, a funky haven for hippies, pensioners, and free souls in general. Busch Dark by the pitcher—which is okay with me.

The King's Head is also in Santa Monica and works very hard to look Olde English. There seems to be an all Empire crowd here, but maybe that was just my New York view of things outside of New York. Still, it's a nice enough room with a comfortable living-room flavor, and you can't fault the selection of beer—Watney's, Bass, Guinness, Courage, and Coors. There are also some excellent choices among the bottled beers, including McEwan's Scotch Ale, Swan Lager from Australia, Newcastle Brown Ale, and Edinburgh Ale. This is a refuge for homesick folks from various ends of the British Empire, and why not.

In what used to be the old Malibu Inn, there's a Western abortion called the Crazy Horse Saloon—which really does strike an Easterner as self-conscious as all hell. But there's a lot of rough old wood around the place—for all I know, it's from some movie set—and a fine big etched-glass mirror behind the bar. Worth a visit, to catch the movie stars who drop in between movies.

Clementine's in Beverly Hills is popular with the sleek set, the "tinted-shades crowd," as one local writer has described them. It has a U-shaped bar that is ideal for all the narcissism that goes on in this community. You can see everyone and be seen by everyone. Lots of space, though, so if you don't feel like looking for celebrities, you can admire the busy decor. Good frothy margaritas, good people gazing—what the hell, when in Rome—and good for one visit.

There is also a Joe Allen's in this part of town—the West Coast branch of the Manhattan Joe Allen's—and it is as much a twin of that place as it was physically possible to make it. The dining room is larger and more comfortable, I thought, but that was the only distinction I could make between the two actors' strongholds. A good friend of mine, novelist and screenwriter David Scott Milton, took me to Allen's and while we were there, he observed, "This is for people who miss New York—it's so hard to find anything that approximates New York here, and you can see them trying to recreate a little of New York here." I wasn't homesick for New York. I didn't have to be, since I was going back in a few days, but Allen's is a real place, if you know what I mean—a real good saloon.

For the ultimate L. A. place, try the Raincheck Room at 8279 Santa Monica Boulevard in West Hollywood. I like the way another friend, writer-author-jazz authority Joe Goldberg, describes it: "This is the place for West Coast Actor's Studio people, for unfamous regular actors; they make a living, but you've never heard of them and probably never will. And it is for people still young enough so that they *may* make it." Behind the bar there is a listing of what actors and actresses are in town, and what actors are appearing locally, and the bar hosts a game whereby winners get a free dinner. The point of the game is to choose the name of one of these actors or actresses and use the letters of that name to come up with the initials of the titles of ten films he or she has been in. It sounds easy, isn't, but is kinda fun. You can cheat by using film refer-ence books, but I'm told the dinners at the Raincheck aren't worth that sort of chicanery. In any case, that would definitely remove any fun from the game. That would be work, research.

The beer at the Raincheck is pretty good—Bud, Coors, Guinness, and (nice surprise) San Miguel from the Philippines, which is a very popular beer around the Pacific and deservedly so. There's a place to play darts, a billiards room, a pinball machine in an adjoining room, but the action centers around the bar, which manages to be noisy and interesting at the same time. If you want anyone to know you're in town, there's a mail drop. If you want to cause a minor fuss, have yourself paged. It's not the same effect as at the Polo Lounge in the Beverly Hills Hotel, but it gets a response. One actor got a call and scurried through the crowd to the phone like Moses parting the Red Sea. "Boy, you got there fast," said his friend when he got back to their table.

Only in L. A. . . .

# 38/Ale to the Silent North!

The only time Canada seems to make news in this country is when they host the Olympics or else their prime minister (or his wife) does something outrageous. Yet Canada, by my lights, is probably the country of the future. It has space in which to grow (east and west, if not north), vast natural resources, and a growing sense of national pride. I have visited, at some length, three of its major cities and they are super-cities—Montreal, Toronto, and Vancouver—urbane as nearly any place in America. These are cities that are expanding in a civilizing manner, remembering that tall buildings not only dwarf people, give them no sense of human scale, but also block out the sky. In Vancouver, the fastest growing city on the North American continent (Toronto, I believe, is next), you can look in almost any direction and still see water and mountains. It's exhilarating to be in the center of this exciting city and be able to see the things that were there before the city began to reach toward the skies.

All this is by way of a perhaps irrational preamble to saying that Canadian beers are also civilized fellows, and we ought to be friendlier toward them. I think their beer is at least as good as ours; speaking in average terms, I'd say *better*. And their ale, which is everywhere available, is just fine with me. I happen to like the taste of ale better than I like the taste of most American lagers, which are brewed to be served very chilled and are often served so damned chilled that you taste the cold, rather than the beer. And if you did taste the beer at a civilized temperature, you might find it doesn't have too much taste at all. American beers

are brewed to satisfy the American mania for *lightness*, whatever that means. We are knocked out by things that are light. J&B Scotch, which is hardly a great scotch, is number one in America because it is light. What does that mean? J&B is hardly one of the smoothest (on the palate) scotches around, so it isn't light in that regard. Is it wonderfully light in color? If so, that means the distiller didn't add as much caramel coloring as do other distillers, because scotch whisky is colorless like gin or vodka unless it's aged in sherry casks. What the success of J&B means is that a good advertising campaign will do wonders.

Lest it sound that way, this is not intended as a tirade against American beer. Let other clods fool with that Sisyphus stone. On a hot summer's day, some American beers taste terrific because they are refreshing. But light means less among other things, and there's simply no disputing that our beer has less taste than it used to, or ought to, I feel. The Canadian product, on the other hand, always seems tasty to me. And, without being a brewer, I suspect that the reason for this is that the Canadians have stuck closer to the classical British brewing tradition than we have to the traditional German methods.

All right, Abel, calm down. Right now there are probably a lot of purists in Canada who are complaining that their beer isn't as tasty as it used to be. And they may be right. But I'd trade them any day—four cases of Rheingold or Schaefer, my local beers (even though they're not brewed here anymore) for four cases of Labatt, Molson's, Moosehead, or Schooner Ale.

The gent in the middle pauses to admire the head on his beer, but his companions appear less reflective in the 1931 film, *Woman of Experience*. Then again, the gent on the right may be complaining about the head on his beer. No fool, he, the gent on the left is going to the head of the class.

What I do know is that their beer is stronger than ours—5 percent alcohol by volume and 4 percent by weight (the average American beer is 3.7 percent alcohol by weight). But I'd leave it to an expert to explain the differences in taste between Canadian and American brews. And I just happen to have one on hand. I found him between the pages of a lively affair called *The Great Canadian Beer Book*, edited by Gerald Donaldson and Gerald Lampert. The two Geralds found just the right person to support my cause, and I thank them for him—Les Jessop, former brewing chief of Canadian Breweries and 1970 President of the North American Master Brewers Association. "If I had to use a specific word to describe the taste of Canadian beer as compared with European, for instance, I'd say it's milder. Less bitter," declares Mr. Jessop. "You can taste the hops more in European beer. The Canadian hop character is more delicate. That's pretty much a nationwide characteristic. There's more fullness in our beers than in American beers. By fullness, I mean, well, the feeling of having a real mouthful."

What's interesting about the Canadian beer story in America is that Canadian beer trails only German beer in terms of our imports. However, its sales are mostly limited to areas adjacent to our long border with our neighbor to the north. In most of our big cities in this part of the country you can find Labatt's and Molson's products and some of the forty plus brews (Carling's Red Cap and Black Horse Ales) made by the giant Carling O'Keefe Limited operation. But there are a number of other Canadian brewers of interest, and even the brewing giants know enough to provide variety and to cater to local tastes. Labatt's division in St. Boniface, Manitoba, produces these brands: White Seal Lager, Club Lager, Kiewel's Ale, Dublin Stout, Banquet Ale, and Triple XXX Stout. Whereas Labatt's brewery in St. John's, Newfoundland, produces these: Jockey Club, Red Label, Blue Star, Black Label, Labatt's "50" Ale, and Gold Keg Malt Liquor. No doubt some of this brewing activity represents a takeover of small local breweries, but the point is that it isn't just Labatt's beer or ale being offered to the public.

In any case, the brewery I'm most interested in is Uncle Ben's, which has breweries in three Canadian provinces. Maybe I'm just intrigued by the name, but I do wonder about Uncle Ben's Tartan Pilsner, Simon Fraser Lager, Gentle Ben's Beer, Old Blue Pilsner, and Red Deer Pil.

I'm curious. Just curious? Hell, no. I think the Canadian beer story should be much better told, so we can all do something to satisfy our curiosity.

# 39/The Super Pub Crawl: Washington, D. C.

(Washington being the special kind of city that it is, it deserves a special kind of pub crawl. The pubs are real. You'll have to make up your own mind about the rest, which comes from a classified report leaked to us by a dissident member of the House Select Subcommittee on Leisure Time Activities. It is based on information gathered by an agent working for the Secret Alcohol Studies Department, Licensed Beverages Division, of the CIA. It is presented here verbatim, as given in testimony before the committee when it was holding closed hearings on the Vices Bill sponsored by Representative Lew D. Vices, Rep., North Dakota.)

I was at my usual 5 P.M. listening post. In The Carroll Arms in the Capitol Hotel. Right near the seat of power in America. Congressmen, government officials, and most important, lobbyists for major industrial concerns and foreign governments, come here. It doesn't look like an important place. It just looks like a nice, comfortable drinking spot; but of course this is deceptive. Any place that is so close to the Capitol is important. You learn a great deal about an important man when he is relaxed.

I spotted them right away. The one from New York and the local operative. "Welcome to Washington, Pub Crawler," said the local man. "Good to be here, Genial Host," said the New Yorker. I knew immediately that these were code names and I will henceforth refer to them in the interests of brevity. I realize that the committee's time is not only valuable, but limited, because I see by my CIA timepiece that it is near the cocktail hour. And, well, as I say, I was immediately suspicious of these two. What was Pub Crawler doing here? I had to know.

One thing, for sure—this was no ordinary meeting. The man known as Pub Crawler seemed inordinately interested in "government girls." He inquired about their whereabouts as the Carroll Arms does not seem to be patronized by young women of whom, as the committee very well knows, there are a multitude in the nation's capital. "All the government girls go home right after work," replied Genial Host, who added the observation that these young women often belonged to car pools and that was their means of getting home. Ah, were these two out to sabotage our local transportation system, causing giant traffic jams and almost surely bringing all government work to a halt?

I noticed that both men were drinking Löwenbräu beer, which added immeasurably to my suspicions. Why were they not drinking good domestic—that is, American—beer?

While I was mulling the ramifications of these developments, they got up and left. I followed them posthaste and hailed a cab after them. Their cab headed off between the New Senate Office Building and the old one—known, of course, to you gentlemen as "new S.O.B." and old S.O.B."—and then past the Library of Congress and the Supreme Court. This was no ordinary cab ride. They were going out of the low-fare zone. Could they be in the pay of a foreign government, with an unlimited expense account? As I watched the meter rise in my cab, my hackles rose.

Their taxi left Pennsylvania Avenue and halted before a place called Whitby's Underground. *Underground,* so that was it! I paid my driver, cursed him, and followed them inside. There were two rooms. They were upstairs. I managed to get a table almost next to them and overheard Pub Crawler say, "This is a nice spacious room, but why'd they put up that ugly red whorehouse wall behind the bar? It's really a handsome bar, otherwise." His companion and he then discussed the decor at some length while drinking another foreign beer—Guinness! This would have to stop. I didn't mind the surveillance, but why couldn't they drink our kind of beer?

"There's a 'Hill' crowd here," Genial Host was saying. "Young people who work in Congress. It's not a university area, but a very liberal area." Then he added, mocking our fine southern American way of speaking, "They're not afraid of blacks here." Were these guys civil rights agitators stoking the fires of new racial unrest? What were they? This was maddening, gentlemen.

The two of them talked about the young Washington women who come to this underground place and their "liberal attitudes," and for the first time I knew that I was not on a fool's errand. These were two hardcore "Lefties," of that I was certain. But then, why the Guinness—were they IRA arms runners as well? The evidence was mounting against them rapidly, on a host of counts.

I had not yet completed my notes—we take notes, you know, for all reports like this—when they were up and out again. Those bastards were trying to give me the slip. Ha! Fat chance they'd do that! I would follow them to the ends of the earth, if that's where Pub Crawler wanted to go.

Fortunately, however, they were still in sight when I hurried out of this Whitby's place. They'd turned right and were walking toward a place called the Hawk and the Dove. I knew, for a certainty in my CIA heart of hearts, that they would surely go in there and sit on the Dove side

. . . but they didn't. They were clearly more clever than I had expected. Hoping to throw me off the track once again, they slipped into a place called Mr. Henry's.

Still, the talk was about a "government crowd," although Genial Host mentioned Roberta Flack and other entertainers who have sung there. He also said that on Sunday afternoons there is gospel singing downstairs, which again raised the civil rights possibilities. This time, at least, they drank some American beer, which made me feel better until I realized that they were probably doing this only to confuse me further. Pub Crawler seemed quite enthused about this place—"a 'must' for any Washington pub crawl . . . friendly . . . homey, rather than self-conscious . . . interesting conversations." It was then, gentlemen, the possibility that he might be setting up a series of bars for message drops first entered my mind. Perhaps there was an entire network of such places around the city, and, if so, the cost of surveillance would be astronomical. But we would do it, if we had to. Pub Crawler was obviously determined to go to all these places, and I would never be far behind.

I prepared my notes once again, making neat erasures, and once again the two men tried to take advantage of this brief pause in my vigilance to duck out. But no one ducks out on me. They'd already hailed a cab when I got outside, and I had to jog after them (good thing I keep myself in neato shape) before another empty cab came along.

This time they went to the downtown area and pulled up to a large place called Le Garage. Aha! the message drop for the French operative in this spy network. When I got up to the door, my entire surveillance system went into "Red Alert" status. What were these two guys trying to pull on me? This was no bar. This was an old warehouse, probably the center for a whole espionage network. Up there on the wall it said: "S.D. HECHT COMPANY." Then in smaller letters, but still capitals: "FURNITURE

& DRAPERIES. SHOW ROOM 1648." What a cover! I had to give them credit. These were two slippery ones, all right.

Inside I was assaulted by a barrage of sound. The place was filled with people. It wasn't a warehouse—at least I was right on that score. It was a place full of people and model antique cars hanging from the ceiling on strings and everyone acting as if they were at a fraternity party. No, maybe not that; at least they were sitting down. Well, it dawned on me that this was another bar and these guys were trying to get lost in the crowd here. Fat chance of that! I found them after bumping into two or three pretty young waitresses; don't worry, I said "Excuse me!" every time. I'm not going to give the old CIA a bad rep for rudeness. And there they were, sitting in the restaurant section having some food and drinking (ugh!) more of that foreign beer. I sat down and ordered another American beer and strained to hear every cotton-pickin' word they were saying. It wasn't easy, but I have very trained ears, you know. "I like it," Pub Crawler was saying. "Little too cutesy on the car motif, but a good place to eat and drink and look and listen." Jeez, he sure talked funny for a secret operative, but then you never know about these kinds of guys. I mean, words like *look* and *listen* are really loaded words when you're in my business.

Woops, here I am still having my beer, and they were paying their bill and cutting out on me again. Well, to tell the truth I did order another one to counterbalance the foreign poison they were drinking. But this time there was no trouble. Now really out to throw me off, they were strolling—can you imagine, strolling!—around that area looking at the buildings. If I didn't know better, I'd say they were a couple of architecture freakos, but at least they had the good sense to admire what a pretty town this town really is. It's my town, and I love it—even though I live in Virginia because of you-know-who and you know-why....

Uh, where was I? Oh yeah, on L Street, where they headed west and strolled up the street a block or so to another goddamned bar. This one was called the Black Rooster. And this time I practically went through the door with them; in fact, Genial Host, a clever duck if ever there was one, even held the door open for me. I sat down at the incredibly long bar. Jeez, you never saw such a long bar, all copper covered, and really nice. I told myself that I wouldn't mind having a drink or two here off-hours, if it weren't such a pinko hangout . . . what's that? How'd I know it was a pinko hangout? Well, you see, one of the first things Pub Crawler said was, "I hear this is a New York *Times* hangout," and Genial Host said it was, and . . . well, yes, maybe I am digressing a bit, but those newspapers really make me see red . . . uh, yeah, sorry, maybe I *am* raising my voice. I'll get back to my report. Sorry, really sorry.

So I'm so close to these guys I'm practically drinking out of their beer glasses, except I wouldn't because one of them is drinking this English stuff, Watney's and the other Bass Ale, and they're yacking away about what a good place this is—"look at the terrific old bar mirrors" and "real pubby atmosphere" and a whole lot of other talk like that. I'd swear, if I didn't know better, that they were all swish. But they're too good at knocking back the beer to be anything but heterosexual. We learn about a man's personal habits in the CIA, and I know a heterosexual drinker when I see one.

To tell you the truth, this place was beginning to get on my nerves because everyone seemed to be having a good time except me, so I was kind of relieved when they got ready to go. I'd noticed that Pub Crawler was taking a lot of notes, and it didn't escape my mind that he might be leaving messages for one of their cohorts to knock me off somewhere along the way, but I'd wait until Pub Crawler dropped off a message before calling in for some more help. I could take these two anytime, even if they were good beer drinkers.

From the Black Rooster they turned right, then left on Connecticut Avenue. Then up Nineteenth. Then M Street. If they were trying to wear me out, they had the wrong guy. But they stopped at a place called Exchange, Ltd. I wondered if they weren't some kind of financial wheeler-dealers for the Rockefellers or guys like that because this place has a real stock trendicator with each day's results from the New York Stock Exchange, and they seemed to be watching it pretty carefully. Or were they just throwing a curve at me? For all I knew at this juncture, they might be racketeers who were laundering their money at all these stops.

Anyway, I was just beginning to enjoy the place. I've got a few stocks myself, you know, although I don't follow the market as closely as I did when I was drawing overseas pay and hazardous duty pay. All-of-a-sudden they're up and out again. I tell you, at that point I wanted to say, "Hey guys, what's the hurry? *This* is a nice place," but that would have meant blowing my cover, which, as you know, is a real no-no for someone in my line of work.

Then those two guys led me a merry chase. They took a cab to Georgetown and went to a place called Nathan's, then another place called Clyde's, then yet another place called Guncher's—which is full of pinball and slot machines. At first I thought Guncher might be a dirty word, but after a little smooth prying I learned that it means "to cheat at pinball," which, I assure you, is something a CIA agent would never do.

I overheard Genial Host say something about "going back to Mr. Henry's to catch the act there," but Pub Crawler just looked kind of grim and said, "No, we have to go on. I haven't seen enough yet."

Jeez, what was he looking for? Nobody in their right mind gathers this much information unless they're into something really big. And they went on, all right, to a place called The Class Reunion, where they met a couple of guys. And then all of them went to a place called Tam-many Hall, five blocks from the White House, no less!

This was getting hairy, I tell you. Now I was clearly outnumbered, and when Pub Crawler went into Tammany Hall, he immediately went over to a bunch of guys lined up at the bar. I recognized one of those guys; he works for the Washington *Post.* So I started to really sniff around and learned that this is practically a vulture's nest of newspapermen from all over—the Los Angeles *Times,* AP, UPI, *Newsweek, Time,* all the rad-lib sheets.

And I knew, at last, what was going on. These guys, all of them—not just Pub Crawler and Genial Host—were out to use the media to subvert the drinking habits of millions of loyal Americans. They were out . . . they wanted us all to come out and get drunk with them!

Well, it didn't work. I went over to the gang of vipers. It turned out that a lot of them were New York expatriates, and you know what an infamous lot of rats they are. And I told them that the CIA was wise to them and the National Security Council and . . . if the FBI wasn't wise to them, well, then, we'd just wise up the FBI to them, too. I was really handing them the riot act when a big, Irish-looking—IRA, probably—bartender came over to me and asked me "to kindly leave the premises." I did so, only because I didn't want to blow my cover, but they didn't win this little game they were playing—especially that Pub Crawler and Genial Host. I left that place on my own two feet. They weren't going to get me drunk. No one gets me drunk. I'll swear to that, under oath, if need be. Maybe I was a little woozy at the end of the evening, but I got back to my room at the YMCA without any trouble, and after some push-ups and a brisk shower, I was as good as new.

And that's my report. I hope you act upon it with dispatch and bring all the powers of Congress to bear on this dastardly situation.

COMMITTEE CHAIRMAN: Any questions?

COMMITTEE MEMBER (*under his breath*): For chrissakes,

Charlie, let's get out of here—I have a date waiting at the Carroll Arms.

COMMITTEE CHAIRMAN: Very well. No questions then. Thank you very much. (then, *sotto voce*) Hey, Bill, whattaya say we call up home and tell them we have another secret hearing tonight, then go out on the town and really tie one on!

(According to additional notes that came into our possession from a committee member who can only be identified as "Deep Gullet," the entire committee then got into a huddle, conferred, and then left the chambers with apparent resolve. There are further reports, much later in the evening, from the Washington police, but that is a different story. . . .)

Cartoon by Peter Paul Porges.

"Make that upper-middle class."

"We got a letter from Johnny saying he's not going back for his senior year."

# 40/A Terrific Night in Becky's Dive Bar

The last time I was in London, Becky—Mrs. Rebecca Willeter—was having some problems with the health authorities. It seem they felt her pub's sanitary facilities weren't exactly sanitary since you had to go to the men's room at some risk to your shoes. The beer cellars in Becky's Dive Bar—not "dive" as we use it, perjoratively, but meaning a downstairs bar, a basement bar—are believed to have once been the cells of the Marshallsea debtors' prison, and in those days they didn't much go in for the amenities. So it is true that you practically need hip boots to visit the loo in Becky's.

I hope all this is cleared up very promptly, however, because Becky's place is a unique institution and *she* is a unique institution. London is full of handsome old pubs—Elizabethan pubs, Victorian pubs, Regency pubs—but Becky's is none of these. It is devoid of any architectural distinction. And no matter. Becky's used to be a kind of private, booze-serving canteen for the hop merchants in this building, but now it is indisputably one of the world's extraordinary watering holes—and no pun intended! Becky's cellars have housed over three hundred kinds of bottled beer and at any one time may be playing host to at least two hundred different kinds of beer. She also always has some outstanding beer on draft, and some of the strongest I've ever drunk—Dutton's of Blackburn, in particular, is to be handled with caution.

Becky, of course, stocks beers from all over the world, and she even has two beers for diabetics—one from Germany and one from Australia. But you don't visit Becky's

for anything you can drink elsewhere in London, you go there for Thwaites of Blackburn and Shepherd Neame's of Faversham, Kent, things like that—the glorious small local beers from all over the British Isles.

"Everything here sells; there's nothing that's not popular here," Becky is saying in response to a question. She is a dark-haired woman, friendly, animated, and really knowledgeable about her beer. "Where else would you get these lovely beers?" she says in response to a question about the Lyons food chain people, who are trying to get her to move out. "The only reward you get is people coming in and trying these lovely beers—all these amenities people can't get anywhere else, and good value for their money, too. . . . And I always watch people—you *have* to watch people—I want to make sure they get home. Business people are afraid of Ruddles. They're falling down the stairs on Ruddles."

My companion and I are drinking the Ruddles. It is our second bottle, here. It is wonderful stuff, but I am aware that it is also powerful stuff, and that I had better switch to something else after this bottle. "Ruddles—it's the strongest in London," Becky goes on. "It's from the Midlands—Rutland County—and it took me three years to get it in here. But I get very good delivery now. It wasn't always that way, but now it is. There's nothing static here. Nothing stays around."

Becky, if you haven't gathered as much, runs a "free house." Her place doesn't belong to any brewer. Asked if she'd like to win the "Pub of the Year Award" given out by the *Evening Standard,* she replies indignantly, "No free house has ever won it, and I wouldn't want to win it—it's so common. This is the last bastion of public houses—beer in the wood—and you get these lovely beers here, and everybody's welcome; the red carpet is out for everyone."

I am now having some Benskin Colne Spring, and my friend is having some Warwick Stout. We are both having a damned fine time. "Newcastle [Brown Ale] was the best seller in bottles," Becky is telling us, "until I got the Ruddles. But I have to watch the sailors on both of them. And the Tiger Beer from Singapore. They take it away in carloads!"

We have now switched to the draft Thwaites, and it is maintaining the standard of the earlier treats. Becky is maintaining the free flow of her conversation. "Dublin Guinness—I'm the only one here that sells it," she says after *I* have remarked on the distinct difference between draft Guinness in Dublin and London. I'd like to talk about this a bit more, but Becky is now explaining the beauty of her draft beers: ". . . it's pure hops and malt, there's no chemical in it at all."

It is getting late, and Becky's is in Southwark, on the other side of the river. Yet the temptation to drink one's way through Becky's beer cellars is very strong indeed. We settle for taking a cab back, not the underground and have two more rounds. We both order a Fremlin County Ale, which sounds like poetry in beer. It is. We are both by now so elated with each new discovery that we decided to have another Ruddles. Wot the 'ell!

Good night, Becky. Lovely beers you have. And good luck, good luck, with the authorities. Tell them you're an authority, too.

Photograph by Berenice Abbott for Federal Art Project "Changing New York." Photo courtesy of the Museum of the City of New York.

The local favorite, the Yanks, were once again champs in 1936 and Billy's Bar, First Avenue and 56th Street, remained the favorite "local" for discriminating drinkers. The author, when he first came to Gotham, used Billy's as a very pleasant antidote to overcrowded P. J. Clarke's (see *New York Super Pub Crawl, East Side*).

# 41/A Sober Look at Beer in America

Old Ox Cart, Eichler's, Edelbrau, Griesedieck, Topper—

Names like these are disappearing from the American vocabulary. . . . The names represent the labels on just a few of the hundreds of local beers once brewed across the U. S.

Now a scant four dozen of the local brands can still be found in taverns and stores, and even they may disappear as rising costs and sharp competition squeeze the regional brewers.

—*U.S. News & World Report*,
September 16, 1974

The rest of this article presents some grim statistics. There were twenty-five breweries in Chicago around 1950. Now there is one. In Wisconsin in the 1950s, there were seventy-two brewers. Now there are nine (the article said twelve, but this is the up-to-date mortality figure). What is happening is that the rich are staying rich while the survivors struggle to stay around—although it should be pointed out, in all fairness, that beer companies operate on a very low profit margin figure in contrast to most large American industries, usually ranging in the below-three-percent category.

In 1975, which, of course, is the most recent year for which we have figures, the leading breweries were as follows: Anheuser-Busch, Schlitz, Pabst, Miller, Coors (this prosperous company got bumped down one notch because of a costly labor strike and because Miller introduced its "Lite" beer to considerable success), Schaefer, Stroh, Olympia (which now owns Hamm's, among other companies), Carling-National (itself a merger of large companies), G. Heileman (which took over Grain Belt in 1975), General Brewing (which has recently acquired Falstaff), C. Schmidt, Genessee, Rheingold, Pearl, Lone Star, and Pittsburgh Brewing. This list may not mean anything to the uninitiated, but the *same* list in 1970 included Falstaff, Hamms, and Associated Brewing, all of whom are now owned by someone else.

At the same time this alarming trend is going on, beer consumption rises each year. It is alarming for the same reasons there are no more Hudsons, Packards, Nashs (individuality and as many choices as possible for the consumer). In 1960 we were drinking, on a per capita basis, about fifteen gallons of beer each, and now we are solidly around twenty-one gallons per person. Moreover, 1975 was the eleventh straight year that beer consumption has risen in this country. The big breweries, in addition to knocking off the competition, must be doing something right to please the public, because that public, unlike England's (see Richard Gilbert's piece on the campaign for real ale), fails to be bothered by the increasing homogenization of American beer tastes. There remains a small loyal market for ale, a stable market for the sweeter, more alcoholic malt liquors, and while you may find some porter in a few regional markets, those days are surely numbered. But most of us drink what most of us drink. We're drinking more beer all the time, and we are enjoying—if that's important to you—less choice all the time. Imported beer, while a slowly growing market, represents perhaps one percent of the beer consumed in America. Eccentric local brews—well, there's no way of telling. Let me remind you that Anheuser-Busch, Schlitz and Pabst, by themselves, represent over forty percent of all the beer consumed in America.

Giantism is no new phenomenon in America, but just to give you some idea of how big the larger American brewers are, I asked an expert in the field to give me à list of the world's ten biggest brewers. Of the ten he named, only Kirin—the incredibly successful Japanese brewery that is itself part of a super-large conglommerate—and Guinness, which exports more beer to more countries than any other brewery, cracked the list. Otherwise, it was an all-American list.

The point of all this is that if you were to take a similar listing of the top ten foreign breweries in the world, you'd find considerable diversity among their products. Lowenbrau and Guinness couldn't be more different. And you *can* taste the difference between a Lowenbrau and a Heineken and a Kirin. This hardly makes our own large brewers into villians. Responding to public and federal and state pressure, they are showing a lot of concern about the ecology problem presented by thrown-away cans and bottles (which is hardly their fault). But it does say something about us as a nation. We drink what we're told we'd like to drink, and most of the beer advertising is directed to that relatively small portion of the total beer drinking public who actually drink (some say three-fourths, some say higher) most of the beer consumed each year in this country. And somehow we seem to drink what they drink.

Well, those guys plopped in front of their TV sets or wherever, don't speak for me. I speak for me. And I want to hear about more and different beers, not fewer and fewer beers that all taste alike. It can be a great drink, beer, but it won't be if it ends up with our having no more choices than the difference between Coca-Cola and Pepsi-Cola.

I am reminded in all of this of the remark made by a friend of mine who works in the beer industry in a capacity which causes him to travel a great deal. He is an absolute Spartan when it comes to drinking nothing but fresh beer in all his moving around the country. In fact, he generally avoids foreign beer because it "gets oxidized. . . . They leave air space in the container, and there's *got* to be some air in it." He sticks to whatever's brewed wherever he finds himself. "What is the freshest is the best, and that's usually the local beer," he says, "but the frightening thing is that Budweiser may be the freshest beer wherever you go in this country."

He meant no disrespect for our national giant; in fact, he was speaking of the number of plants the company has around the nation and how they are designed to operate on a rapid turnover basis. But it could well be that one day our local beers will all be Bud or Schlitz or Pabst or a very few others. And when that day comes, it will be a very sad one indeed because we'll have lost yet again a little of the individualism that America was once all about.

# Acknowledgments

This book, quite honestly, could not have been written without (more than) a little help from my friends. I talk about them inside, but I'd like to thank them all—out here, in public—for their generous gifts of time and talent. Bartender, the very best beer in the house for Brian Boylan, Gary Blumberg, Stuart Brown, Richard Gilbert, Craig McGregor, Jay Robert Nash, Ray Puechner, and Bill Ryan. Carole Abel, my bride of 6,324 days, helped research this book, typed almost all of it, tested (and invented) recipes, and in various devious wifely ways helped cajole—and command—its completion. Other friends wrote dandy pieces for which there was, alas, no room when the final pruning of a very large manuscript took place. More beers, bartender, for Gene Walter, who contributed much; George Mettler, teacher, novelist, and my favorite ex-FBI agent; and Louis Hoover, who should finish his novel whenever he's not writing those real fine C&W songs. Happily, five of America's greatest cartoonists, Eldon Dedini, Herbert Goldberg, Bill Murphy, Peter Paul Porges, Brian Savage, and Norman Lindsay *are* represented at their usual literate level within these pages, and I'm more than pleased with their presence. As for Jack Looney, who concocts puzzles—Jack, *I* couldn't use the "beer puzzle," but that's okay, Jack, we're still friends.

Additional thanks, surely, belong to Noel Fox, for on-the-spot taping and tippling in Copenhagen and to Carol Schwalberg for jetting around' Los Angeles and environs on my behalf. I received all sorts of other help in researching this book, and special thanks are herewith launched in the directions of John Baker, Irv Greenfield, Mike Hamilburg, 'Maddy' Hochstein, Herbert M. Kallman, Seymour Krim, Angus McGill Norris and Ross McWhirter, Tom O'Toole, John Segal, Linda Shapiro, Marty Solow, Arthur Ribeck, and Shari and Clyde Steiner. David Williams substituted accurate German translations for my *gasthaus Deutsch*, and Gene Light and Bill Murphy chipped in with some invaluable graphic gifts. Maureen Baron, John Gallagher, and Rose Sommer added to my beer reference library when the occasion required yet *another* book, and Brenda Taylor provided emergency typing. Then, too, since no man is either an island or a decent pub crawler all by his lonesome, I was gleeful for the endurance and expert company provided by Joe Goldberg, John Flory, John Modi, Dick Opie, and Alice Turner. John Modi provided other areas of expertise as well, including production advice and editorial suggestions.

I am also indebted to certain individuals and organizations in or associated with the brewing industry. In particular, I am grateful for the terrific help afforded me by Morgan Guenther and Dolly Wright of the United States Brewers Association, Peter Evans and David Smith of The Brewers' Society in London, and Alan Montgomery, Billy Porter, and Paul Mitson of the Arthur Guinness Son & Co. organizations in both London and Dublin. In addition to Guinness, other brewers on both sides of the

Atlantic were quite helpful, and these include: Anchor Steam Beer; Adolph Coors; Allied Breweries, Ltd.; Anheuser-Busch; Bass Charrington and Charrington & Co.; Carling National; Carlsberg; Courage Barclay & Simmonds; Jos. Schlitz; Kirin; Löwenbräu; Olympia; Pabst; Rheingold; F. & M. Schaefer; C. Schmidt & Sons; Scottish & Newcastle; Tuborg; Watney Mann; and Whitbread. Still more thanks go to the German American Chamber of Commerce, Deutscher Brauer-Bund e.V., *Brewers Digest,* the Beer Museum in Barnesville, Pennsylvania, the British Tourist Authority, and the Irish Tourist Board. Finally, although all illustrative material is credited elsewhere, I want to express the gratitude all authors using graphics must feel toward the splendid Picture Collection of the New York Public Library and the very cooperative Photo Library Department of the Museum of the City of New York,

If I have failed to acknowledge the help provided by any person and/or organization, blame it on faulty memory—and the avalanche of research materials on top of my rolltop desk. It's home, all right, but so is the corner pub.